FOUR YEARS UNDER
MARSE ROBERT

Drawn by Wm. L. Sheppard.

MARSE ROBERT.

FOUR YEARS UNDER MARSE ROBERT

by

Robert Stiles
Major of Artillery,
Army of Northern Virginia

A *Bellum Edition*
R. Bemis Publishing, Ltd.
Marietta, Georgia 30007
1995

ISBN: 0-89176-046-8

Cover Concept by David Productions
Cover Design and Graphics by
Penstroke Graphics, Atlanta, GA

Printed in the United States of America

First Printing: September, 1995

Bellum Editions
is a registered trademark of
R. Bemis Publishing, Ltd.
PO Box 71088
Marietta, GA 30007

ROBERT STILES DURING THE WAR YEARS

TO

THAT GREAT CAPTAIN

TO WHOM THE WORLD TO-DAY ATTRIBUTES MORE OF THE
LOFTIEST VIRTUES AND POWERS OF HUMANITY, WITH
LESS OF ITS GROSSNESS AND LITTLENESS, THAN
TO ANY OTHER MILITARY HERO IN HISTORY; AND

TO

MY COMRADES

LIVING AND DEAD—WHO COMPOSED

THAT IMMORTAL ARMY

WHICH FOUGHT OUT FOR HIM

HIS MAGNIFICENT CAMPAIGNS

CONTENTS

CHAPTER XXI. - - - - - - - - Cold Harbor of '64.

CHAPTER XXII. From Cold Harbor to Evacuation of Richmond
and Petersburg.

CHAPTER XXIII. The Retreat from Chaffin's Bluff to Sailor's Creek.

CHAPTER XXIV. Fatal Mistake of the Confederate Military Authorities.

FOUR YEARS UNDER MARSE ROBERT

CHAPTER I

"Four years under Marse Robert."

At the first blush this title may strike one as inaccurate, lacking in dignity, and bordering on the sensational. Yet the author prefers it to any other and is ready to defend it; while admitting, though this may seem inconsistent, that explanations are in order.

Not one of his men was an actual follower of Robert Lee for four full years. In fact, he was not himself in the military service of Virginia and of the Confederate States together for that length of time, and he did not assume personal command of what was then the Confederate "Army of the Potomac" and later, under his leadership, became the "Army of Northern Virginia," until June 1, 1862.

But more than a year before, indeed just after the secession of the State, Governor Letcher had appointed Lee to the chief command of the Virginia troops, which, under his plastic hand, in spite of vast obstacles, were turned over in a few weeks in fair soldierly condition to the Confederate Government, and became the nucleus of the historic Army of Northern Virginia; and their commander was created one of the five full generals provided for by law in the military service of the Confederate States.

As full general in the Confederate service, Lee was not at first assigned to particular command, but remained at Richmond as "Military Adviser to the President." In that position, as also in his assignment, somewhat later, to the conduct, under the advice of the President, of the operations of all the armies of the Confederate States, he of course had more or less supervision and control of the armies in Virginia. Such continued to be Lee's position and duties, and his relations to the troops in Virginia, until General Joseph E. Johnston, commanding the army defending Richmond, was struck down at Seven Pines, or Fair Oaks, June 1st, 1862, when President Davis appointed Lee to succeed him in command of that army.

From this brief review it appears clearly that the men who, after June 1st, 1862, followed Lee's banner and were under his immediate command were, even before that time and from the very outset, in a large and true sense his soldiers and under his control; so that, while strictly speaking no soldier followed Lee for four years, yet we who served in Virginia from the beginning to the end of the war are entitled, in the customary and popular sense, to speak of our term of service as *"Four years under Lee."*

But our claim is, "Four years under MARSE ROBERT." Why "Marse Robert?"

So, in Innes Randolph's inimitable song, "A Good Old Rebel," the hero thus vaunts his brief but glorious annals:

> "I followed old Mars' Robert
> For four year, near about;
> Got wounded in three places
> And starved at Pint Lookout."

Again, why "Marse Robert?"

The passion of soldiers for nicknaming their favorite leaders, re-christening them according to their unfettered fancy and their own sweet will, is well known. "The Little Corporal," "The Iron Duke," "Marshall Forwards," "Bobs," "Bobs Bahadur," "Little Mac," "Little Phil," "Fighting Joe," "Stonewall," "Old Jack," "Old Pete," "Old Jube," "Jubilee," "Rooney," "Fitz," "Marse Robert" —all these and many more are familiar. There is something grotesque about most of them and in many, seemingly, rank disrespect. Yet the habit has never been regarded as a violation of military law, and the commanding general of an army, if a staunch fighter, and particularly if victory often perches on his banner, is very apt to win the noways doubtful compliment of this rough and ready knighthood from his devoted troops. But however this may be, "Marse Robert" is far away above the rest of these soldier nicknames in pathos and in power.

In the first place, it is essentially *military*.

Though in form and style as far as possible removed from thàt model, this quaint title yet rings true upon the elemental basis of military life—unquestioning and unlimited *obedience*. It embodies the strongest possible expression of the short creed of the soldier:

> "Their's not to reason why,
> Their's but to do and die."

I do not believe an army ever existed which surpassed Lee's ragged veterans in hearty acceptance and daily practice of this soldier creed, and there is no telling to what extent their peculiar nickname for their leader was responsible for this characteristic trait of his followers. Men who spoke habitually of their commanding general as "Master" could not but feel the reflex influence of this habit upon their own character as soldiers. This much may certainly be said of this graphic title of the great captain; but this is not all.

"Marse Robert!" It goes without saying that the title is distinctively *Southern*.

The homely phrase was an embodiment of the earliest and strongest associations of the men applied in reverent affection, but also in defiant yet pathetic protest. It was, in some sense, an outcry of the social system of the South assailed and imperilled by the war and doomed to perish in the great convulsion. The title "Marse Robert" fitted at once the life of the soldier and the life of the slave, because both were based upon the principle of absolute obedience to absolute authority.

In this connection it may not be uninteresting to note —what is perhaps not generally known—that during the last months of the war the Confederate authorities canvassed seriously the policy of arming the Southern slaves and putting them in the field as soldiers. I was told by a leading member of the Senate of Virginia that, by special invitation, General Lee came over from Petersburg and appeared before, as I remember, a joint committee of the two Houses, to which this matter had been referred, and gave his opinion in favor of the experiment upon the ground, mainly, that unhesitating and unlimited obedience—the first great lesson of the soldier—was ingrained, if not inborn, in the Southern slave.

Yet once more—to christen Lee "Master" was an act of homage peculiarly appropriate to his lofty and *masterful personality*.

There never could have been a second "Marse Robert;" as, but for the unparalleled elevation and majesty of his character and bearing, there would never have been the first. He was of all men most attractive to us, yet by no means most approachable. We loved him much, but we revered him more. We never criticised, never doubted him; never attributed to him either moral error or mental weakness; no, not even in our secret hearts or most audacious thoughts. I really believe it would have strained and blurred our strongest and clearest conceptions of the distinction between right and wrong to have entertained, even for a moment, the thought that he had ever acted from any other than the purest and loftiest motive. I never but once heard of such a suggestion, and then it so transported the hearers that military subordination was forgotten and the colonel who heard it rushed with drawn sword against the major-general who made it.

The proviso with which a ragged rebel accepted the doctrine of evolution, that "the rest of us may have descended or ascended from monkeys, but it took a God to make Marse Robert," had more than mere humor in it.

I am not informed whether the figure of speech to which I am about to refer ever obtained outside the South, or whether its use among us was generally known beyond our borders. It undoubtedly originated with our negroes, being an expression of their affectionate reverence for their masters, by metaphor, transferred to the one great "Lord and Master" of us all; but it is certainly also true that Southern white men, and especially Southern soldiers, were in the habit—and that without the least consciousness of irreverence—of referring to the Divine Being as "Old Marster," in connection especially with our inability to comprehend His inscrutable providences and our duty to bow to His irreversible decrees.   There is no way in which I can illustrate more vividly the almost worship with which Lee's soldiers regarded him than by saying that I once overheard a conversation beside a camp fire between two Calvinists in Confederate rags and tatters, shreds and patches, in which one simply and sincerely inquired of his fellow, who had just spoken of "Old Marster," whether he referred to "the one up at headquarters or the One up yonder."

We never compared him with other men, either friend or foe.   He was in a superlative and absolute class by himself. Beyond a vague suggestion, after the death of Jackson, as to what might have been if he had lived, I cannot recall even an approach to a comparative estimate of Lee.

As to his opponents, we recked not at all of them, but only of the immense material force behind them; and as to that, we trusted our commanding general like a providence. There was at first a mild amusement in the rapid succession of the Federal commanders, but even this grew a little trite and tame.   There was, however, one point of great interest in it, and that was our amazement that an army could maintain even so much as its organization under the depressing strain of these successive appointments and removals of its commanding generals.   And to-day I, for one, regard the fact that it did preserve its cohesion and its fighting power under and in spite of such experiences, as furnishing impressive demonstration of the high character and intense loyalty of our historic foe, the Federal Army of the Potomac.

As to the command of the Army of Northern Virginia, so far as I know or have reason to believe, but one man in the Confederate States ever dared to suggest a change, and that one was Lee himself, who—after the battle of Gettysburg, and again, I think, though I cannot verify it, when his health gave way for a time under the awful strain of the campaign of '64—suggested that it might be well he should give way to a younger and stronger man. But the fact is, that Lee's preeminent fitness for supreme command was so universally recognized that, in spite of the obligation of a soldier to undertake the duties of any position to which he may be assigned by competent authority, I doubt whether there was an officer in all the armies of the Confederacy who would have consented to accept appointment as Lee's successor in command of the Army of Northern Virginia— possibly there was one—and I am yet more disposed to question whether that army would have permitted Lee to resign his place or any other to take it. Looking back over its record, from Seven Pines to Appomattox, I am satisfied that the unquestioned and unquestionable preeminence, predominance, and permanence of Lee, as its commander-in-chief, was one of the main elements which made the Army of Northern Virginia what it was.

I have said we never criticised him. I ought, perhaps, to make one qualification of this statement. It has been suggested by others and I have myself once or twice felt that Lee was too lenient, too full of sweet charity and allowance. He did not, as Jackson did, instantly and relentlessly remove incompetent officers.

The picture is before you, and yet it is not intended as a full picture, but only as such a presentation of him, from the point of view of his soldiers, as will explain and justify the quaint title which they habitually applied to their great commander. I have not attempted and shall not attempt a complete portrait. Why should I, when the most eloquent tongues and pens of two continents have labored to present, with fitting eulogy, the character and career of our great Cavalier. It is our patent of nobilty that he is to-day regarded—the world over—as the representative of the soldiery of the South.

Not only is it true of him, as already intimated, that he uniformly acted from the highest motive presented to his soul—but so impressive and all-compelling was the majesty of his virtue that it is doubtful whether any one ever questioned aught of this. It is perhaps not too much to say that the common consensus of Christendom—friend and foe and neutral—ranks him as one of the greatest captains of the ages and attributes to him more of the noblest virtues and powers, with less of the ordinary selfishness and littleness of humanity, than to any other great soldier. This is what is meant by our dedication—that the world has come to view him very much as his ragged followers did in the grand days when they were helping him to make history.

Can you point to another representative man upon whom the light of modern day has been focussed with such intensity, of whom these supreme things may be said with so little strain; or rather, with acquiescence practically universal? For our part, we say emphatically—we know not where to look for the man.

The scheme of this book is a modest one. The author makes no pretense that he is qualified to write history or to discuss learnedly, from a professional standpoint, the battles and campaigns of armies; while of course an old veteran cannot be expected always and absolutely to refrain from saying how the thing looked to him. All that is really proposed—and the writer will be more than content if he acquit himself fairly well of this limited design—is to state clearly and truthfully what he saw and experienced as a private soldier and subordinate officer in the military service of the Confederate States in Virginia from '61 to '65.

It is not proposed, however, to give a consecutive recital of all that occurred during these four years, even within the narrow range of the writer's observation and experience; but rather to select and record such incidents, arranged of course in a general orderly sequence, as are deemed to be of inherent interest, or to shed light upon the portrait of the Confederate soldier, the personality of prominent actors in the war drama upon the Southern side, the salient points of the great conflict, or the general conditions of life in and behind the Confederate lines.

Again, such are the imperfections of human observation and such the irregularities and errors of human memory, especially in the record of events long past, that many may be disposed to question the value of such a book as this, written to-day, relating to our civil war. I can only reply that not a few of the incidents recorded were reduced to writing years ago, indeed soon after they occurred; while perhaps as much has been gained in perspective as has been lost in detail, by waiting. Certainly it can be better determined to-day what is worthy of preservation and publication than it could have been immediately after the war.

The slips and vagaries of memory, however, cannot be denied or excluded. It can only be said, "forewarned is forearmed." I shall endeavor to exercise that conscientious care which the character of the work requires, but cannot hope to attain uniform and unerring accuracy in every detail. In the record of conversations, interviews, and speeches I shall sometimes adopt the form of direct quotation, even where not able to recall the precise words employed by the speakers and interlocutors—if I am satisfied this form of narrative will best convey the real spirit of the occasion.

And as the writer is, in the main, to relate what he saw and heard and did, he craves in advance charitable toleration of the first personal pronoun in the singular number.

CHAPTER II

INTRODUCTORY SKETCHES

Ante-war History of the Author—The Fight for the "Speakership" in 1860—Vallandigham, of Ohio—Richmond After the John Brown Raid—Whig and Democratic Conventions of Virginia in 1860.

There are features of my antecedent personal history calculated, perhaps, to impart a somewhat special interest to my experiences as a Confederate soldier. I was the eldest son of the Rev. Joseph C. Stiles, a Presbyterian minister, born in Georgia, where his ancestors had lived and died for generations, but who moved to the North and, from my boyhood, had lived in New York City and in New Haven, Conn. I was prepared for college in the schools of these two cities and was graduated at Yale in 1859. It so happened that I had never visited the South since the original removal of the family, which occurred when I was some twelve years of age; so that practically all my education, associations and friendships were Northern. True, I took position as a Southerner in all our college discussions and debates, but never as a "fire-eater" or secessionist. Indeed, I was a strong "Union man" and voted for Bell and Everett in 1860.

After my graduation in 1859 I passed the late summer and autumn in the Adirondack woods fishing and hunting with several classmates, and devoted the rest of the year to general reading and some little teaching, in New Haven; until, becoming deeply interested in the fierce struggle over the Speakership of the House of Representatives, I went to Washington, and from the galleries of the House and Senate eagerly overhung the great final debates. I had paid close attention to oratory during my college course and I doubt whether there was another onlooker in the Capitol more deeply absorbed than I. On more than one occasion

the excitement and pressure of the crowd in the galleries
of the House was fearful, and once at least persons were
dragged out, more dead than alive, over the heads of others
so densely packed that they could not move; but I never
failed to secure a front seat.

I grew well acquainted—that is, by sight—with the party
leaders, and recall, among others, Seward and Douglas and
Breckenridge, Davis and Toombs and Benjamin, in the Senate; Sherman and Stevens, Logan and Vallandigham,
Pryor and Keitt, Bocock and Barksdale, and Smith, of Virginia, in the House. It became intensely interesting to me
to observe the part some of these men played later in the
great drama: Seward as the leading figure of Lincoln's
Cabinet; Davis as President of the Southern Confederacy;
Benjamin, Toombs, and Breckenridge as members of his
Cabinet, the two latter also as generals whom I have more
than once seen commanding troops in battle; "Black Jack"
Logan,—hottest of all the hotspurs of the extreme Southern
wing of the Democratic party in the House in 1860,—we all
know where he was from '61 to '65; and glorious old "Extra
Billy" Smith, soldier and governor by turns; Barksdale, who
fell at Gettysburg, was my general, commanding the infantry brigade I knew and loved best of all in Lee's army and
which often supported our guns; and poor Keitt! I saw him
fall at Cold Harbor in '64 and helped to rally his shattered
command.

The Republican party had nominated John Sherman for
Speaker, and he was resisted largely upon the ground of his
endorsement of Hinton Rowan Helper's book, which was
understood as inciting the negro slaves of the South to in-
surrection, fire, and blood. The John Brown raid had occurred recently, and Col. Robert E. Lee had led the party of
United States Marines which captured the raiders and their
leader. They had just been convicted and executed as mur-
derers. The excitement was frightful and ominous, and
scenes of the wildest disorder occurred in the House. One
of these was in every way so remarkable that I ask leave to
describe it somewhat fully.

The Republican leaders had become convinced they could
not elect Sherman, and about the same time the Demo-

crats, seeing there was no possibility of electing their original candidate, Thomas S. Bocock, of Virginia, had put up William N. H. Smith, of North Carolina, an old line Whig, or Southern American, and it seemed certain they would elect him. Indeed, he was elected and his election telegraphed all over the land; but before the result of the ballot could be announced, Henry Winter Davis, of Maryland, and E. Joy Morris, of Pennsylvania, as I recollect, Northern Americans or Republicans, who had voted for Smith, changed their votes and everything was again at sea. It was then openly proposed to withdraw Sherman; and John Hickman, of Pennsylvania, who had been elected as an anti-Lecompton Democrat, but had gone over to the Republicans, took the floor to resist what he characterized as cowardice and treachery. Hickman had not voted for Sherman until the crisis was reached, 'but had been openly charged, on the floor of the House, with secretly desiring and plotting to elect him. Pryor and Keitt and other hot-headed Southerners had attacked Hickman fiercely, and leading Northern Democrats had upbraided him for his desertion. Under these taunts and thrusts he had become the bitterest man upon the floor.

In the gloom which seemed to overshadow the House, Hickman, as he rose, looked pale, repellent, ghastly, almost ghostly. Repeatedly during his harangue, which was really one of great power, he walked from his seat in the back part of the House, down the narrow aisle toward the Clerk's desk, his right arm lifted high above his head, his fist clinched and his whole frame trembling with passion, and as he reached the open space in front of the desk he would shriek out the climax of a paragraph, simultaneously smashing his fist wildly down upon a table that stood there.

The speech produced a profound, almost awful, impression. I remember the peroration as if it were yesterday, as he shouted, on his last stride down the aisle, glaring around upon his Republican associates: "I know not and I care not what others may do, but as for me and my house, we intend to vote for John Sherman—until Gabriel's last trump, the crack of doom, and the day of judgment."

In spite of this powerful protest, as soon as the dilatory tactics of the opposition were exhausted and the ballot was called, it became evident that Sherman had been withdrawn; indeed he withdrew his own name, and Pennington, of New Jersey, a moderate Republican, and personally an unobjectionable man, was put up in his place. There was nothing that could now be done; this call of the roll would end it all.

The Democrats went wild and every moment wilder, as the Republicans—even John Sherman's most devoted friends as their names were called—one after another fell into line and voted, full-voiced, for "Pennington." That is, all the Democrats went wild except Vallandigham, of Ohio. He sat coolly in his seat, while Barksdale, Keitt, Houston, Logan, and the rest surged around him. When they appealed to him, with excited gesticulations, he simply brushed them aside and kept his eyes fixed on a particular spot on the Republican side. As Hickman's name was called and he rose and voted for Pennington, Vallandigham sprang to his feet and, stretching out his right arm toward the Clerk's desk, in a long, resonant drawl that would not be drowned, he shouted: "Mr. Clerk, I move that this House do now adjourn!"

Cries from the Republican side: "Sit down! Sit down! Order! Order! You can't interrupt the ballot! Sit down!"

But Vallandigham went right on. He would not sit down, and he would interrupt the ballot—and he *did*.

"Mr. Clerk, I move that this House do now adjourn, especially, sir"—both arms now extended, mouth wide open, eyes wide staring—"especially, sir, since we have just had Gabriel's last trump, the crack of doom and the day of judgment!"

I question if anything like it ever occurred in the history of legislative bodies; or if any speech or stroke of daring leadership ever produced such an effect. A yell went up from the entire House—Democrats and Republicans joining in it. There was a wild burst and bolt, of perhaps half the delegates, out of the chamber, and then a rush of the rest for Vallandigham.

I remember that old Houston, of Alabama, who weighed about a ton, ran up, puffing like a porpoise, and threw his immense bulk into Vallandigham's arms, rolling him upon the floor. Poor Barksdale lost his wig in the scrimmage. In a twinkling the hero of the moment was lifted high upon the shoulders of his party friends, who marched triumphantly all over the House, bearing him aloft and almost waving him like a banner.

By this flash of lightning out of the heavens, as it were, the Democrats gained another day, though they did not win the fight.*

I cannot forbear another anecdote of this remarkable man; for while not an eye and ear witness to it as to that just related, the utterance attributed to him bears so unmistakably the impress of his vigorous, incisive intellect and his power of crushing sarcasm, that I am almost willing to vouch for the truth of the recital.

As the story goes, some time during the first half of the war Mr. Thaddeus Stevens, or some other equally single-hearted patriot, alarmed at the rapid depreciation of the currency, offered in the House a measure providing in substance that gold should not be sold at a premium; when from

---

*It is proper to say that the Congressional *Globe* makes no mention of this remarkable episode—that is, of the startling culmination of it—though the facts and circumstances leading up to this culmination are there set out substantially as above related. The proceedings of the House, as recorded in the *Globe* at and about the date, are orderly and consecutive and the adjournments regular. The record, however, does show an adjournment over a day, and it may be well that the unparalleled occurrence above described took place upon that day. Those familiar with Congressional proceedings are aware of the usage or rule preventing any trace upon the record of an irregular or illegal session or adjournment of the House; e. g. the House has occasionally met for business on Sunday and even remained in session all that day, but the entire Sunday session—with everything transacted thereat—is entered as of the preceding day. Therefore, while not assured precisely how the thing was done in this instance, it is not unlikely that the irregular, illegal and abortive proceedings above described took place upon the day covered by the adjournment, and that the entry of the adjournment over that day was an after-thought.

the back benches, where the little Democratic contingent was then wont to abide, Vallandigham arose and drawled out: "Mr. Speaker! I move you, sir, the following amendment to the bill: 'Provided that, during the pendency of this act, the laws of nature and of finance and of common sense be, and they are, hereby suspended.' "

I do not know whether any biography of Vallandigham has been published, but one should be. We realize, of course, that his attitude, actions, and utterances during the war must have been as offensive and irritating to the bulk of the people of the Northern States as they were refreshing and delightful to us of the South; but we believe the time has come when men of all parties would be able to appreciate his tremendous vitality, his unconquerable courage, his unquenchable brilliance.

And, by the way, his death, as the circumstances were narrated at the time in the public press, was even more marvelous and startling than any incident of his checkered life. As I recall the facts, some years after the close of the war he was senior counsel for the defense in a murder trial which excited great popular interest. There had been a collision between the supposed murderer and his victim, at the close of which the latter had fallen mortally wounded by a pistol shot.

Vallandigham's theory was that he had been killed by the accidental discharge of his own weapon, and during an intermission in the trial, taking up a pistol, he proceeded to illustrate to his associate counsel just how the thing might have occurred, when, shocking to relate, it did so occur again—the pistol was accidentally discharged into his own person and Vallandigham fell dead.

At the close of the prolonged fight over the Speakership I left Washington and ran down to Richmond, with a view of "spying out the land" as a place in which to try my fortune when I should have acquired my profession. My father had been pastor of a church in that city for four years during my childhood, and had been much beloved by his people, who received me with more than old Virginia hospitality. I was charmed with everything I saw and every one I met,

except that I was shocked and saddened by meeting everywhere young men of my own age in military uniform. They
had not long since returned from the camp at Charlestown
and the execution of John Brown, and it chilled me to see
that they regarded themselves, as they proved indeed to be,
the advance guard of the great army which would soon be
embattled in defence of the South. I loved the Union pas-
sionately, and while I had seen a great deal at Washington
that made me tremble for it, yet I had not there seen men
armed and uniformed as actual soldiers in the war of dis-
union.

It was not a little singular that most of these young men
—that is to say, those whom for the most part I met in a
social way—belonged to the Richmond Howitzers, the very
corps which, without choice on my part, I joined in 1861,
and with which I served during the greater part of the war.

State conventions, both of the Whig and Democratic
parties, sat in Richmond during my visit and discussed, of
course, mainly the one absorbing issue. I was an eager
observer of the proceedings and much impressed with the
high average of intelligence and speaking power in both
bodies. This seemed especially true of the Whig Convention—perhaps because I was so much in sympathy with that
party in deprecating the disruption of the Union. I confess, however, the question has since been often pressed
home upon me whether, after all, the Democrats of Virginia did not, in this great crisis, exhibit a higher degree of
prescient statesmanship.

Among the Whig leaders I distinctly recall William Bal-
lard Preston, A. H. H. Stuart, Thomas Stanhope Flournoy,
and John Minor Botts. I do not remember whether John
B. Baldwin was a member of this convention of 1860. If
so, I did not happen to hear him speak. Mr. Preston, Mr.
Stuart, and Mr. Flournoy, as well as Mr. Baldwin, were,
later, members of the Secession Convention of Virginia, but
all were Union men up to President Lincoln's call for troops.
Mr. Preston and Mr. Stuart were not only finished orators,
but statesmen of ability and experience. Both had graced
the Legislature of their State and the Congress of the United

States, and both had been members of the Federal Cabinet —Mr. Preston during General Taylor's and Mr. Stuart during Mr. Fillmore's administration.   Mr. Preston was afterwards a member of the Confederate Senate and Mr. Stuart one of the commissioners appointed by Virginia to confer with Mr. Lincoln as to his attitude and action toward the seceded States.

Mr. Botts made a very powerful address before the convention, but the spirit of it did not please me. He belittled the John Brown raid, at the same time accusing Governor Wise of having done everything in his power to magnify it.   He ridiculed the Governor's military establishment and his "men in buckram," while dubbing him "The un-epauletted hero of the Ossawattomie war."   He said that old John Brown certainly did a good deal against the peace and prosperity of the commonwealth and the country, but added, "Whatever he left undone in this direction has been most effectually carried out by his executor, the late Governor of Virginia."

CHAPTER III

At the close of this, my first visit South, I turned Northward, filled with admiration and affection for the Southern
people and feeling that I had found my future home. Notwithstanding the dark shadow that impended, I little fan-
cied that I would so soon again see the fair city of my
choice and under circumstances changed so sadly. I was
young, and as I turned my back upon Virginia and the
John Brown raid, which were then the points of greatest
tension, my strained nerves relaxed, and what I had seen and
heard of evil portent faded away like a disturbing dream
when one awakes.

I found my dear ones well and the practical New Eng-
landers, at least most of them, deeply immersed in business
and finance. Like many wiser men, I felt reassured by the
comforting conviction that the material interests of this
rapidly developing country were too vast, too solid and
priceless to be shattered and sacrificed in these superficial
popular excitements.

In the quiet of the family circle we discussed my plans
and determined that I should enter the Law School of
Columbia College in the approaching fall. I do not remember where I went or what I did during the summer
vacation, but in the early autumn I came back thoroughly
quieted, rested and refreshed, went promptly to New York
City and entered with enthusiasm upon the study of my
chosen profession under that admirable teacher, Professor
Theodore W. Dwight, of Columbia.

For a time all went well. True, the ground swell of a mighty revolution was gradually rising at the South, but no one about me believed it would ever break in the angry waves of actual war, and I was not wiser than my fellows. Indeed I purposely turned my thoughts away, which for the time was not difficult to do, enamored as I was of the law.

Three or four of us, Yale graduates and classmates, were in the same boarding-house on Washington Square. Ed. Carrington, a youth of uncommon power and promise, who lost his life during the war in an obscure skirmish in Florida, like myself, was studying law, but he roomed with Joe Twichell, who was then studying theology; dear Joe, who preached the bi-centennial sermon at Yale, and is to-day, as he has always been, the most admired and best beloved man of the class of '59. My room-mate was Tom Lounsbury, then employed in literary work on one of the great encyclopedias, to-day the distinguished incumbent of the Chair of English in Yale University.

But this peace was not to last long. The election of Lincoln, the rapid secession of the Southern States, the formation of the Southern Confederacy, the inauguration of the Presidents, first of the new and then of the old federation; the adoption by the Southern States of a different and a permanent Constitution—all this tended strongly to convince thoughtful men that the two sections, or the two countries, were deeply in earnest and differed radically and irreconciliably as to the construction of the United States Constitution. Then came the strained situation in Charleston harbor, and the futile efforts of the Peace Congress called by Virginia, and later, of her commissioners and those appointed by the Confederate Government to wait upon President Lincoln.

It is unnecessary to say that, though striving hard to maintain my hold upon the law, I was yet far from an indifferent spectator of this majestic march of events. I went repeatedly to talk with two or three of the leading business men of New York, who had been friends and parishioners of my father while pastor of a church in that city, and was delighted to find them hopeful; relying not only upon the weight and influence of material and business interests to avert actual war, but also, and especially, upon the noble intervention and mediation of Virginia.

It made my heart glow to hear how these great financiers and merchant princes spoke of my adopted State. They said in effect, that it had always been so; that Virginia was undoubtedly the greatest and most influential of all the States; that she had been the nursing mother of the Union and of the country and would prove their preserver; that Virginians had really made the United States in the olden days,—Washington, Jefferson, Madison, Marshall,—and Virginians would save the United States to-day. They declared that they had always worshiped the Old Dominion, and now, more than ever, for the noble position she had assumed in this crisis.

How could I help glowing with pride and brightening with hope! Alas! the shriek of the first shell that burst over Sumter shattered these fair hopes—and pandemonium reigned in New York.

It is not within the province of this book to discuss the responsibility for that shell. I will, however, be candid enough to say that I never entertained a doubt as to the South having the best of the Constitutional argument; and yet, so strong was my love for the Union and my affection for my friends, at least nine-tenths of whom were on the Northern side, that I often felt, and more than once said, I could never strike a blow or fire a shot in the conflict, if it should come. Nevertheless, I was inexorably led in the sequel to give myself unreservedly and whole-heartedly to the defense of the South.

One link in the chain that led to this decision was the conviction that forced itself upon me that I could not remain in New York. After the firing upon Sumter the whole city was in an uproar. A wild enthusiasm for "the flag" seized and swept the entire population which surged through streets hung with banners and bunting, their own persons bedecked with small United States flags and other patriotic devices. It is not worth while to go further into these de-

tails. Enough to say that it was manifestly as uncomfortable and impracticable, at that time, for me to remain in
New York as for an able-bodied young man, of strong convictions on the Northern side of the controversy, to remain
in Richmond.

Therefore I returned to New Haven, where, with the entire family assembled, we conferred over the situation and
decided that father and his three boys must go South as soon
as possible, leaving mother and the girls to follow when the
way should be clear and we ready to receive them. As there
was no assurance of reaching our destination in safety without passports, father, who knew General Scott well, applied
to him for passes South for himself and his three boys. The
General replied, sending my father a pass, but refusing to
furnish passports for his sons, and it then became necessary
for us boys to devise some route, other than the railroads,
for reaching our Southern friends.

My next younger brother was an expert sailor, having
followed the sea for years, and was recognized as perhaps
the most daring and skilful manager of a small sailing
craft to be found about New Haven harbor, or indeed anywhere in that part of Long Island Sound. As there seemed
to be no other way to Virginia open to us, we bought a
staunch, swift sail-boat, had her carefully caulked and overhauled, and set to work to make her some extra sails which
my brother thought we might need during our voyage. We
procured a copy of a detailed survey of the coast along that
part of the Eastern Shore of Virginia where we proposed to
land, and also letters to gentlemen living along that coast.
The preparation of the boat and the working up of our expedition was a great relief, not only in giving us something
to do, but also in holding out the prospect of interesting adventure accompanied by a reasonable spice of peril.

About this time I discovered, in taking a sort of spiritual
inventory of myself, that I had passed to another and distinct stage of feeling and of purpose. I believed firmly my
people in the South were right; I knew well they were weak;
I saw clearly they were about to be invaded; and I was striving to get to them. To what end? With what purpose? To

give them another mouth to feed, or to give them another man to fight? Right, weakness, invasion!—how could there be any save one inference from such a trinity of propositions? I did not fully realize this process as it was wrought out in me; but when I came to find my scruples and my shrinking gone—though not my sorrow—I looked back and plainly saw the path along which I had been led. From that hour, throughout the four years of my service as a Confederate soldier, never did I entertain a doubt as to my being where I should be and doing what I should do.

While our boat was making ready for the trip, some one called at the house and asked for me, but sent no card, so I went to the reception-room, having no idea who my visitor was.

"Why, Beers!" I cried, "what are you doing here?" He was very pale, and had evidently been subjected to severe mental and moral tension—nevertheless, Yankee-like, he answered my question by asking another, "What are you going to do?" "O," said I, "we are going South by sail-boat; General Scott won't let us go by railroad." Instantly he replied, "I am going with you."

Who was the man who thus, without hesitation, reservation or condition, cast in his lot with us?

The story is in every way so remarkable that I cannot forbear a full recital of it. It should not be forgotten, however, that while the peace of death has, years agone, passed upon the chief actor in this strange, sad drama, and probably also upon most of his relatives living when he died —there may yet be others now living to whom the record of his life and death must needs be somewhat painful; therefore I shall endeavor to tell the story simply and quietly.

When I first knew James H. Beers he was an intelligent young mechanic—originally, I think, from Bridgeport, Conn., but at the time living in New Haven, where I was a college student. We were both members of a Bible-class connected with a church of which my father was then pastor, and Mr. Gerard Hallock, of the New York *Journal of Commerce*, the most prominent member.

Soon after my first acquaintance with Beers, Mr. Hallock became interested in him, attracted by his regular attendance at church and Bible-class, and his modest yet self-respectful and intelligent bearing, and he took him to New York in some subordinate capacity connected with his paper. This was a few years before the war, but Beers continued to visit New Haven often, perhaps regularly. We heard from time to time that he had exhibited unusual facility for journalism and had been rapidly advanced, until he had come to be an assistant to the night editor of Mr. Hallock's great paper. It was probably through his connection with the leading Democratic daily that he imbibed the views he held as to the construction of the Federal Constitution and the relations between the Federal Government and the States; views which he followed to their logical conclusion and in defense of which he ultimately laid down his life.

As the sectional excitement increased and civil war became more and more imminent, Beers grew more and more restless and unhappy, until actual hostilities began with the bombardment of Sumter, when he informed Mr. Hallock that it would be impossible for him to continue to discharge his duties upon the paper. Thereupon he left New York and appeared in New Haven, as above described.

When he announced his determination of going with us I discouraged it, reminding him that he was a Northern man and had, besides, a wife and two little girls to provide for; mentioning also his fine position and prospects, all of which would necessarily be sacrificed. He replied that he had some money which he would leave with our mother, trusting her to use it for his wife and children and to bring them South when she came; adding that God never gave a man a wife and children to stand in the way of the discharge of his plain duty, and that it was plainly his duty to go with us and aid the South in defense of her clear and clearly-violated rights.

I cut the matter short by referring him to my father, and he at once went to his room and saw him. Father afterwards told me it was obvious that Mr. Beers' mind was irrevocably made up and that it would be worse than useless to resist him further; so it was settled he was to go with us. I do not remember whether his wife and children were then in New Haven, but they were committed by him to the care of our mother and sisters, and later followed Beers to Virginia, as I now recollect, in company with the ladies of our family.

Everything was arranged and we were to embark and sail on a certain night, but during the preceding day a telegram was received from a friend who was standing guard for us in Washington, which by a sort of prearranged cipher we understood to mean that we could slip through safely if we left New York by a certain train the next day. My recollection is that it was deemed best to divide the party,—Beers, my next younger brother, and I getting off so as to catch the train indicated; father and my youngest brother, then below fighting age, following later.

We reached Washington and got safely across the river and to our destination, but, by some untoward accident, Beers was left behind and experienced some difficulty in dodging the provost guard and completing the last stage of his "on to Richmond." We were very uneasy, met every train from the North, and were unspeakably relieved when he arrived. We had told his story to our friends and he was welcomed into the same hospitable family circle which was entertaining us. The city was crowded with people, but the sons of Virginia were flocking home to her defense and every heart and every door was open to receive them.

A day or two after his arrival a most unpleasant experience befell poor Beers. Walking by himself in the street, he was arrested as a spy and locked up in the negro jail. For hours we were unable to ascertain what had become of him, and when we did find out it was too late to procure his release on *habeas corpus;* so with profound mortification and profuse apologies we had to content ourselves with doing what we could to make him comfortable where he was, he protesting that he needed nothing and could suffer no real inconvenience that one night. Indeed, noble fellow that he was, he met me with a manly smile at the door of his cell, expressing mingled amusement and approbation; saying that while the charge of his being a spy was a little wide of the mark, yet the mistake was a very natural one, that there were doubtless numbers of such characters about, and he was glad to see that we were on the alert for them.

Next morning when his case was called in the Mayor's Court something of the truth with regard to him had gotten abroad and the court-room was crowded with the first gentlemen of Richmond. I was the main witness, and it goes without saying that the dramatic points of Beers' strange story, especially those that would most commend him to the Southern people, lost nothing in the telling. He was not only honorably discharged, but he was vociferously cheered by the entire audience, and he walked out of the court-room the idol of the hour—the rest of the last rebel reinforcement from the North shining somewhat in his reflected light. Thus, to our great relief, the awkward contretemps of his arrest contributed rather to the reputation and advantage of our friend.

I recall this additional incident: Mr. John Randolph Tucker—"Ran. Tucker"—then Attorney-General of Virginia, was an intimate friend of my father, who had now arrived in Richmond, and suggested to him that Mr. Beers and I, as we were citizens of the State of Connecticut where I had recently cast my first vote, were in rather an exceptional position, as bearing upon a possible charge of treason, in case we should enlist in the military service. The suggestion was deemed of sufficient importance to refer to Mr. Benjamin, then Attorney-General of the Confederate States, and Mr. Tucker and I interviewed him about it. These two great lawyers concurred in the view that the principles which protected citizens of the Southern and seceded States were, to say the least, of doubtful application to us, and that it would probably go rather hard with us if we should be captured. Notwithstanding, I enlisted, and Beers would probably have done so with equal promptness had he not been an expert mechanic—men so qualified being then very scarce in Richmond and very much needed. He was asked to assist in changing some old flintlocks belonging to the State of Virginia into percussion muskets, and all of us insisting that he could thus render far more valuable service than by enlisting in the ranks, he reluctantly yielded and went to work.

How long he was thus employed I do not know. My youngest brother went on to our relatives in Georgia, but soon after his arrival there insisted upon enlisting in one of the battalions for coast defense. My sailor brother and I enlisted in Richmond and joined the army at Manassas. I saw but little of Beers after this. Just when he entered the army I cannot say, but it must have been some time before the battles around Richmond in the early summer of 1862; for on the battle field of Malvern Hill I met some of the men of the "Letcher Artillery," to which he belonged, who told me that my "Yankee" was the finest gunner in the battery and fought like a Turk. Between Malvern Hill and Chancellorsville I saw Beers perhaps two or three times—I think once in Richmond, after his wife and children and my mother and sisters arrived from the North.

I have seldom seen a better-looking soldier. He was about five feet eleven inches in height, had fine shoulders, chest and limbs, carried his head high, had clustering brown hair, a steel-gray eye and a splendid sweeping moustache. Every now and then I heard from some man or officer of his battery, or of Pegram's Battalion, some special praise of his gallantry in action, but as he was in A. P. Hill's command and I then in Longstreet's, we seldom met. I am confident there is no battle-scarred veteran of Pegram's Battalion living to-day but stands ready to vouch for Beers as the equal of any soldier in the command, and some of them tenderly recall him as a good and true soldier of Jesus Christ as well as of Robert Lee. He was in the habit of holding religious services with the men of his battalion on every fitting occasion—services which they highly appreciated.

Just after the battle of Chancellorsville I was in Richmond, having recently received an appointment in "engineer troops." I am unable to recall the details, but I was notified to meet poor Beers' body at the train. Colonel, afterwards General, R. L. Walker (Lindsay Walker), commanding A. P. Hill's artillery, hearing that Beers had been killed on the 3d of May and buried upon the field, had the body exhumed and sent to me at Richmond.

It is strange how everything connected with the burial, except the sad scene at the grave, seems to have faded out of my recollection. I know he was buried in our family lot in Hollywood, and as no one of us was buried there for long years after this, we must have bought the lot for the purpose. I remember, too, that we laid him to rest with military honors, Captain Gay's company, the "Virginia State Guard," acting as escort; and I must have ridden in the carriage with the stricken widow and his two little girls, for I distinctly recall standing between the children at the side of the open grave and holding a hand of each as the body of their hero-father was lowered to its last resting place. I remember, too, that not a muscle of their pale, sweet faces quivered as the three volleys were fired over the low mound that covered him. They were the daughters of a soldier.

There stands to-day over the grave a simple granite marker bearing this inscription:

JAMES H. BEERS,
of Connecticut,
Who Fell at Chancellorsville,
Fighting for Virginia and the South,
May 3, 1863.

My story is done, and I feel that it is worthy of recital and remembrance. Indeed it embodies the most impressive instance I have ever known of trenchant, independent thought and uncalculating, unflinching obedience to the resulting conviction of duty—"obedience unto death."

Observe, Beers had never been South and had no idea of ever going there until the Southern States were invaded. Observe again, he was not a man without ties, a homeless and heartless adventurer; but a complete man—a man blessed with wife and children and home, and withal a faithful and affectionate husband and father. Observe once more, he was not an unsuccessful or disappointed man. On the contrary, I have seldom known a man who had a position more perfectly congenial and satisfactory to him or whose prospects were brighter or more assured. It was simply and purely his conviction of right and of duty which led him to us and to his brave death.

One feature of the poor fellow's story, of intense color, has been purposely omitted. I refer to his parting with his parents. It is my strong desire that this sketch shall not contain one word calculated to bring unnecessary pain to the heart of any relative of my dear friend under whose eye it may chance to fall. If being a Southerner you would pass just and charitable judgment upon his family, try for a moment to conceive what would have been the feelings of a Southern father and mother and family circle toward a son and brother who, in 1861, had proposed to go North for the purpose of fighting against his people and his State.

My recollection is that Mrs. Beers did not long survive her husband. It gives me pleasure to say that, so far as I know, the family of Mr. Beers did their duty by his children. I tried to have the little girls adopted in the South, and came very near succeeding, yet perhaps it was, after all, well that their friends sent for them and that they finally returned to the North.

It is well, too, that there are not more men like Beers in the world. The bands of organized society are not strong enough to endure many such. They are too trenchant, too independent, to be normal or safe. It is well that most of us believe and think and feel and act with the mass of our fellow-beings about us. If it were not so, quiet and harmonious society would be impossible; it would dissolve and perish in fierce internecine strife. And yet, when every now and then God turns out a man of different mould, a man brave enough and strong enough not to be dominated in opinion, in conscience, or in action by his associates—we ordinary men, of average human stature and strength, realize how almost pitifully small and weak we are.

The mound that covers James H. Beers is indeed low and humble, yet where will you dig in earth's surface to find richer dust? I rejoice that he lies where he does, hard by my dear ones and where my own body will soon rest, so that when the resurrection trump shall call us all forth, after running over the roll of my beloved and finding them "all present or accounted for," I can turn my eyes to the right and greet the hero whose sacred dust I have guarded all these years.

CHAPTER IV

FROM CIVIL TO MILITARY LIFE

Off for Manassas—First Glimpse of an Army and a Battle-field—The
Richmond Howitzers—Intellectual Atmosphere of the Camp—Essential Spirit of the Southern Volunteer.

The exact dates of the personal movements and experiences thus far narrated cannot be determined. This is
largely due to a habit of destroying family letters, and this
to a weak dread of opening them, or even of looking upon
them, after the lapse of years.

Up to this point the lack of such letters has signified
little. It can make little difference just when I left New
York for New Haven, or when we left New Haven for
Richmond, or Richmond for Manassas. This book is not
intended to be a rigid record of the daily succession and the
precise dates of camp and march and battle; and yet there
is no gainsaying the almost inestimable value of letters to
a book of reminiscence, furnishing contemporaneous record
and comment so much more vivid and accurate than memory. In the absence of these I shall have to rest largely, for
the elements of time and date, upon the relation of what I
may record to the general movement of the campaigns,
which will, for the most part, prove sufficient for my purpose. For example, I know that Beers' funeral was just
after the battle of Chancellorsville, May 3, 1863; that we arrived in Richmond a short time before the battle of Bethel,
June 10, 1861; that we left Richmond almost immediately
after the battle of Manassas, July 21, 1861.

It was not our fault that we did not leave earlier. My
brother and I had volunteered in an infantry company called
after a favorite corps which had left the city for the front,
"Junior Company F," which was being drilled in awkward

squads in a large basement room under the Spotswood
Hotel. We felt that the Juniors were hanging fire too long.
The city was crowded with troops from all over Virginia
and the South, pressing to the front, and with swarms of
gaily dressed staff officers and military attachés and hang-
ers-on, and we longed to be away, out of this martial show,
and off to the real front. We grew daily more restless, especially after the affair at Bethel—sometimes spoken of as
"Big Bethel," "Great Bethel," or "Bethel Church." The
main armies were facing each other in central Virginia, and
as day after day and week after week passed, we began to
feel that it would be a personal reflection upon us if another
fight should occur without our being in it.

Suddenly the great battles of Manassas shocked the city
and shook the continent, and we could stand it no longer. As
I remember, it was but a day or two after the main fight of
July 21 that my brother and I met two soldiers of the First
Company, Richmond Howitzers, who were in the city on
business for the company, and were to return next day. So
without saying "by your leave" to any one, we boarded the
cars next morning with these men. They undertook to
conceal us on the train till it started and to secure our en-
rollment in the company when we arrived—undertakings
skilfully and faithfully performed.

The ride to Manassas was certainly not a reassuring experience. The train was crowded almost to suffocation with
troops from a far Southern State. They had been long on
the way and were worn with travel in the heat of summer.
Some of the men were sleepy and sprawling, others restless
and noisy, and both men and cars were very dirty. It was a
tedious trip, but it ended at last, and we were glad to make
our escape. As we stepped from the train we were met by
two or three more of the Howitzers, to one of whom was
committed the duty of piloting us to the camp of the battery.

We were very much struck with our guide. Scarcely
more than a half-formed country lad, he was yet a fellow of
genuine, transparent nature, healthy and hearty and strong
in body and mind; one of the sturdiest, manliest figures and

faces I ever looked upon. He seemed to be exceptionally right-minded, broad-minded, and intelligent, was evidently glad to see us and "to tell us all about it"—the army and the battle and the service, as he saw them—and we heard much from him during our brief walk of just what we wanted to know.

Such he was then. For the next four years he was the equal of any soldier in that incomparable army. To-day, thank God! he still lives, is perhaps the best beloved and most trusted friend I have on earth, one of the best citizens and farmers in Virginia—a man whom everybody knows and trusts and looks up to and leans upon.

At last we were in "the army;" and what was it after all? We walked perhaps a mile or more through the camps, and the prominent ideas borne in upon me were—multitude, overloading, lack of cohesion and of organization, absence of women and children, and a general sense of roughness and untidiness, of discomfort and confusion. Of course these impressions were soon to give way to others; but it was not alone my impressions that changed, it was the army itself. During the few months next ensuing it dispensed with useless baggage and equipment, acquired cohesion, organization, power and endurance, and men learned to do fairly well for themselves what women had theretofore invariably done for them. Under the discipline of the next twelve months, imperfect as it was, we trained down and trained up, just as the fighting men do, to a condition of bare, hard flesh; compact yet supple muscles; clean, clear lungs; sound, strong hearts; and perfect possession and control of all our fighting powers.

In connection with this process of training down to fighting weight, it occurs to me that the wagon train of the First Company, Richmond Howitzers, during the first nine months of the war was, I verily believe, quite as large as that of any infantry brigade in the army during the grand campaign of '64. Many of the private soldiers of the company had their trunks with them, and I remember part of the contents of one of them consisted of a dozen face and a smaller number of foot or bath towels; and when the order came for trunks to be sent back to Richmond or abandoned, the owner of this elaborate outfit, although but a "high private in the rear rank," actually wrote and sent in to the captain an elegant note resigning his "position." Yet this curled and scented gentleman became a superb soldier and used to laugh as heartily as any of us when, in after years, at some point of unusual want and stringency and discomfort, some impudent rascal would shout out, "Jim, old fellow, don't you think it's about time for you to resign again?"

As to the battle-field, if it showed marked traces of the conflict that had taken place I do not recall them. One scene and incident, however, I do recall, which made a very tender impression upon me. Not long after our arrival the battery was about to change its position, indeed I think the head of the column was already in motion, when some one said to me, "Captain ——— is lying in that house over yonder seriously, or it may be mortally, wounded; don't you want to go and see him a moment?" I did not want to go, but I knew the poor fellow's sisters and felt as if I ought to go, and I went. Few interviews have ever made deeper impression upon me. The heroic Christian man had been a prominent member of the Richmond bar and the mainstay and support of his sisters. He was now lying seriously wounded, in a deserted house, from which, as I remember, even the doors and windows had been carried off, and in which there seemed to be little or no furniture save the bed he occupied. The attendant who took care of him was not at the moment in the building. My comrade and I entered and I walked to the bedside, made myself known to the Captain and told him that I had seen his sisters within a day or two and that they were well, but very anxious about him. He did not seem to be suffering greatly at the time, but was evidently death-struck and I think fully aware of it. Yet there was no shrinking and no tremor. His voice was firm and clear and he was entirely self-possessed. I took his hand, or he took mine, and my recollection is that my comrade and I knelt by the bedside and we all prayed together for a few moments, and then we left him there in that desolate place to meet the last enemy; but I felt, and I am sure he did, that he would not meet him alone.

I had helped to take wounded men from the trains in Richmond, but they were surrounded by relatives and friends, or by admiring, almost worshiping crowds, and the entire city, with all it contained of sympathy and help, was at their feet. Here, however, was an entirely different picture, and for a long time my mind every now and then reverted to it with a sadness I could not dispel.

The intellectual atmosphere of the Confederate camps was far above what is generally supposed by the people of this generation, even in the Southern States, and this intellectual aspiration and vigor of the men were exhibited perhaps equally in their religious meetings and services and in their dramatic representations and other exhibitions gotten up to relieve the tedium of camp. But however this may be in general it cannot be denied that the case of the Richmond Howitzers was exceptional in this regard. The corps was organized at the time of the John Brown raid by George W. Randolph, afterwards Secretary of War, and has never been disbanded. In 1861 it was recruited up to three companies and formed into a battalion, but unfortunately the first company was never associated with the other two in the field. The composition of the three companies was very similar; that is, all of them were made up largely of young business men and clerks of the highest grade and best character from the city of Richmond, but included also a number of country boys, for the most part of excellent families, with a very considerable infusion of college-bred men, for it was strikingly true that in 1861 the flower of our educated youth gravitated toward the artillery. The outcome was something quite unparalleled, so far as I know. It is safe to say that not less than one hundred men were commissioned from the corps during the war, and these of every rank from a Secretary of War down to a second lieutenant.

Few things have ever impressed me as did the intellectual and moral character of the men who composed the circle I entered the day our guide led my brother and myself to the Howitzer camp. I had lived for years at the North, had graduated recently at Yale, and had but just entered upon the study of law in the city of New York when the war began. Thus torn away by the inexorable demands of conscience and of loyalty to the South, from a focal point of intense intellectual life and purpose, one of my keenest regrets was that I was bidding a long good-by to congenial surroundings and companionships. To my surprise and delight, around the camp fires of the First Company, Richmond Howitzers, I found throbbing an intellectual life as high and brilliant and intense as any I had ever known.

The Howitzer Glee Club, trained and led by Frederick Nicholls Crouch, author of "Kathleen Mavoureen," was the very best I ever heard, and rendered music at once scientific and enjoyable. No law school in the land ever had more brilliant or powerful moot court discussions than graced the mock trials of the Howitzer Law Club. I have known the burial of a tame crow to be witnessed not only by the entire command, but by scores, perhaps hundreds, of intelligent people from a neighboring town, and to be dignified not only by salvos of artillery, but also by an English speech, a Latin oration, and a Greek ode, which would have done honor to any literary or memorial occasion at old Yale.

There was a private soldier in the battery—not the poet of the crow's death either—a Grecian of such finished skill that I have known him keep, for months together, a diary of the movements of the battery, in modern Greek; and have watched him—wondering if there was anywhere to be found another man of scholarship and scholarly enthusiasm so great—as he dodged the persistently pursuing smoke of a camp fire and by its wretched, flickering light, with painstaking care, jotted down his exquisite, clear Greek lettering that looked like the most perfect output of the most perfect Greek press in Germany. So much for the intellectual life of our camp and march.

What now of the essential spirit of these young volunteers? Why did they volunteer? For what did they give their lives? We can never appreciate the story of their deeds as soldiers until we answer this question correctly.

Surely it was not for slavery they fought. The great majority of them had never owned a slave and had little or no interest in the institution. My own father, for example, had freed his slaves long years before; that is, all save one, who would not be "emancipated," our dear "Mammy," who clung to us when we moved to the North and never recognized any change in her condition or her relations to us. The great conflict will never be properly comprehended by the man who looks upon it as a war for the preservation of slavery.

Nor was it, so far as Virginia was concerned, a war in support of the right of secession or the Southern interpretation of the Constitution. Virginia did not favor this interpretation; at least, she did not favor the exercise of the right of secession. Up to President Lincoln's call for troops she refused to secede. She changed her position under the distinct threat of *invasion*. This was the turning point. The Whig party, the anti-secession party of Virginia, became the war party of Virginia upon this issue. As John B. Baldwin, the great Whig and Union leader, said, speaking of the effect of Lincoln's call for troops, "We have no Union men in Virginia now." The change of front was instantaneous, it was intuitive. Jubal Early was the type of his party—up to the proclamation, the most extreme anti-secessionist and anti-war man in the Virginia Convention; after the proclamation, the most enthusiastic man in the Commonwealth in advocacy of the war and personal service in it.

But coming closer down, let us see how the logic of these events wrought itself out among my comrades of the Howitzer Company. We will take as a type in this instance the case of a brilliantly endowed youth of excellent family in Richmond, who, like the guide who piloted us to the battery upon the field of Manassas, became one of my closest and dearest friends, but unlike him and most unhappily for his family and his comrades, sealed his fate and his devotion with his life at Gettysburg.

He was a student at the University of Virginia in the spring of '61, and perhaps the most extreme and uncompromising "Union man" among all the young men gathered there. Indeed, so exaggerated were his anti-secession views and so bold and aggressive was he in advocacy of them, that he became very unpopular, and his friends feared serious trouble and even bloody collision. The morning President Lincoln's proclamation appeared he had gone down town on personal business before breakfast, and while there happened to glance at a paper. He returned at once to the University, but not to breakfast; spoke not a word to any human being, packed his trunk with his belongings, left a note for the chairman of the faculty explaining his conduct, boarded the first train for Richmond and joined a military company, before going to his father's house or taking so much as a morsel of food.

What was the overwhelming force which thus in a moment transformed this splendid youth? Was it not the God-implanted instinct which impels a man to *defend his own hearth-stone?*

There were 896 students at Harvard in 1861, there were 604 at the University of Virginia. Why was it that but 73 out of the 896 joined the first army that invaded the South, while largely over half of the 604 volunteered to meet the invaders? It was manifestly this instinct of defense of home which gave to the Confederate service, from '61 to '65, more than 2,000 men of our University, of whom it buried in soldiers' graves more than 400; while but 1,040 Harvard men served in the armies and navies of the United States during the four years of the war, and of these only 155 lost their lives in the service.*

Here, then, we have the essential, the distinctive spirit of the Southern volunteer. As he hastened to the front in the spring of '61, he felt: "With me is Right, before me is Duty, *behind me is Home."*

---

*Figures taken from catalogues of the two institutions, for 1860-61. Prof. Schele's Historical Catalogue of Students of the University of Virginia, a careful statement by Prof. (Col.) Charles S. Venable of the same institution; and Francis H. Brown's "Roll of Students of Harvard University Who Served in the Army or Navy of the United States During the War of the Rebellion," prepared by order of the Corporation.

CHAPTER V

Inadequacy of General Equipment—Formation During First Two Years
—High Character of Men Accounted For—An Extraordinary Story.

The writer having served almost exclusively with the artillery, what he has to tell must necessarily refer largely to that arm. Some general observations upon field artillery in the Army of Northern Virginia will therefore not be out of place.

With the exception of a couple of long-range Whitworth guns, run in from England through the blockade and which I never saw, the artillery of General Lee's army consisted of old-fashioned muzzle-loading pieces, for the most part 12-pounder brass Napoleons and 3-inch rifles. Batteries were usually composed of four guns. For the equipment and operation of such a battery about seventy-five officers and men were required and say fifty horses. Every old artilleryman will recall the difficulty we experienced in keeping up the supply of horses. After Gettysburg it was our habit, when a piece became engaged, to send the horses to the rear, to some place of safety, preferring to run the risk of losing a gun occasionally rather than the team that pulled it.

During the earlier stages of the war our artillery corps was very inadequately provided with clumsy ordnance and defective ammunition, manufactured for the most part within the Confederate lines; but as the struggle went on this branch of our service, as well as our infantry, was, to a constantly increasing degree, supplied with improved guns and ammunition captured from the armies opposed to us. We also learned to make better ammunition and more reliable fuses, but never approached the Federal artillery either in these respects or in general equipment.

For the first two years the armies of the Confederacy adhered to that very defective organization in which single batteries of artillery are attached to infantry brigades. Two evils resulted: the guns were under the command of brigadier-generals of infantry, who generally had very little regard for artillery and still less knowledge as to the proper handling of it; and the scattering of the batteries prevented that concentration of fire in which, upon proper occasion, consists the great effectiveness of the arm. At and after Chancellorsville, however, the artillery of the Confederate armies, certainly that of the Army of Northern Virginia, began to be massed into battalions composed of, say, four or five batteries and fifteen to twenty-five guns, and these placed under the command of trained and experienced artillery officers. From that time the artillery began to be really reckoned and relied upon in estimating the effective strength of the army.

So much for the physical aspect of the artillery of General Lee's army. A word now as to the character of the men who composed that corps. It will of course be admitted by every man of intelligence and candor who served under Lee, that his infantry was essentially his army; not alone because it constituted the bulk and body of its fighting strength, but also because it did the bulk and body of the fighting; and yet I think even the infantry itself would admit that the artillery, though appearing to afford least opportunity for personal distinction, yet furnished, in proportion to its numbers, perhaps more officers below the rank of general who were conspicuous for gallantry and high soldiership than either of the other two arms. Their names rise unbidden to my lips—Pegram and Pelham, and Breathed and Carter, and Haskell, and many, many more. Every veteran of the Army of Northern Virginia is familiar with the splendid roll.

If this claim be challenged, it may perhaps best be tested by asking this question: admitting that the fact be so, *can any satisfactory explanation of it be suggested?*

For one, I answer unhesitatingly—yes, I think so; explanation amounting to demonstration. I believe that any man

who looks into the matter without prejudice will be ready
to admit that it is to be expected that artillery soldiers
should excel in four great soldierly qualities—*intelligence,
self-possession, comradeship, loyalty to the gun.*

I will not stay now to prove that these qualities characterized our artillery in an eminent degree. The remaining
chapters of this book will furnish abundant demonstration.
As to *intelligence,* the chapter last preceding would seem to
be all-sufficient; but apart from these positive exhibitions of
intelligence and even culture of a high order, it is obvious
that the very nature of the arm and its operation, its comparative mechanical elaboration and complexity, and the
blending of scientific knowledge and manual and bodily dex-
terity required for its most effective use, must in large degree influence the original selection and the after development of the men of the artillery branch of the service.

Again, an artilleryman, officer or private soldier, should
be a broader-gauged man, especially as to his view and
comprehension of battle and campaign, than an infantryman of corresponding grade. An infantry company in the
Army of Northern Virginia, during the latter part of the
war, averaged certainly not over fifteen or twenty men,
and covered but a small space on the line. A captain of
infantry saw and touched little outside these narrow limits.
Two or three strides, so to speak, would cover all of the
line he was familiar with and responsible for, and he came
in contact with no officer of wider domain and control, save
his colonel, under whose eye and immediate direction he was
always, save when on picket duty.

A captain of artillery, on the contrary, was often separated from his colonel by the stretch of several brigade
fronts; for a battalion, as usually placed, would cover about
the front of a division, and as he received no orders—after
the organization of the artillery into battalions—from any
infantry officer of less rank than a major-general, he was
necessarily thrown in great measure upon his own resources
in the management of a command which, including all its
departments, was really of greater complexity and difficulty
than an infantry brigade.

I trust I may not be misunderstood, or regarded as attempting to magnify over-much myself or my office, when I say that all this applies with special force to the adjutant of an artillery battalion.   This officer,—if he does his full duty,—as adjutant of the command, as personal staff and aide to the commanding officer, and often as battalion chief of the line of caissons—familiarizing himself with the positions of all the guns in battle, seeing that all are fully supplied with ammunition and anything and everything else that may be required, and passing from one to another as the exigencies of the fight may demand—covers as wide a stretch of the line, sees as much of the campaign, and comes as much into contact with officers of high grade as any officer of his rank in the service.   To-day, more than a generation after that heroic Olympiad, it is a deep satisfaction to be able to say that I endeavored to do my full duty as adjutant of Cabell's Battalion—to attend to all my duties in this broader and fuller construction of them, and in battle, as far as possible, to be with that one of our batteries which was most heavily engaged.   The campaign of 1864 was the only one in which I acted as adjutant of an artillery battalion from the outset to the end, and in consequence my knowledge of that campaign is at once more comprehensive and more detailed than of any other, and what I have to tell of it is of greater value.

The training of the artillery service in the development of imperturbable *self-possession,* in emergency and crisis, is self-evident and requires no comment.   To appreciate it to the full, it was only necessary to look at one of our guns, already overmatched, at the moment when a fresh gun of the enemy, rushing up at a wild gallop, and seizing a nearer and enfilading position, hurled a percussion shell, crashing with fearful uproar against our piece, and sweeping almost the entire gun detachment to the earth.   At such a moment I have marked the sergeant or gunner of such a piece coolly disengage himself from the wreck and, stepping to one side, stoop to take his observations and make his calculations, of distance and of time, free from the dust and smoke of the explosion; then, with ringing voice, call out to No. 6

at the limber,—whose duty it was to cut the fuse,—"three seconds!" then, stepping back and bending over the trail handspike, doggedly aim his strained and half-disabled piece, as the undisabled remnant of the detachment step over the dead and dying bodies of their comrades, each in the discharge of the doubled and trebled duties now devolving upon him. The story I have to tell is full of kindred scenes.

Another of the most marked and developing features of the artillery service is *comradeship*.

I do not mean that lighter sense of happy and kindly association which certainly did characterize the artillery, of General Lee's army at least, in very high degree. I refer now to an element far deeper and more powerful—the *interdependence,* the reliance upon each other, which inheres in the very nature of artillery service, and is indispensable of the effective working of the gun.

The unit of the infantry is the man; of the cavalry, the man and horse; of the artillery, the detachment. While co-operation is a duty and in some degree a necessity in infantry service, yet a single infantry soldier operates his arm perfectly, indeed each one is complete in himself—more than one cannot operate the same arm at the same time. If one runs away he only renders himself useless, he deprives his country of his services alone.

No so with the artillery. It takes ten cannoneers (exclusive of drivers) to make a gun detachment. Each man has his special part to perform, but all indispensable to the perfect working of the piece, so that each man is dependent upon all the rest. If one fails, all the rest are affected, and even the piece itself is rendered so far inefficient. Upon each man rests the responsibility for the effective service of the detachment and the gun.

It is impossible not to perceive this distinction, and equally impossible not to admit the importance of it, in the development of a soldierly character. Again, I say, my story will not fail to furnish apt and impressive illustration.

But the strongest sentiment, aye, passion, of the true artillerymen is *loyalty to the gun.*

The gun is the rallying point of the detachment, its point of honor, its flag, its banner. It is that to which the men look, by which they stand, with and for which they fight, by and for which they fall. As long as the gun is theirs, they are unconquered, victorious; when the gun is lost, all is lost. It is their religion to fight it until the enemy is out of range, or until the gun itself is withdrawn, or until both it and the detachment are in the hands of the foe. An infantryman in flight often flings away his musket. I do not recall ever having heard of a Confederate artillery detachment abandoning its gun without orders.

Nor were the Federal artillerymen one whit behind in this loyal devotion to their pieces. One of the Haskells, who, as I remember, served on General McGowan's staff, told me this vivid story. It seems almost incredible, yet I have no reason to question its truth; at all events, it is too good not to be told.

In one of the late combats of the war, far away down on the right of our line, Pegram, passing ahead of his infantry support, had advanced his entire battalion against the enemy strongly entrenched—showering double-shotted canister into their infantry line and belching solid shot across the narrow ditch, in the very faces of their gunners and into the very muzzles of their guns. The Federal artillerymen, as was their wont, fought him fiercely, muzzle to muzzle—until McGowan's infantry coming up, Pegram passed around the work, to the right and front, after the retiring Federal infantry, while the artillerymen and their pieces fell into McGowan's hands.

Most of the horses of the staff had been killed or disabled, and they had mounted Federal artillery horses from which in some cases the harness had not been removed, so that, as the staff officers rode to and fro delivering orders, the trace chains rattled and jingled merrily.

The Federal gunners had done what they could on the instant to disable their pieces for the time, throwing away the lanyards and running the screws down low, so that the muzzles pointed high in the air. Having rooted out a few friction primers from a gunner's haversack and fished a

string or a handkerchief out of someone's pocket, for a lanyard, McGowan's infantry managed to load one of the captured pieces and, turning it in the direction of the retreating
Federals, sent two or three shots whizzing over their heads,
to seek the quartermasters and wagon camps in the rear.

Meanwhile, the gunner of this particular piece, a tall,
splendid-looking fellow, stood hard by, with his lip curled in
scorn and his arms twitching convulsively; until at last,
unable to stand it longer, he sprang into the midst of the
blundering infantry and hurled them right and left, shouting:

"Stand aside, you infernal, awkward boobies! Let me at
that screw!" meanwhile whirling it rapidly up, until the gun
came down into proper range. Then, seizing the trail hand-
spike and aiming the piece, he sprang back, yelling out:
"Now, try that! Let 'em have it! Fire!"

Away flew the shell on its flight of death, until it tore
through the line of his own friends. And he continued thus
to direct the movement of the awkward squad of rebel cannoneers, and to sight and fire the piece, until the Federal infantry were out of range. Then, stamping his great foot
upon the ground and gesturing wildly with his great clenched fist, he exclaimed:

"Damned if I can stand by and see my gun do such shooting as that!"

CHAPTER VI

March and Counter-march—Longstreet and Prince Napoleon—Leesburg —The Battle—The Mississippians—D. H. Hill—Fort Johnston.

During the first few days of wild hurrah, uncertainty, and drift which followed our victory at Manassas, the guns of our battery were marched and counter-marched on scouting expeditions, first with one brigade and then with another. Our most noteworthy experience was with Longstreet's, then known as the "Fourth Brigade," in connection with which we were reviewed by Prince Napoleon at Centreville. The Prince did not strike me as an impressive man, but I recall the ease and confidence with which Longstreet handled both his artillery and infantry commands in the various maneuvers, and the riding of one of the young officers of his staff, who sat his beautiful thoroughbred superbly, dashing at full speed from point to point, leaping ditches and obstructions without being once jarred in his seat, though using a flat English saddle and that *without stirrups*. I remember, too, that it was so hot on the sun-scorched plain that the metal-covered tops of the ammunition chests actually burned us cannoneers, as we mounted and dismounted at command, in the battery drill.

The generals in the ranks, of whom there was, even at this early stage, an abundant supply, being still of the opinion that we ought to be and soon would be ordered to occupy Washington, regarded these several movements as in execution of or preparation for that grand objective—an objective which our commanding generals, for reasons doubtless satisfactory to themselves, seem to have soon given up—if indeed they ever seriously contemplated it. Within a short time all idea of a general offensive seeming to have been abandoned, even by the staff contingent in the ranks, we were, on the 11th of August, '61, ordered to Leesburg, under Brigadier-General N. G. Evans, of South Carolina, whose force consisted of the Thirteenth, Seventeenth and Eighteenth Mississippi Regiments, the Eighth Virginia Infantry, our battery, and two companies of cavalry.

Leesburg, the county seat of Loudoun, was at this time, perhaps, the most desirable post in our lines, on account of the character both of the country and its people—the former beautiful and rich, full of everything needed by man and beast, and the latter whole-hearted and hospitable, ready to share with us all they had. If ever soldiers had a more ideal time than we enjoyed at Leesburg, then I cannot conceive when or where it was. During the war, in hunger and thirst, in want and weariness and blood, our thoughts would often turn fondly back to our bucolic Loudoun paradise. "When this cruel war was over" more than one of our boys went back there to get "the girl he left behind him" from '61 to '65, but would never leave again; and to-day many a grizzled, wrinkled, burdened man feels his heart grow young again and breaks into sunny smiles when a comrade of the long ago slaps him on the back and reminds him of the good times we had at Leesburg. It was here we buried the crow, with honors literary and military; nor was this by any means the only camp entertainment with which we returned the many civilities extended to us by our fair friends in the good little burg.

Of course, where there were so many brave knights all could not always succeed with the fair ladies. One of the defeated took this startling and original revenge upon his successful rival. "The captain with his whiskers" had repeatedly run him off from a new-found Dulcinea, and this same result happening once more, our hero returned to camp weary and disgusted and threw himself down to sleep. Owing to some abnormal condition of mind or body, he was at the time much given to talking in his sleep and, dreaming himself on guard and inquiry made as to the commanding officer of the force, he electrified his half-slumbering companions by shouting out:

"Halt! You want to know who commands this battery, do you? Well, sir, General Susceptibility commands this battery, with a numerous staff of volunteer aides!"

Poor fellow; but he was soon promoted to a captaincy and commanded a battery of his own, and doubtless avenged his grievous wrongs by perpetrating the like on his own boys upon occasion. Very recently he received his last promotion, having fought a good fight for many years as a faithful Christian minister.

We saw no really hard service at Leesburg, though the activity of the force gradually increased. Our horses being in fine condition with the abundant forage, and the great, open fields affording a fine arena for it, we devoted ourselves assiduously to battery drill. There was also considerable scouting up and down the river and some little firing across. One of our own men was wounded in one of these affairs and one or two cavalrymen killed.

About the middle of October, however, General Evans withdrew his force and made a feint of retreat, which drew the enemy across to our side of the river. Their plan of attack seems to have been well conceived and came very near being successfully executed. They landed in two columns, one at Edwards' Ferry and another at Ball's Bluff, considerably nearer to the town, the latter point, especially, being concealed by thick woods. Our little army returned in the very nick of time, but were misled as to the disposition and designs of the enemy, regarding the Edwards' Ferry force as the main and dangerous body, and were either entirely ignorant of the crossing at Ball's Bluff, or at least did not regard that as of any magnitude or moment. Indeed, as I recollect, the presence of these latter troops was discovered as it were by accident, just as they emerged from the forest, and were practically between us and Leesburg. But General Evans acted with vigor after the true condition of things was developed, rapidly concentrating his force to meet the advance from Ball's Bluff; first checking and then staggering it, and finally driving the entire body back in bloody repulse upon and into the river, where many were drowned.

To us it seemed a mistake not then to have attacked the Edwards' Ferry force, but there may have been good reason for not doing so. The gallant Eighth Virginia, under its staunch Colonel, afterwards General, Eppa Hunton—since the war both a Congressman and a Senator of the United States from Virginia—took a prominent and honorable part in the fight, which was hotly contested and one of the most remarkable of the minor battles of the war in the disproportion of the enemy's loss to the number engaged on our side. No part of the honor, however, belongs to our battery, as the fighting took place in heavy woods, where it was impracticable to carry our guns.

To me the battle of Leesburg, or Ball's Bluff, as the Federals called it, presented several points of rather special interest. First, the gallant and almost marvelous escape of a young Federal officer, named Crowninshield, who had been the strongest man on the Harvard boat crew about the time I held the like prominent position among the boating men of Yale. In the account of the battle, given by one of the Northern papers, I noticed, with great interest and pleasure, that Crowninshield, rather than surrender, swam the river and made good his escape, after his right arm had been shattered by a Minie ball. It was really a plucky and splendid feat.

Then, too, I very much enjoyed a newspaper report of a speech of Roscoe Conkling, delivered in the House of Representatives at Washington, upon this battle, in the course of which, extolling the valor of the Federal troops, he quoted from Tennyson's "Charge of the Light Brigade" the lines:

> "Cannon to right of them,
> Cannon to left of them,
> Cannon in front of them,
> Volleyed and thundered."

This was at once amusing and aggravating, as we had felt peculiarly chagrined at not being able to fire even so much as one shot while the battle roared in the thicket in front of us. The enemy, on the contrary, did have and use at least one gun, a brass three-inch rifle, which was captured and turned over to our battery.

A third incident was of a more personal nature. I had broken my knee-cap by a heavy fall during our feigned retreat, and the limb had become as rigid as a bar of steel. My gun detachment was very anxious I should take part in the fight, and, of course, I was eager for it, as I had seen no service, and it had been agreed I should act as gunner and sight the piece. We changed position several times during the action, in the vain hope of finding a point from which we might fire upon the enemy without imperilling our own men, and I was carried from one to another of these positions, or as near as might be, in an ambulance, driven by a half-witted youth named Grover, employed for that purpose.

As I was getting out of the vehicle, for the third or fourth time, and preparing to hobble painfully up the hill to take my place at the gun, I said to him: "Grover, why don't you go up yonder with me to fight? You are better able to do it than I am."

"Yes," said he, "but there's a differ."

"Well, what is it?" I asked; "what is the differ?"

"Why," said he, "you see, you 'listed ter git killed and I 'listed ter drive a avalanche."

It is of course familiar to students of the financial history of the Confederacy, yet it may not be devoid of interest to the general public, to note that, in the South during the war, banks, municipalities, companies, and, even in some cases, individuals issued fractional notes or shin plasters which passed as currency supplementary to the Treasury notes issued by the Confederate Government. I am confident every surviving member of our battery, who was with us at Leesburg, will recall the little "dog money" notes issued by the town, ornamented by a picture of a majestic Newfoundland dog lying down before a massive iron safe supposed to be full of currency. No one, so far as I know, ever questioned the validity of Leesburg's fiat money; certainly we Howitzers experienced no difficulty whatever in getting rid of all we could get our hands upon.

About the middle of November, pursuant to a policy of brigading together, so far as possible, troops from the same State, the Eighth Virginia Regiment was ordered back to

Manassas, and the Twenty-first Mississippi, commanded by Col. B. G. Humphreys, was sent to fill its place—the entire Mississippi brigade, consisting of the Thirteenth, Seventeenth, Eighteenth and Twenty-first Regiments, being then, or shortly after, put under the command of General Griffith, of that State, who was killed at Savage Station in June, '62, when Barksdale, theretofore colonel of the Thirteenth, was made brigadier-general and took command of the brigade, which bore his name up to Gettysburg, where he met his gallant death. Thereupon Colonel Humphreys, of the Twenty-first, was promoted to the rank of brigadier, and in turn commanded and christened this fine body of soldiers. It may be well to mention that Colonel Featherstone, of the Seventeenth, was made brigadier in the spring of '62, so that three out of the four original colonels of this brigade became generals, the fourth, Colonel Burt, of the Eighteenth, having been killed at Ball's Bluff. I may also add that General Humphreys was elected Governor of Mississippi shortly after the close of the war.

For more than a year after the battle of Leesburg, we were closely associated with these sturdy fellows and became strongly attached to them; indeed, up to the very end, the two commands never crossed each other's path without hearty cheers and handshakes.

This Mississippi brigade was, in many respects, the finest body of men I ever saw. They were almost giants in size and power. In the color company of the Seventeenth Regiment, when we first met them, there were thirty-five men more than six feet one inch high, and in the Twenty-first there was one man six feet seven inches in height, and superbly formed, except that his shoulders were a trifle too square and too broad in proportion. They were healthy and hardy, even ruddy, which was surprising, coming as they did from a region generally regarded as full of malarial poison. They were bear hunters from the swamps and cane brakes and, naturally enough, almost without exception fine shots.

As a body, they were very young men and brimful of irrepressible enthusiasm, equally for play and for fight. The laugh, the song, the shout, the yell of the rebel charge burst indifferently from their lips; but in any and every case the volume of sound was tremendous. It was a common saying that the "sick men" left in Barksdale's camp, when the brigade was away on duty, made more noise than any other full brigade in the army. The only comment I have to make upon this statement is that I cannot recall ever having seen onè of them sick or "ailing" in any way, except when suffering from hunger or from wounds. At times they seemed about as rough as the bears they had hunted, yet they were withal simple-minded and tender-hearted boys, and at Fredericksburg hundreds of them became Christians.

I knew almost every man in the brigade and often attended their religious meetings. Many a time, after I became adjutant of our battalion of artillery, Col. H. C. Cabell's, as I galloped past their lines awaiting the order to charge, my heart has been cheered and strengthened by a chorus of manly voices calling after me, "God bless you, Brother Stiles, and cover your head in the day of battle!" How could I help loving these simple, brave, great-hearted fellows.

Early in December, '61, General Evans was relieved of the command at Leesburg and sent, I think, to South Carolina, his native State, to take charge of some troops there, and Gen. D. H. Hill, of North Carolina, was put in his place. He was a brother-in-law of Stonewall Jackson and, like him, a thorough Christian and thorough Calvinist. That he was likewise a thorough soldier may be inferred, as the logicians would say, *"a-priori* and *a-posteriori,"* from the two facts, that he was a graduate of West Point, and that he attained the rank of lieutenant-general in the Confederate service. He was, moreover, a man of intellect and culture, with a decided taste for scholarship and letters, having been, both before and since the war, connected with educational institutions of high grade and a writer of books, both scientific and religious.

Like Jackson he was, too, a born fighter—as aggressive, pugnacious and tenacious as a bull-dog, or as any soldier in the service, and he had a sort of monomania on the subject of personal courage.

It is certainly worthy of note that this fighting zeal is so frequently combined with a high degree of spiritual religion.

Almost countless stories are told of the grim courage and grit of General Hill. In the first Maryland campaign he held the pass at Boonsboro for many hours with a mere handful of troops against McClellan's overwhelming numbers, thus giving time for Jackson to complete his capture of Harper's Ferry and join Lee at Sharpsburg. It is said that toward the close of the Boonsboro fight, riding down his short line, his men reported that they were out of ammunition, and that the stern old North Carolina Puritan replied: "Well, what of it? Here are plenty of *rocks!*"

His habit was, when his skirmishers were firing wildly, to ride out among them, and if he noticed a man lying down or behind protection and firing carelessly, he would make him get right up and come and stand out in the open, by his horse, and load his musket and hand it to him. Then he would crane his neck until he saw a Federal skirmisher, when he would point him out to his man, but would fire at him himself, not only taking long, portentous aim before pulling trigger, but making equally long examination afterwards to determine whether he had hit him; and he would continue and distribute these blood-curdling object-lessons until his men settled down to a style of firing that suited him.

Very amusing accounts passed around the army about "old D. H." every now and then *"treating"* the non-combatant officers of his staff—the quartermasters, commissaries, and doctors—to what he called "a little airing in a fight," when he thought they stood in need of it, or heard that they had been "airing," a little freely, their own martial experience and prowess.

Occasionally, in his official reports, he gave the tartest and most amusing expressions to his strenuous views and standards of soldierly courage and devotion. I recall one in which, in commenting upon the flight of a body of cavalry before overwhelming numbers, he remarks incidentally, that it takes a good man to stand and fight against heavy odds, when he has only two legs under him; but that if you put six legs under him to run away with, it requires the best kind of a man to stand and fight.

In another report, in describing a stampede and the crush and jam of fugitives in the highway, he says, "Not a dog; no, not even a sneaking exempt, could have made his way through."

As early in the drama as the Leesburg campaign he had begun to indulge and exhibit these rather peculiar notions and habits. Soon after taking command, desiring to know the number, calibre, and character of the Federal guns across the river, he gathered a large escort and rode up and down the river bank in a manner calculated to attract the fire of artillery, and when the enemy accepted his invitation and the shell came singing over and buried itself in the earth hard by, he called for a pick and shovel, dismounted and dug it up with his own hands, apparently unconscious that other shells were shrieking and bursting about him and his improvised and somewhat nervous staff. Of course this impressed us no little; exactly how, it would be difficult to say. One thing, however, was clear—that this apparent unconsciousness of personal peril was in no degree "put on," that our general was undoubtedly "to the manner born."

Our company had special reason for desiring to make a good impression upon General Hill. At the battle of Bethel, or "Big Bethel," where he commanded a regiment and won the spurs and stars of a general, he had with him the other two companies of our "Howitzer Battalion," which unfortunately never materialized in the field. We did not wish him to draw unfavorable comparisons and gave him no reason for doing so, though we had no opportunity, while under him, of distinguishing ourselves.

He was a man of strong likes and dislikes, and in some way was led to notice and to conceive a decided liking for me. Not long after he assumed command he ordered Captain Shields to send, I think, a sergeant and some fifteen or twenty men, of whom I was one, to take charge of Fort Johnston, a considerable, closed earth-work, on a commanding eminence about a mile out of town, which mounted two or three siege pieces of rather clumsy construction, fired by friction primer like field pieces. In addition to this, we generally had one and, much of the time, two, of our field pieces also with us at the fort. About the same time, the general ordered about the same number of Mississippians— that is to say, enough for two gun detachments—to report at the fort and to be under my special charge. I have an indistinct recollection that I selected these men. The idea was that we light artillerymen should adapt our drill to the heavy guns and then teach the Mississippians the manual and use of both field and siege pieces, so that all of us could work effectually all the pieces in the fort.

The Mississippians were glad to come. They liked the noise and smoke and uproar of the guns. There never were two such field artillery detachments as they made after a brief period of drill. They would shove the pieces up almost any hillside, however steep, and would even hold them against the recoil when inclined to roll too far back. We passed a good deal of time running up and down the river with the field pieces, the captain sometimes with us and sometimes not, appearing first on one commanding hilltop and then on another, and firing across at the railroad trains and canal boats on the other side. On two or three occasions we stirred up a hornet's nest in the shape of Federal batteries which happened to be drilling in the neighborhood, and once were compelled to withdraw with more speed than dignity; but my irrepressible Mississippi artillerymen made fun of it all, actually playing leap frog down the steep Loudoun hillside, under a galling fire, from perhaps eight or ten guns. I was quite an athlete at the time, having been considered the strongest man at Yale while there, and had reason to deem myself an expert in matters involving physical achievement and endurance. I have no hesitation in saying that I never witnessed an exhibition of bounding, buoyant power and unshakeable bodily soundness and stamina that compared with this performance of the Mississippians. The men were all, or most of them, over six feet in height and averaged, I should say, over 200 pounds in weight, and yet they ran down the steep slope, keeping abreast of galloping horses, and leaping over each other's shoulders, the head of course inclined, but the column of the body almost upright; and as the leaper would strike far below, with a jar calculated to jolt a man's vital organs out of gear forever, he would instantly assume position again, with a shout, while two hundred pounds of yelling, human trap-ball would in turn execute the perilous flying leap over his head.

The situation at Fort Johnston, from the view-point of rank, command, and subordination, was mixed and delicate enough already, though I had no real difficulty, with my own company officers, in keeping up my little *imperium in imperio*. But just about the time matters had settled into working order with the existing elements, a militia regiment from a neighboring county was orderd into the fort for the purpose of improving and strengthening, as well as more fully manning it. This regiment, as I remember, was afterwards broken up and the men entered as individual recruits in veteran regiments, as was the almost unvarying mode of recruiting in the Confederate service; but at this time—late winter of '61-'2, or early spring of '62—this regiment seems to have retained its original organization under its original officers. I have spoken of it as a militia regiment, as we all did at the time, but I do not know what its real status was. The regimental officers were of course jealous of us—private artillery soldiers seeming to be set over even infantry officers, and the general being in the habit of communicating with us directly in matters concerning the fort and everything in it. To add to the uneasiness and discontent, the idea got abroad that this small force was thus isolated with the view of sacrificing it in case the enemy should cross over, to enable the other troops to withdraw in safety.

At one of the evening dress parades of the regiment, at which of course the colonel was in charge, I attempted, with his permission, to show the absurdity of this rumor, and at the same time to pour oil generally on the troubled waters; but a little before midnight one of my Mississippians, "Buck Denman," a man marked even among those heroes for courage and power, who was corporal of the guard that night, came and woke me up with the startling intelligence that the "melish" were formed and about to leave the fort. I rose instantly and ordered Denman to call out his entire squad and have them rendezvous at once at the outlet of the fort with *loaded muskets.*

He yelled like a Comanche as he sprang to execute the order, and by the time I reached the centre of the parade, passing by the head of the regiment on the way, the bear hunters were at their posts "loaded for b'ar" or "melish," as the case might be, and shouting for the battle. The "colonel commanding" hesitated what command to give, and I at once assumed his place and did not hesitate. The men were in column and ready to march out, but they front-faced readily at my command, and I briefly laid the situation before them, emphasizing—but never mind what I empha-sized, the moon gave light enough to shed a gleam on the musket barrels of the Mississippians formed right across the only outlet, and these added the emphasis; but I did appeal also to the better judgment and better feeling of the men and closed with an invitation to their colonel to call on General Hill with me in the morning.

While I was speaking I noticed immediately in front of me, standing on a sort of irregular front line of officers, a remarkable and grotesque figure. He was a tall, gaunt man, dressed in an old Continental uniform or something very like it. I recall the cocked hat, blue, buff-faced coat, of that cut, fa'-top boots, and a drawn sword in his hand of about the length and model of a scythe blade. It was not a very bright night, but his whole attitude showed absorbed and sympathetic attention. I had hardly ceased when he stepped briskly toward me, saluted, wheeled and faced the regiment and his, the leading company, and uttered, in quite a sol-dierly tone, just these words: "Snickersville Blues, fall out! Mr. Stiles is right, and I am going to stand by him!" The example was contagious, and in a few moments the strained situation was entirely relieved.

In the morning General Hill decided that I was right, commended the course I had pursued, and said he would send for a commission for me (which I presume he forgot) ; but suggested that it might interest and conciliate the regiment if we would pick out two or three detachments and drill them in the manual of the heavy pieces. We did so with admirable result, of course offering to the gallant captain of the "Snickersville Blues" the place of gunner of the first detachment. The old fellow, whose name I think was Moore, took the greatest interest and delight in the drill and showed some proficiency at it; so that in a few days he asked me to allow him to drill his detachment before General Hill, who rode out almost every evening to see how we were getting on. I never saw anything quite so irresistibly funny as Moore's dress and bearing as he formed his detachment, marched them to the gun and put them in position about it. He got on fairly well until a primer failed and he could not recall the appropriate command—"Don't advance, the primer has failed!"

As No. 2 first hesitated and then started to advance, Moore, gasping with excitement and stretching out his right arm deprecatingly toward the cannoneer, blurted out, "Don't go up, the thing's busted!" Of course there was an explosion, though not of the primer, but as Moore seemed so genuinely mortified, it was soon hushed. General Hill seemed to appreciate the situation, and assured the gunner that his improvised command answered every purpose and was far preferable, in such an emergency, to not saying anything because unable to recall exactly what to say.

Soon after this, in the early spring of '62, the General directed us to have a large number of flannel powder bags made up, a few for the heavy guns, but most of them of a size suited to our field pieces, and gave such additional orders as satisfied me that the army was about to abandon its present lines and take position somewhere in the low country near Richmond. The young ladies of Leesburg had offered repeatedly to do anything they could for us, and so we held, for several successive nights, a regular sewing bee over these powder bags, which, as fast as made, were taken up to Fort Johnston and filled in the magazine there. We had a lively, lovely time, making the bags, but I felt all the while as if I were guilty of the vilest deception; for of course these sweet girls were led to believe these powder bags were to be used in their defense, while I well knew we would abandon them to their fate about as soon as the bags were finished, filled, and packed for transport. At last the time for our departure actually came, and a sad leave-taking it was, for some of these dear people had treated us as no strangers were ever treated before; and besides, we all felt not only the pain of parting but also something akin to the disgrace of desertion.

With D. H. Hill, worship of Stonewall Jackson held a place next after and close alongside his religion. He had the greatest admiration for Jackson's genius and the greatest confidence in his future. He honored me with frequent and sometimes very extended interviews; and as there was nothing else he so much delighted to talk about or I to hear, I absorbed much that prepared me for his brother-in-law's marvelous career. Even at that early day, Hill predicted that if the war should last six years and Jackson live so long, he would be in supreme command.

It is fair to add that the pure white star of Robert Lee had not yet fairly appeared above the Southern horizon.

CHAPTER VII

THE PENINSULA CAMPAIGN.

Reenlistment and Reorganization in the Spring of '62—Gen. McClellan
—The Peninsula Lines—The Texans—The Battle of Williamsburg
—The Mud.

We left Leesburg about the 7th of March, '62, for Culpeper C. H., which was the place of rendezvous of the army before taking up the line of march for the Peninsula, whither we were ordered to repair to meet McClellan. Only two things of interest occurred on the way—the reenlistment and reorganization of the battery and a hurried glimpse at our friends in Richmond. The former, as I remember, took place at or near Culpeper C. H., about the 15th of March, and deserves more than casual mention.

In the spring of 1862, throughout our service, the men reenlisting were allowed to elect their own officers; so that for weeks about this time the army, and that in the face of the enemy, was resolved—it is the highest proof of its patriotism and character that it was not also dissolved—into nominating caucuses and electioneering meetings. This compliment, by the way, is as well deserved by the men voluntarily reenlisting and electing their own officers, on the Federal side as the Confederate, if, as I presume, the same system was adopted by the Federals.

I do not say this is not the usual mode of organizing a volunteer army, at least in this country; nor do I deny that the result was better, on the average, than might have been anticipated, but it was bad enough. Our friend, Gen. D. H. Hill, in a report of a little later date, says, "The reorganization of the army, at Yorktown under the elective system, had thrown out of service many of our best officers and had much demoralized our army."

In short, the selection of military officers by the elective method is a monstrosity, an utter reversal of the essential spirit of military appointment and promotion. It ought to be enough to immortalize it as such that, about the time of or soon after the original enlistments, the men of one of the Virginia regiments, in the exercise of their volunteer right to choose their officers, protested successfully against the assignment of General, then Colonel, Jackson to command them.

It is fair also to add that the result, in the case of our own company—as I have abundantly shown an exceptionally intelligent corps,—so far as the newly-elected captain was concerned, could not have been more satisfactory, as he was a man of the noblest nature and every inch a soldier. But this was not by any means the case with all the officers elected by us. Our two preceding captains were promoted, the one to be colonel commanding "Camp Lee"—the camp of instruction at Richmond—and the other, at a later date, to be surgeon of that post, with rank of major.

We seemed to be in no sort of hurry to get at McClellan; that is, we took our time on the road, feeling sure, from past experience, that he would take his. Our army and people invariably regarded that general as "an officer and a gentleman" and a fine soldier, too, except that he was a little slow and prone to see double as to the number of his foes. The Richmond *Examiner,* by far the most vigorous journal published in the South during the war, epitomized "little Mac" in the following graphic sentence, "Accustomed in peace to the indecent haste of railroad travel, McClellan adopted in war the sedate tactics of the mud turtle." He certainly did seem to have a penchant for *mud,* Peninsula mud, Chickahominy mud, James River mud—any sort of mud; but he was too much of a gentleman to "sling" any of it, even at us "rebels."

The only point of the march down at which we were made to hurry was the only one at which we would have demurred to doing so if it would have done any good, and that was Richmond, where, as I remember, we arrived about the 10th of April, and left by steamer down James River a day

or two later. I remember, too, that as the boat left the
shouting thousands on the shore and swept out into the
stream our glee club burst into the rollicking stanzas of
"Mynheer von Dunck"—a song as good in verse and in
music as it is bad in morals:

> "Mynheer von Dunck,
> Though he never got drunk,
> Sipped brandy and water gaily;
> And he quenched his thirst
> With two quarts of the first
> To a pint of the latter, daily.
> Water well mingled with spirit, good store,
> No Hollander dreams of scorning;
> But of water alone he drinks no more
> Than the rose supplies
> When the dew drop lies
> On its bloom of a summer morning—
> For a Dutchman's draft should potent be,
> Though deep as the rolling Zuyder Zee."

And as we steamed out of hearing of the pier the stout
voices of the singers were publishing, with metrical and musical elaboration, the somewhat shady proposition that—

> "A pretty girl who gets a kiss and runs and tells her mother,
> Does what she should not do and don't deserve another."

These revelling, rollicking songs came later to be prime
favorites with sundry brigadier, major and even lieutenant-
generals in the Army of Northern Virginia, and they cheered, too, many a comfortless camp and relieved many a
weary march of the old battery.

In due time we made our landing and found our place in
the peninsular lines of Yorktown and Warwick River, which
were admirably adapted to the purpose for which General
Magruder designed and located them; namely, to enable a
small body of troops to hold the position—but for occupation by a large army they were simply execrable. There was
scarcely solid ground enough accessible to afford standing,
sleeping, or living room for the men.

Our boys had their first taste of actual war in these abominable lines. Soon after our arrival the enemy attempted a crossing in force. Our guns being called for, we made an inspiring rush for the point of attack and were loudly cheered by the long lines of waiting infantry as we thundered by with our horses at a wild gallop. We got in only at the end of the fight, but our pieces were soon placed in the works and in situations about as trying as any we ever occupied. Our positions were commanded by those on the other side, our earth-works were utterly insufficient, we were heavily outnumbered in guus, and the Federal sharpshooters were as audacious and deadly as I ever saw them. For the most part they were concealed in the tops of tall pine trees and had down shots upon us, against which it was almost impossible to protect ourselves. When we attempted to do so by digging holes back of and beneath our works, the water rose in them and drove us out. Then, too, the enemy had opposite to us several rapid-firing guns of the earlier models, which we dubbed "the hopper mine," "the putty machine," etc., and which ground out a stream of bullets almost equal to the fire of a line of battle. The guns were not, however, really effective, and I do not recall ever encountering them again. But our boys showed excellent pluck and did some fine shooting, dismounting one of the guns of a Rhode Island battery which we had the luck of meeting several times during the war.

The only relief we had from the sharpshooters was when the marvelous Texan scouts got to work upon them, which was as often as their "impudence" got to be unbearable. This was the first time we had met those greatest of all soldiers, the Texas brigade. I question whether any body of troops ever received such a compliment as General Lee paid them in his letter to Senator Wigfall, written later in the war, in which he asked him, if possible, to go to Texas and raise another such brigade for his army. He said that the efficiency of the Army of Northern Virginia would be thereby increased to an incalculable extent, and that he would be relieved of the unpleasant necessity of calling on this one brigade so often in critical junctures. I have not the letter before me, but I have read it several times and feel substantially sure of its contents.

In the present instance the work of these worthies appeared little less than miraculous. They were apparently unconscious of danger and seemed to bear charmed lives. When the pressure of the Federal sharpshooters became intolerable, the Texans would pass the word that it was time to go out "squirrel shooting." Then they would get up, yawn and stretch a little, load their rifles and take to the water, disappearing from view in the brush. Then everything would be still a few minutes; then two or three shots, and the sputter of the sharpshooters would cease. After a while the Texans would straggle back, and report how many "squirrels" they had got.

Notwithstanding this relief, or it may have been for the lack of it,—for our guns were separated by considerable distances,—one of our detachments broke down utterly from nervous tension and lack of rest. I went in as one of the relief party to bring them out and take their places. It was, of course, after nightfall, and some of these poor lads were sobbing in their broken sleep, like a crying child just before it sinks to rest. It was really pathetic. The men actually had to be supported to the ambulances sent down to bring them away.

Amongst the unpleasant experiences of these lines were the night attacks, or perhaps, to speak more accurately, I should say, the night alarms. Down in these swamps at night it was incredibly dark and musketry never roared and reverberated as terribly anywhere else. These exhibitions reached the dignity at least of fully developed "alarms." Especially was this the case when, one black night, a sudden outburst of fire—infantry, artillery, machine guns and all—stampeded a working party of some two hundred negroes who had just begun the much-needed strengthening of our very inadequate fortifications. The working party not only fled themselves, but the frantic fugitives actually swept away with them a part of our infantry support.

I was sent back to the drivers' camp to see that the horses were harnessed and ready in case it should be necessary to withdraw our pieces, and I met a line or mass of troops advancing to our support. Hearing some one call "Stiles!" I asked, "Who said 'Stiles' and who are you speaking to?" A voice answered, "I called Stiles," and another, close beside me, said, "He's speaking to me. Stiles is my name. I'm Capt. Edward Stiles, of Savannah, Georgia." I grasped his hand, unable to see him, and having only time to say, "Then I'm your cousin, Robert Stiles, of Richmond, Virginia. Look you up to-morrow." Until that moment I did not know I had a relative in the Virginia army, knowing that some and supposing that all of my cousins were in the armies of the coast defense.

It was, of course, well understood by all of us that the Federal commander, having complete control of the navigable rivers, by virtue of his overwhelming naval power, could at any time turn either of our flanks or land a heavy force between us and Richmond, and that therefore our present line could not be a permanent one. We were not surprised, then, at receiving orders, about the 2d of May, to withdraw and march toward Richmond, which we did.

The enemy followed, but not vigorously. My recollection is that our company was the rear battery during the next day and that we several times unlimbered our pieces, but never fired a shot; so the evening of the 4th of May found us on the Richmond side of Williamsburg, hitched up and ready to fall in behind our brigade. We heard firing in the rear, but thought little of it until a mounted officer rode up with orders from competent authority to bring up as rapidly as possible the first battery he could find ready hitched up, and so we passed rapidly back through Williamsburg, and became at once hotly engaged, doing good service, as we also did the next day. Indeed our action the first evening might, without much strain, be termed *"distinguished."* The enemy, under a heavy fire from our battery and another, abandoned a three-inch rifled gun and a caisson of ammunition, and the general at whose orders we had entered the fight calling for volunteers to bring them into our lines, our boys volunteered and brought them off the field, using the captured gun with fine effect the following day.

Williamsburg was not in any sense a decisive battle, perhaps not designed to be so on either side. Upon our side certainly, perhaps upon both sides, it accomplished its limited purpose, which upon our part was to let General McClellan see that it would not be well for him to seriously interfere with or molest us in our "change of base," or "retreat," if one prefers that term, though, as above remarked, it cannot be contended that the line we were leaving could ever have been designed for permanent occupation.

It is obvious, I say, that McClellan did learn the lesson we intended; for after Williamsburg our army was allowed to pursue its march very leisurely up the peninsula—a considerable part of it stopping to finish the reenlistment and reorganization by the election of new officers.

But it is not a satisfactory battle to contemplate, because the administering of this lesson cost too much in blood, and this because, as so often happens, some one blundered. Col. Richard L. Maury—son of Commodore M. F. Maury—and an exceptionally intelligent officer, who at the close of the fight commanded the Twenty-fourth Virginia, Early's old regiment, the colonel and lieutenant-colonel having been shot down—has written a brief but strong memoir on this battle, from which it would seem well nigh impossible to draw any other conclusions.

He makes substantially the following points:

General Magruder had built, and was commended for building, a chain of redoubts across the Peninsula from the York to the James, as a second line; Fort Magruder, a strong closed work, about a mile from Williamsburg, on the main road running down the Peninsula, being the key of the entire line. The battle was fought in and from these fortifications, we occupying Fort Magruder, but, incredible as it may seem, not occupying the other works, and not even those within a short distance of the main road along which lay our route to Richmond. Indeed General Hancock was allowed, without firing a shot, to possess himself of one or more of these works, and yet the heaviest loss in the action was entailed in the attempt to dislodge Hancock, which failed. Several of the general officers, by whose apparent neglect all this hap-

pened, have publicly defended themselves by stating that
they did not know and were not informed as to the location
of these works. It seems to go without saying that they
ought to have been informed. Furthermore, it is evident that
if a single general officer upon our side was fully informed
as to the entire line, it was General Magruder, who built it,
and who, it seems, took no part in this battle. Indeed, as I
remember, he had been sent on toward Richmond. As
above intimated, it would seem impossible that all these facts
should co-exist with prudence and generalship upon the part
of all our leading officers.

There is, however, one relief to the rather sombre picture.
Our troops, whether prudently and wisely led or not, certainly fought well. "Hancock the Superb" was generous
enough to say that the Twenty-fourth Virginia and the
Fifth North Carolina, the two regiments which attacked his
strong force in its fortified position, deserved to have the
word "immortal" inscribed upon their banners.

Two of the most vivid pictures in the gallery of my memory are set in the framing of this battle—the one the most
shocking instance of the unhuman demoraliation of war, the
other the most inspiring illustration of the noblest traits developed by it.

During a lull in the fighting our guns were withdrawn
and were in column parallel to the road, in a common on
the outskirts of the town, resting and awaiting orders, when
a number of wounded Federal prisoners were brought up in
an ambulance and laid temporarily on the grass, while a
field hospital was being established hard by. Among them
was a poor wretch, shot through the bowels, who was rolling
on the ground in excruciating agony and beseeching the by-
standers to put him out of his misery. There did not appear
to be anything that could be done for him, at least not in
advance of the coming of the surgeons, so I was in the act
of turning away from the painful spectacle when a couple of
Tureos, or Louisiana tigers, the most rakish and devilish-
looking beings I ever saw, came up and peered over the
shoulders of the circle of onlookers.

Suddenly one of them pushed through the ring, saying:
"Put you out of your misery? Certainly, sir!" and before

any one had time to interfere, or even the faintest idea of his intention, brained the man with the butt of his musket; and the bloody club still in his hands, looking around upon the other wounded men, added glibly, "Any other gentleman here'd like to be accommodated?"

It is impossible to express my feelings. I fear that if I had had a loaded musket in my hands I should have illustrated the demoralization of war a little further by shooting down in his tracks the demon, who suddenly disappeared, as a gasp of horror escaped the spectators.

For the honor of human nature, let me quickly give you the other picture.

At the crisis of the battle we were stationed in Fort Magruder, as above explained, the key of our position. I was standing, sponge-staff in hand, awaiting the firing of my gun, the next piece to the left being a gun of the Fayette Artillery. As my eye fell upon it, No. 1 was sponging out, No. 3, of course, having his thumbstall pressed upon the vent. Suddenly I saw No. 3 stoop, clapping his right hand upon his leg below the knee, and then I saw him topple slowly forward, never, however, lifting his thumb from the vent, but pressing it down close and hard—his elbow strained upward as his body sank forward and downward. The heroic fellow had been first shot in the calf of the right leg, and as he bent to feel that wound a bullet crashed through his skull; but his last effort was to save No. 1 from the loss of his hands by premature explosion as he rammed home the next charge. I have never witnessed more sublime faithfulness unto death than was exhibited by the downward pressure of that thumb as it was literally dragged from the bole of the piece by the weight of the sinking body of the noble cannoneer.

This incident reminds me of another which well illustrates how receptive and retentive of pictorial impression are the minds of men—especially men of a certain type—at moments of intense excitement. It is this faculty, in great measure, which imparts special interest and value to the personal reminiscences of men of this character.

Nearly three years after the battle of Williamsburg, I think in March, '65, entering the office of the provost-marshal of the city of Richmond for the first and only time during the war, I found an officer, in a new uniform of a colonel of cavalry, in an unpleasant altercation with one of the employees of the office. As I approached he turned to me, saying:

"It's a hard case, Major, that a veteran colonel of the Army of Northern Virginia is bearded in this way by a beardless boy of a provost-marshal's clerk, and that he cannot have even the poor satisfaction of slapping his jaws as he is entrenched behind this partition."

While pouring out this complaint the Colonel gazed at me with increasing interest and, as he ceased—starting a little—said abruptly:

"I have seen you before, sir!"

"Yes, Colonel," I replied, "or at least, I have seen you, and I recall just when and where it was; but as you are the ranking officer won't you be good enough to say first, if you can, when and where you saw me?"

"Certainly, sir," said he; "it was at the battle of Williamsburg, in May, '62. You were then a private soldier in an artillery company and were standing, bare-headed, at the angle of Fort Magruder with a sponge-staff in your hand as I led a charge of cavalry past the fort."

My recollection exactly coincided with his. The officer, I think, was Col. J. Lucius Davis, who commanded a body of Virginia troops at Charlestown or Harper's Ferry during the John Brown raid; but, whoever he was, he was not a colonel at Williamsburg, but I think a captain; and, as I remember, then wore a brown-gray tunic belted around his waist, and his hair, which was then quite long, swept back from his forehead as he gallantly led his men, sabre in hand, at full speed against the enemy.

We never met save on the two occasions mentioned and could not possibly have seen each other at Williamsburg more than a moment. The rank, dress, bearing—everything, indeed, save the essential personality of the two men—was entirely different at the two meetings, and yet neither of us felt the slightest hesitation as to mutual identification or the time, place, and circumstances of the first meeting.

The one feature of the march up the Peninsula was mud. Even the great "Mud turtle" himself must have been satiated with it. As for me, I had never imagined anything approximating to it. The ground had been saturated by recent heavy rains, which seemed to have brought down with them myriads of diminutive green frogs, the only living organisms, except of course the mud turtle, which could enjoy the big lob-lolly puddles into which the road-bed had been churned by the multitude of houghs and wheels and the feet of the trampling thousands. Our company wagon, containing a present supply of commissary and quartermaster stores and all our extra clothing, sank to the hubs and had to be abandoned. We feared for the guns and could not think of wasting teams on wagons. The danger was really imminent that the guns themselves would have to be abandoned, and the captain instructed me to have at hand a haversack with hammer and spikes and to keep near the rear of the battery, and if a gun could not be dragged through the mud, then to "spike it" as thoroughly as I could, slip the trunnions from the sockets and let the piece drop into the deepest mud I could find, and mark the spot. By dint, however, of fine driving, and heavy lifting and shoving at the wheels, we managed to save our brazen war dogs, for which we were beginning to feel a strong attachment.

The poor horses often sank to their bellies, and we were several times compelled to unhitch a stalled horse, tie a prolonge around him, hitch the rest of the team to the rope and drag him out. I mean just what I say when I aver that I saw a team of mules disappear, every hair, under the mud, in the middle of the road. Of course they had first fallen, in their impotent efforts to extricate themselves, and they afterwards arose and emerged from their baptism of mud, at once the most melancholy and the most ludicrous-looking objects that could be imagined. It was wretched, and yet it had its funny side.

We mounted upon the gun and caisson horses, for the emergency, the very best men, regard being had to the single requisite of skill and experience in handling draft horses and heavy loads, and no regard whatever as to whether or not they had theretofore been battery drivers. In this way it happened that two of the finest soldiers in the command were driving at my gun, the one the wheel team and the other the lead, there being at the time six horses to the piece. It was stalled, and two or three unsuccessful efforts having been made to start it, the wheel driver declared that it was the fault of the leader. The latter retorted, and the war of words waxed hot, until suddenly the wheel charioteer dismounted in the thigh-deep mud and, struggling up abreast of the lead team, dared the driver of it to get down and fight it out then and there. It is possible the other would have accepted the challenge if a glance down at his friend and foe had not brought the absurdity of the entire thing so vividly before him that he simply threw his head back in a burst of laughter, saying, "Why Billy, you must take me for an infernal fool, to expect me to get down in that infernal mud to fight you!" Whereupon the gentleman in the mud laughed, too, as did everybody within sight and hearing, and Billy struggled back to his wheelers, remounted, and with "a long pull, a strong pull, and a pull altogether"—out she came.

Another gentleman—he who had "resigned" when all trunks were sent to the rear from Manassas—having gotten at the company wagon this day, just before it was abandoned, had on a beautiful new suit of "Crenshaw gray," and, thus arrayed, was making a perilous passage out in the woods parallel to the road, dodging behind the big pine trees and springing from tussock to tussock of swamp grass and bushes. The boys had been watching him for some time, but he begged so hard, by cabalistic signs, that they had not "told on him." But finally the lieutenant saw him and called to him to come and get in the mud and help start a stalled gun. Of course he had to come, but he came very slowly, meanwhile beseeching the boys to "put on a little more steam and get the gun out!"

But the fellows had now come to appreciate the fun of the thing, as had also the lieutenant, and he ordered them to do nothing until Jim should get down in the mud with them. He wriggled and squirmed, his comrades standing in the mud about the gun jeering and jibing at him, as he mounted and walked upon a big pine log which projected out to the slough of despond in which the gun was stuck, till, getting about squarely over it, he stopped and begged once more; but the boys shouted derisively, and the lieutenant called out, "Get down to it, sir; nobody's going to shove a pound until you get in and shove with the rest!" Poor Jim! He lifted his foot and stamped it down in vexation on the wet bark, which parted and slipped from the smooth, slick bole of the tree, and down came Jim, with a great splash like the mules, hide and hair and Crenshaw gray, all into and under the mud. I don't think I ever heard such a shout as greeted this "knight of the sorrowful figure" as he emerged, from his thighs up, the liquid mud dripping from every part of the upper half of his person. But it cured him and his suit as well, the beautiful Crenshaw gray thenceforward exhibiting a sickly, jaundiced, butter-nut hue, like the clothes some backwoods cracker regiments wore when they first came to Virginia.

Only one other feature of our march up the Peninsula merits notice, and that was our almost actual starvation on the way. The cause of this was separation from our brigade, which was probably ten miles from Williamsburg before we were ordered to follow. In the condition of the roads already described, catching up with any particular body of troops was of course out of the question. We really had nothing to eat for two days and nights, except, that, as we were compelled to impress corn for the horses—of course old, hard corn—we roasted a little of it for ourselves.

On the third day we overhauled a commissary train, in a by-road we were traveling to escape the jam and the mud, and Captain McCarthy, making known the extreme need of his men, begged rations enough to give them just one meal; but the officer in charge answered:

"I cannot issue you anything, Captain, except upon the order of General Griffith, your brigadier, or my commanding officer."

To which our captain replied:

"General Griffith is somewhere between here and Richmond, I don't know where your commanding officer is; but if you can't give me anything, except upon the order of one of these two officers, then I can take what my men need, on my own order, and I'll do it. Here, boys, drive a gun up here in the road ahead of this train, unlimber it and load it. Now, sir, you shan't pass here without issuing three days' rations for my men; but I'll give you a written statement of what has occurred, signed by me!"

We sprang with a shout to execute the Captain's order, and in a few moments had our three days' rations, cooking them in the few utensils we always kept with us, and soon made a good square meal. I suppose Captain McCarthy's conduct was deemed justifiable, as no notice of a court-martial or a court of inquiry was ever served upon him.

It was, however, some days before the supply departments were thoroughly organized, after the disorganization and paralysis of the fearful mud deluge, and meanwhile not only did we artillerymen once more come down to hard pan and hard corn, but one evening General Griffith, who was a charming gentleman, rode over to where our battery was parked, saying to our captain that he came to beg three favors—a couple of ears of corn for himself, a feed for his horse, and a song from our Glee Club—to all of which he was made royally welcome, and he sat right down about our camp fire and roasted and ate his corn with us.

The boys used to say, "ten ears to a horse, two to a man—which shows that a horse is equal to five men." Later in the war this ratio was practically vindicated, for the supply of horses got to be in every sense a prime necessity with the field artillery of the Confederate armies. Many a time, during the campaign of '64, have I heard artillery officers of the Army of Northern Virginia—belonging to different corps—meeting for the first time after heavy fighting, in which the commands of both had been engaged, exchange some such greeting as this:

"Well, old fellow, how did you come out? How many horses did you lose? Lose any men?"

CHAPTER VIII

SEVEN PINES AND THE SEVEN DAYS' BATTLES

Joseph E. Johnston—The Change of Commanders—Lee's Plan of the
Seven Days' Battles—Rainsford—the Pursuit—Playing at Lost Ball
—"Little Mac's Lost the Thrigger"—Early Dawn on a Battle-field—
Lee and Jackson.

I turn back a moment to the mud and the march up the
Peninsula in order to relate a reminiscence illustrative of
several matters of interest, aside from the mud, such as the
state of the currency, the semi-quizzical character and bearing of the Confederate soldier and his marked respect for
private property, as well as the practical limitations to that
respect.

The column had halted at New Kent Court House, a little
hamlet in the great pine forest, then and now boasting not
over a half dozen houses, in addition to the tavern and the
temple of justice. The infantry had broken ranks and most
of them were resting and chatting, seated or reclined upon
the banks of the somewhat sunken road. On one side had
been a large cabbage patch from which the heads had been
cut the preceding fall, leaving the stalks in the ground, which
under the genial spring suns and rains,—it was the middle
of May,—had greened out into what I think are termed
"collards" or "sprouts." They were just what the soldiers
longed for and required, and an enterprising fellow saun-
tered up to the fence and offered an old woman, who stood
near by, "a dollar for one of them green things."

The price was fixed not by the seller but by the purchaser
and clearly under the combined influence of three considerations: he thought so much of the sprout, and so little of the
dollar, and then that dollar was probably the smallest money
he had.

No sooner said than done, and by the time the fellow paid his dollar and began browsing upon his sprout, the fence, which was about breast high and a very flimsy affair, was lined with soldiers, each with his right arm extended toward the old woman, a one-dollar Confederate Treasury note fluttering in his fingers.

I can see and hear them now: "Here, miss, please let me have one; I'm a heap hungrier'n these other men." "But, mother, I'm a sick man and *such* a good boy; you ought to 'tend to me first." And so it went; and so went the old woman, backward and forward, jerking the sprouts out of the ground with wondrous speed, and as fast as she gathered an armful, striding along the fence, distributing them and raking in the dollars. I never witnessed a brisker trade in cabbage; but the buyers were so eager and the pressure of the leaning men became so great, that the fence, the frail barrier between *"tuum* and *meum,"* suddenly gave way, and quicker than I can tell it there wasn't a sprout left in the patch.

The men had no intention of breaking into the enclosure, but Providence having removed the fence, they followed up the Providential indications by removing the sprouts. It is not easy to say just what the purchasing power of these dollars was, but at that comparatively early date it is easy to see that the old woman, counting only the money she actually got, made an astounding sale of her entire crop of sprouts.

At last we arrived and took our places in the outer line of defenses of Richmond, McClellan at first establishing his lines behind the Chickahominy—his base of supplies being White House, on York River;—but he soon threw across, that is to our side, the Richmond side, of the Chickahominy River and swamp, a considerable force, strongly fortifying its position. Still it was manifest, or seemed to be, that this force on the Richmond side was not strong enough, without drawing aid from the other side, to repel an attack by the entire army of Johnston. The water in the swamp suddenly rose and apparently cut off communication with the other side. Seven Pines was an attack upon the Federal force on the Richmond side of the stream and swamp, with the view of destroying it while it could not be reinforced from the main body beyond the stream, and, as is well known, General Johnston was struck down and totally disabled just at the crisis of the action.

When the commanding general of an army, especially upon the attacking side, is struck down while his plans are developing, it is ordinarily not possible to say with confidence what would have been the result of the engagement if no such calamity had befallen the attacking force. Seven Pines is therefore what may properly be termed an indecisive, if not an abortive battle. While the determined fighting on the Confederate side probably contributed to delay a general advance by McClellan, thus giving time for Lee to get thorough hold upon his army, to acquire their confidence, to mature his plans generally, and in particular to arrange for the withdrawal of Jackson from the valley, yet it must be admitted that, as to the main design of the Confederates, the battle was a failure.

To the Southern people and soldiers generally I have no doubt that, after the Seven Days' battles, Seven Pines seemed to measure up to its chief significance as the fight which resulted in removing Joseph E. Johnston from the command of the main army of the Confederacy and putting Robert E. Lee in his place; and I think likely it did so present itself to me at the time—indeed such is my recollection. But after the war it was my good fortune to be honored with the close and intimate friendship of General Johnston,—closer and more intimate than I ever enjoyed with any other of the great Southern leaders,—and the knowledge thus acquired of the man himself has imparted to the strange fatality of his being stricken down at Seven Pines, *with the tenth honorable wound received in battle,* and to other unfortunate features of his career, a new and almost pathetic interest.

I found him, both as a man and a soldier, to be very different from my previous estimate of him and in every way above that estimate; so that, in looking upon the glorious career of Lee, I have sometimes felt inclined to say in behalf of my friend what he never said for himself: "Who can tell? It might have been!" And I do here say of him, in a single sentence, that as a trained, professional soldier, I do not believe he ever had his superior, if indeed his equal, on this continent; while as a man he was one of the purest and strongest I ever knew, and perhaps the most affectionate.

When he ran for Congress in 1878 against the candidate of the combined Greenback and Republican parties, in a district including Richmond City and several counties, I was chairman of his campaign committee, and heartily wish it were appropriate to relate many of the incidents of the campaign so graphically illustrating how world-wide apart are the soldier and the politician. I must, however, be pardoned for telling one.

He came to his headquarters one morning much outraged at what I had not heard of and, of course, had not authorized—the erection of a banner, the night before, in the strongest manufacturing ward in the city, with his name upon it and some popular catchword or phrase squinting obscurely at "protection." Upon military principles he held me responsible, but I soon ascertained that it had been done with the approval of a shrewd and experienced practical politician, who was also an influential member of the committee, and I deemed it proper to call that body together. Upon their assembling the General took the matter entirely out of my hands, saying substantially and with very hot emphasis: "Gentlemen, this is a matter about which I do not propose to ask your advice, because it involves my conscience and my personal honor. I spoke yesterday, at Louisa Court House, under a 'free-trade' flag. I have never ridden 'both sides of the sapling,' and I don't propose to learn how at this late day. That banner in Clay Ward comes down to-day or I retire from this canvass by published card to-morrow."

I have said he was the most affectionate of men. It will surprise many, who saw only the iron bearing of the soldier, to hear that we never met, or parted for any length of time, that he did not, if we were alone, throw his arms about me and kiss me, and that such was his habit in parting from or greeting his male relatives and most cherished friends. I will only add that he and General Lee entertained the most exalted estimate and opinion of each other, and when—very late in the war, I think in February, 1865—Lee was made practical dictator and commander-in-chief of all the armies of the Confederacy, his very first act as such was the restoration of Joseph E. Johnston to the command of the army from which he had been removed when Hood was put in his place.

As to the actual fighting at Seven Pines, we took part in it, yet not a very prominent part. Among the heroes of the day were our old Leesburg acquaintance, now Major-General D. H. Hill, whose division covered itself and its commander with blood and glory by one of the most dogged and deadly fights on record; and Captain, afterwards Colonel, Tom Carter, of the King William Artillery—yesterday the ideal artillerist, the idol of the artillery of the Army of Northern Virginia, to-day an ideal Southern gentleman and the efficient Proctor of our State University. He is a cousin of Robert E. Lee, and combines more of the modesty, simplicity, purity, and valor of his great kinsman than any other living man of my acquaintance.

At Seven Pines his battery made a phenomenal fight against an overwhelming weight of metal, and while Carter was sitting on his horse, with one foot in the stirrup and the other thrown across the pommel of his saddle, directing the undismayed fight of the undestroyed fragment of his battery, up rode our old friend "D. H.," and in the midst of the awful carnage and destruction once more gave expression to his monomania on the subject of fighting pluck by rising in his stirrups, saluting Carter and his men and declaring he had rather be captain of the King William Artillery than President of the Confederate States. But, as before said, this battle lives and will live in history, mainly as that which brought together for the first time the great Captain and the tattered soldiery, which ere long made the world ring with their fame.

Lee's grand plan of the Seven Days' battles has been so often expatiated upon by able soldiers and writers that I could scarcely hope to add anything of intrinsic value to the discussion, so I propose to give what I have to say on the topic by way of post-bellum reminiscence.

It has been noted with surprise how many distinguished and devout clergymen of the Church of England have admitted an irrepressible lifelong yearning for the army. My recollection is that this feeling crops out more or less in Kingsley; I am sure it runs like a refrain through Frederick William Robertson's life and letters and appears perhaps in his sermons. Years ago, when he who is now Rev. Dr. Rainsford, of St. George's, New York, was a glorious youth, he conducted a most successful mission in St. Paul's Church, Richmond, Va., and drew some of us very close to him. Toward the close of his work he asked Col. Archer Anderson and myself to walk with him over the field of the Seven Days' battles, or as much of it as we could "do" on foot in a day. We started early one crisp February morning, the Colonel and I full of interest, but fearful that we could not keep up with the giant stride of our comrade, who was a trained athlete and one of the most heroic looking specimens of young manhood I ever beheld. We could not help thinking what a soldier he would have made. He was not then a Reverend Doctor and will, I am sure, pardon me for speaking of him on this occasion as "Rainsford."

We explained to him the positions of the two armies just before the opening of the battle; that Lee's was on this, the Richmond side of the Chickahominy, which was generally impassable, except where the various roads, running out of Richmond like the spokes of a wheel, crossed it; that McClellan's army was on both sides of the stream or swamp, the bulk of it perhaps at this time on the Richmond side, but he had established and fortified free communication between his two wings; also that Jackson had been secretly drawn down from the Valley, and was now hovering, hawk fashion, somewhere over beyond and back of McClellan's right flank.

We next showed him the disparity in numbers, McClellan, by his own report, dated June 20, 1862, six days before the fighting began, having "Present for duty one hundred and five thousand eight hundred and twenty-five (105,825) men;" and as he was anticipating battle and calling lustily for reinforcements, his force was probably substantially increased during these six days; while Lee, as demonstrated by Col. Walter H. Taylor, adjutant-general of his army, and Gen. Jubal A. Early, both better informed on the subject than any other man ever was, had a little under or a little over eighty thousand (80,000) men present for duty when the fight opened, including Jackson's forces. Moreover, our inferiority in artillery, both as to number and character of guns, and as to ammunition also, was shocking.

Meanwhile, we were walking out, to and across the Chickahominy, by the Mechanicsville turnpike or the Meadow Bridge road, the last of which debouched on the other side of the stream, a little to our left of the end of the Federal lines, this being the road by which Lee's first attacking column filed out on the 26th of June, '62, swung around McClellan's right flank and burst like an electric bolt upon the besieging army; the next and supporting column marching out by the Mechanicsville pike as soon as the first had cleared that road.

We explained Jackson's part in the plan, entering the fight the next day, on the left of the troops from Richmond and further in rear of McClellan's right flank; our combined forces driving his right wing—which was most ably handled and gallantly fought—back upon his centre, from which troops had been already drawn to support his right.

We pointed out to him the audacious boldness of Lee's plan in withdrawing approximately two-thirds of his army from the lines about Richmond for this attack, so that barely 28,000 men were left between the Federal army and the Confederate capital.

And when at last McClellan succeeded in getting all of his hard-pressed troops across to the Richmond side, this 28,000 men, who had not yet been engaged, uniting with their victorious comrades, fell like an avalanche (or rather had orders to fall—nearly one-third of them did not fire a shot) upon his wornout, beaten, and dispirited troops, drove them pell-mell under the guns of their James River fleet, and but for failure of subordinates to carry out instructions Lee would undoubtedly have dictated terms of surrender to his gallant foe.

We went out on the Meadow Bridge or Mechanicsville road, made the entire sweep, and returned, I think, by the Williamsburg road, the York River Railroad, and the New

Bridge road—at all events, we could scarcely have walked much, if any, less than twenty-eight to thirty miles. It was one of the most enjoyable days of my life. Rainsford caught the plan instantly. Going over it in detail with him, upon the very spots, and climbing the very slopes up which Lee's legions had rushed to the charge, he was thrilled to almost savage excitement, yelling like a rebel infantryman, his giant frame and his grand face absolutely inspired. In his martial ecstasy he threw his great arms about us, hugging us, to our imminent peril; declaring he had loved us both at first sight, but could never forget us now, and that to have lived in and been a part of those days and those battles was enough to lift men forever to heroic stature and character.

Our battery was among the 28,000 men left on the Richmond side of the Chickahominy to defend the capital, to occupy the attention of McClellan's troops on this side, and to prevent their recrossing to the aid of their hard-pressed comrades on the other; but the real defenders of the city were the men who stormed the bloody heights at Gaines' Mill and the positions at Mechanicsville and Cold Harbor. We were in General Magruder's command and were kept most of the time hitched up and ready to move at a moment's warning. We were subjected now and then to fire from Federal batteries, suffered some loss of horses and equipment, and several of our men were wounded, but there were no serious casualties.

On the 29th of June—Sunday, I think it was—General Magruder advanced his troops along the Nine-Mile road to feel the enemy, when the main thing that struck us was the immense quantity of abandoned stores and equipment, indicating how abundant had been the supply of the Federal forces and how great the demoralization of their retreat. Near Savage Station there must have been acres covered by stacks of burning boxes of bacon, crackers, and desiccated vegetables—"desecrated vegetables," our boys called them. To us poorly-equipped and half-starved rebels it was a revelation. Here and elsewhere we picked up a few rations and a few choice equipments of various kinds, but had really

neither time nor taste for plunder. There were other mementoes of their stay and of their hasty departure left by
"our friends the enemy," not quite so attractive or appetizing
—the ghastly leavings of numerous field hospitals; pale,
naked corpses and grotesque piles of arms and legs.

At one of these hospital stations we found an Irishman,
whom we at first thought dying, as perhaps he was; but a
swallow or two of the "crathur" revived him, and when,
under such inspiration, did Pat ever fail to be communica-
tive and witty? He seemed to grasp the situation perfectly,
and upon someone asking if the apparent flight might not
after all be a trap—"Be dad," said he, "an' ef it's a thrap,
thin shure *an' little Mac's lost the thrigger!*"

At or near Savage Station, I think on this 29th of June,
our brigade commander, General Griffith, was killed. In a
shower of projectiles turned loose upon us by an unseen foe,
at least half a shell from a three-inch rifled gun lodged in his
body. The marvel is he did not die instantly, but I noted a
desperate clinch of his fingers and the pallor of his face as he
clasped his hands back of his head after he had fallen from
his horse. He was a genial and cultured gentleman and regarded as a very promising officer. Colonel Barksdale, of
the Thirteenth, at once took command of the brigade, and
was soon commissioned brigadier.

We then crossed over to the York River Railroad, upon
which we had what our men called our "railroad gun," a
siege piece, mounted on a flat-car with an engine back of it,
the front of the car being protected by rails of track iron
fastened upon an incline, the mouth of the gun projecting a
little as from an embrasure. As it puffed up, a number of
Federal batteries, invisible to us, opened upon it and upon
the troops, and General Magruder sent an order for our
guns to cross the railroad by the bridge hard by and come
into battery in the smooth, hard field beyond.

We executed this dashing feat in gallant style, our captain riding ahead, the pieces in a wild gallop and the men on
a wild run following. Again we seemed to be in full sight
of an unseen enemy, for the bridge was raked and swept by
a fearful storm of shot and shell. I distinctly remember the

shells bursting in my very face, and the bridge must have
been struck repeatedly, the great splinters hurtling past and
cutting the air like flashes of lightning, yet no one was hurt.
Once across, we were ordered, "Forward into battery, left
oblique, march!" which elaborate movement was executed by
the men as if on drill. I could not refrain from glancing
around, and was amazed to see every piece, limber, caisson
and man in the exact mathematical position in which each
belonged, and every man seemed to have struck the very attitude required by the drill-book. And there we all stood,
raked by a terrific fire, to which we could not reply, being
really a second line, the first—consisting of infantry alone—
having passed into the dense, forbidding forest in front,
feeling for the enemy. And so it was most of the way to
Malvern Hill. The country not admitting of the use of
cavalry to any extent, we were constantly playing at "lost-
ball," and exposed to galling fire from a foe we could not see,
and to whom we generally could not reply because our infantry was in the woods in front of us.

But two things delighted us greatly: Our old brigade
had been in our rear when we dashed across the bridge,
taking the fire from them—and not only did they witness
this, but they were lying down behind us when we executed
the beautiful movement and made the staunch, soldierly
stand in the open field beyond; so they cheered us enthusias-
tically the next time we moved by them.

The second morning after,—just as we came into battery
on the field of Frazier's (or Frayser's) farm, where the
fighting had closed after dark the preceding day, and which
on that morning presented perhaps the most ideal view of a
battlefield I ever saw—captured cannon, exploded limbers
and caissons, dead horses and dead men scattered over it in
most picturesque fashion,—Col. Stephen D. Lee, of the artillery, afterwards lieutenant-general, rode out in front of our
guns, took off his hat to us and said that he had witnessed
and remarked upon our performance of two days ago, at the
railroad bridge and in the field, as General Magruder had
also; that nothing could have been more soldierly, and having thus shown ourselves equal to the most trying duty of the

soldier, the duty of standing and receiving fire without re-
plying to it, he had determined we should certainly have the
opportunity of seeing how well we could perform the easier
part of returning fire, blow for blow—an opportunity we
certainly did have at Malvern Hill, *ad satietatem,* or *ad
nauseam,* as the case might be, according to the degree and
intensity of a man's hankering and hungering for fight. As
for our own feelings upon this subject, just at this time, we
had but that moment turned our backs upon a scene no ways
calculated to impart hot stomach for battle.

The six brigades of General Magruder's command—
Barksdale's, to which we were attached, being one—had arrived at Frazier's farm the preceding night after dark and
too late to take part in the engagement. We were overpow-
ered with fatigue, intent only on sleep, and sank to rest amid
the wreck and death of the hard-fought field. In the shadowy
dawn, as our guns, moving into position to reopen the fight,
threaded their way through the confused bivouac of the slumbering, the dying and the dead—the mysterious hush of the
battlefield resting over all—we saw, side by side, upturned
together to the bleaching dew, the pale faces of the breathing and the breathless sleepers, not distinguishable in the
dim morning twilight. Suddenly the drums beat to arms
and the living rose,—and then the stolidest veteran in that
vast multitude shuddered as he left the side of his ghastly
bedfellow who had rested with him so quietly all that summer night, and by whose side the frame that now shrank
away with horror might rest to-night as ghastly as he.

All of us had been longing for a sight of Jackson. It is
impossible to exaggerate or even to convey an adequate idea
of the excitement and furor concerning him about this time,
both in the army and among the people.

On Sunday evening, not far from Savage Station, I had
been struck directly over the heart by a spent ball, which
glanced from a buckle, but blackened my breast and nau-
seated me somewhat. Next morning, still feeling badly and
the battery remaining stationary for a time, I had retired a
little from the line and was half reclining at the foot of a huge
pine that stood on the edge of the Williamsburg road. Hear-

ing the jingle of cavalry accoutrements toward the Chickahominy, I looked up and saw a half-dozen mounted men, and
riding considerably in advance a solitary horseman, whom I
instantly recognized as the great wizard of the marvelous
Valley Campaign which had so thrilled the army and the
country.

Jackson and the little sorrel stopped in the middle of the
road, probably not fifty feet off, while his staff halted perhaps a hundred and fifty yards in his rear. He sat stark and
stiff in the saddle. Horse and rider appeared worn down
to the lowest point of flesh consistent with effective service.
His hair, skin, eyes, and clothes were all one neutral dust
tint, and his badges of rank so dulled and tarnished as to be
scarcely perceptible. The "mangy little cadet cap" was pulled
so low in front that the visor cut the glint of his eyeballs.

A ghastly scene was spread across the road hard by. The
Seventeenth and Twenty-first Mississippi, of our brigade,
had been ordered into the woods about dusk the evening before and told not to fire into the first line they met; but the
poor fellows ran into a Federal brigade and were shocked
and staggered by a deadly volley. Splendid soldiers that they
were, they obeyed orders, held their own fire, laid down and
took the enemy's. Almost every man struck was killed, and
every man killed shot through the brain. Their comrades
had gone into the woods as soon as it was light, brought out
the bodies and laid them in rows, with hands crossed upon
the breast, but eyes wide-staring. A sickly summer rain had
fallen in the night and the faces of the dead were bleached
with more than death's pallor. Every eyeball was strained
upward toward the spot where the bullet had crashed through
the skull, and every forehead stained with ooze and trickle
of blood. Men were passing through the silent lines, bending low, seeking in the distorted faces to identify their
friends.

Jackson glanced a moment toward this scene. Not a
muscle quivered as he resumed his steady gaze down the
road toward Richmond. He was the ideal of concentration,
—imperturbable, resistless. I remember feeling that if he
were not a very good man he would be a very bad one. By

a ludicrous turn of the association of ideas, the old darkey minister's illustration of faith flashed through my brain: "Bredren, ef de Lord tell me to jump through a stone wall, I's gwine to jump at it; jumpin' at it 'longs to me, goin' through it 'longs to God." The man before me would have jumped at anything the Lord told him to jump through.

A moment later and his gaze was rewarded. A magnificent staff approached from the direction of Richmond, and riding at its head, superbly mounted, a born king among men. At that time General Lee was one of the handsomest of men, especially on horseback, and that morning every detail of the dress and equipment of himself and horse was absolute perfection. When he recognized Jackson he rode forward with a courier, his staff halting. As he gracefully dismounted, handing his bridle rein to his attendant, and advanced, drawing the gauntlet from his right hand, Jackson flung himself off his horse and advanced to meet Lee, little sorrel trotting back to the staff, where a courier secured him.

The two generals greeted each other warmly, but wasted no time upon the greeting. They stood facing each other, some thirty feet from where I lay, Lee's left side and back toward me, Jackson's right and front. Jackson began talking in a jerky, impetuous way, meanwhile drawing a diagram on the ground with the toe of his right boot. He traced two sides of a triangle with promptness and decision; then starting at the end of the second line, began to draw a third projected toward the first. This third line he traced slowly and with hesitation, alternately looking up at Lee's face and down at his diagram, meanwhile talking earnestly; and when at last the third line crossed the first and the triangle was complete, he raised his foot and stamped it down with emphasis, saying, "We've got him;" then signalled for his horse, and when he came, vaulted awkwardly into the saddle and was off. Lee watched him a moment, the courier brought his horse, he mounted, and he and his staff rode away.

The third line was never drawn—so we never "got" McClellan.

I question if any other man witnessed this interview—certainly no other was as near the two generals. At times I could hear their words, though they were uttered, for the most part, in the low tones of close and earnest conference. As the two faced each other, except that the difference in height was not great, the contrast between them could not have been more striking—in feature, figure, dress, voice, style, bearing, manner, everything, in short, that expressed the essential individuality of the two men. It was the Cavalier and the Puritan in intensest embodiment. These two great roots and stocks of British manhood had borne each its consummate flower in the rank soil of the New World.

CHAPTER IX

MALVERN HILL AND THE EFFECT OF THE SEVEN DAYS' BATTLES

Not a Confederate Victory—The Federal Artillery Fire—Demoralization of Lee's Army—"McClellan Will Be Gone by Daylight"—The Weight of Lee's Sword—Stuart—Pelham—Pegram—"Extra Billy" —To Battle in a Trotting Sulky—The Standard of Courage.

I have said nothing as yet about Malvern Hill. No Confederate cares to say anything about it. If McClellan had done nothing else in the seven days to stamp him as a general, and his army nothing else to stamp them as soldiers, beyond the selection of this position, the disposition and handling of his artillery, and the stubborn and successful stand there made, after and in spite of the experiences of the six days preceding—the reputation, both of general and of soldiers, might well be rested on this basis alone. If it had been a single, isolated battle, it would have gone down into history simply and squarely as a defeat for the Confederates, and even when viewed in its historic connection, it must yet be admitted that all our assaults were repulsed and our pursuit so staggered that the Federal general was allowed to withdraw his army without being closely pressed.

Upon our side there was not a single relieving feature in the picture. In the first place, the battle ought never to have been fought where it was. If the orders of Lee had been carried out, it would not have been, for McClellan would never have reached this position. The "third line," of which Lee and Jackson spoke in the interview described in the preceding chapter, was never drawn. The understanding in the army at the time was that Huger and Holmes were to have drawn it, but that their commands lost their way in the almost trackless forest.   In an address on "The Campaigns of Gen. Robert E. Lee," delivered at Washington and Lee University in 1872, on January 19th, Lee's birthday, Gen. Jubal A. Early says: "* * * Holmes' command, over six thousand strong, did not actually engage in any of the battles."   But Col. Walter H. Taylor, in his "Four Years with General Lee," published in 1877, already referred to, repeats three times—on pages 51, 53, and 54—that Holmes' command numbered ten thousand or more; and it is obvious, upon a comparison of the two statements, that Early's figures, "over six thousand," did not include Ransom's brigade, which numbered thirty-six hundred.

It seems incredible, yet it appears to be true, that General Holmes was very deaf; so deaf that, when heaven and earth were shuddering with the thunder of artillery and the faces of his own men were blanched with the strain, he placed his hand behind his ear, and turning to a member of his staff, said, "I think I hear guns."   The story was told by one of his own brigadiers, and if anything approximating to it was true, then a great responsibility rests upon some one for putting an officer so far disabled in charge of troops,—especially at such a crisis and for such a service,—whatever his other qualifications may have been.

As before stated, General Lee left but twenty-eight thousand men on the Richmond side of the Chickahominy when he crossed to the other side to attack McClellan, and of course looked to these fresh troops, when his victorious but decimated and worn-out soldiers had driven the enemy into their arms, to fall upon the Federal general and gather the fruits of victory.   But here are more than one-third of these fresh troops, and the very ones Lee had arranged should cut off the retreat of his gallant foe, that never got into action at all, and McClellan was permitted to reach and occupy the strong position which saved his army and cost the lives of thousands of ours.   And even this was not all.   Magruder, a most vigorous officer, to whose command we were attached, lost his way and thus delayed the attack and gave McClellan further time for his dispositions.   And when at last we did attack, it was in a disconnected and desultory

fashion, which even to a private soldier seemed to promise
no good result.   But I cannot give a fairer or better idea
of our view of the battle than by quoting from pages 48, 49
of Colonel Taylor's admirable book:

> From these extracts I think it will be clear to the candid reader that
> the retreat to the James River was a compulsory one, and due to a defeat
> then acknowledged by General McClellan himself.
>
> The fighting, however, was not invariably attended with success to
> the Confederates; notably, the defense of Malvern Hill by the Federals
> was in favor of the latter, which result was as much due to the misman-
> agement of the Confederate troops as to the naturally strong position
> occupied by the Federals and their gallantry in its defense.
>
> Considerable delay was occasioned in the pursuit from the fact that
> the ground was unknown to the Confederate commanders. On this occa-
> sion General Magruder took the wrong route and had to be recalled,
> thereby losing much precious time; and when after serious and
> provoking delay the lines were formed for attack, there was some mis-
> understanding of the orders of the commanding general, and instead of
> a spirited, united advance by the entire line, as contemplated, the
> divisions were moved forward at different times, each attacking inde-
> pendently, and each in turn repulsed.   Moreover, owing to the peculiar
> character of the ground, artillery could not be advantageously placed to
> aid the assaulting columns; whereas the Federal batteries, strongly
> posted and most handsomely served, contributed in a very great degree
> to the successful stand made by McClellan's retreating army at Malvern
> Hill.

I have characterized the foregoing as a fair statement,
as it certainly is, and yet even this fails to convey an adequate impression of the stunning and temporarily depressing
effect of this battle upon our army.   As to my own experience and feelings, the revelation I am about to make may
be a damaging one, yet I have no desire to sail under false
colors, and then, too, my own case may serve to confirm and
in part to explain the remarkable statements below made as
to the sudden and fearful deterioration in the condition of
our army which this battle, for the time, effected.

Three of the guns of the old battery were put in action
against McClellan's majestic aggregation of batteries, by
way of at least making a diversion in favor of our assaulting

infantry, a diversion which I presume we to some extent accomplished; for I never conceived anything approximating the shower and storm of projectiles and the overwhelming cataclysm of destruction which were at once turned upon our pitiful little popguns. In the short time they existed as effective pieces they were several times fired by fragments of Federal shell striking them after the lanyard was stretched and before it was pulled; and in almost less time than it takes to tell it the carriages were completely crushed, smashed, and splintered and the guns themselves so injured and defaced that we were compelled to send them to Richmond, after the battle, to be remoulded.

We were put in action, too, after a long, hot run. I was as sound and strong as human flesh could well be, and yet my lungs seemed to be pumped out, my brain reeled and my tongue clave to the roof of my mouth, which was burnt so dry that I experienced great difficulty in swallowing. Nevertheless, I managed to do my part in serving my gun, until, in a few moments, it was completely disabled, when I fell to the earth, a horror of great darkness came upon me, and the only distinct impression I can recall is that I felt I would be glad to compromise on annihilation.

When I roused myself from this semi-stupor or swoon the detachment seemed to have disappeared, but in a few moments I found most of the men. I remember catching by the collar one who had dropped down, "all in a heap," in an unnecessarily exposed position on the projecting root of a large tree and jerking him up; when on the instant a shell tore to pieces the root upon which he had been seated, and yet he sank down again but a step or two from the spot. It was the first battle in which members of the company had been killed outright. The wonder is that any survived who were working these three pieces; but I suppose it is to be accounted for by the fact that the guns were quickly disabled and put out of action.

According to his own report of June 20, 1862, McClellan had three hundred and forty pieces of field artillery. I see no reason for doubting that a very large proportion of these were massed upon Malvern Hill. Nothing human can long withstand the fire of such a mass of artillery concentrated, as the Federal guns at Malvern Hill were, upon very short attacking lines of infantry. Colonel Taylor says divisions were marched forward at different times, each attacking independently and each in turn repulsed. I think it was even worse than this, and that in some cases single brigades advanced to the attack and were almost literally swept backward by what seemed to be the fire of a continuous line of battle of artillery.

The effect of these repeated bloody repulses can hardly be conceived. One fearful feature was the sudden and awful revulsion of feeling among our soldiers, inspired by six days of constant victory and relentless pursuit of a retreating foe. The demoralization was great and the evidences of it palpable everywhere. The roads and forests were full of stragglers; commands were inextricably confused, some, for the time, having actually disappeared. Those who retained sufficient self-respect and sense of responsibility to think of the future were filled with the deepest apprehension. I know that this was the state of mind of some of our strongest and best officers; in fact, I do not know of any general officer in the army, save one, who did not entertain the gloomiest forebodings, and I recall hearing at the time, or rather a day or so afterwards, substantially the same story of that one which within the last few years and a short time before his own death was related by Dr. Hunter McGuire, Jackson's medical director, a man whom of all men he loved and trusted next after his great chief, Robert Lee. I quote from an address first delivered by Doctor McGuire at Lexington, but repeated several times afterwards by special request:

At Malvern Hill, when a portion of our army was beaten and to some extent demoralized, Hill and Ewell and Early came to tell him that they could make no resistance if McClellan attacked them in the morning. It was difficult to wake General Jackson, as he was exhausted and very sound asleep. I tried it myself, and after many efforts, partly succeeded. When he was made to understand what was wanted he said: "McClellan and his army will be gone by daylight," and went to sleep again. The generals thought him mad, but the prediction was true.

The Hill here referred to is probably not our old friend "D. H.," but A. P. Hill, a more brilliant soldier, yet, perhaps, not so peculiarly distinguished for imperturbable grit. The story illustrates two of the greatest and most distinguishing traits and powers of Jackson as a general: he did not know what demoralization meant, and he never failed to know just what his adversary thought and felt and proposed to do. In the present instance, not only did all that Jackson said and implied turn out to be true, that McClellan was thinking only of escape, and never dreamed of viewing the battle of Malvern Hill in any other aspect, but in an incredibly short time our army had recovered its tone and had come to take the same view of the matter. Indeed, as I believe, nothing but another untoward accident prevented McClellan's surrendering his entire army to Lee, notwithstanding his successful defense at Malvern Hill. The matter will be found circumstantially set out in Colonel Taylor's book, pages 41-44, substantiated and confirmed by a full extract from General Stuart's manuscript of "Reports and Notes on the War," and also by extracts from the report of the "Committee on the Conduct of the War," and is in outline as follows:

Stuart, Lee's chief of cavalry, following up McClellan's movements after Malvern Hill, from the heights above West-over, overlooked the entire Federal army huddled together in the river bottoms of and adjacent to Westover plantation, apparently in a state of utter disorganization and unpreparedness, and he could not resist the temptation of dropping a few shells among them, which produced a perfect stampede among the troops and wagons, but at the same time had the effect of calling the attention of the Federal commanders to the fact that the position of their army was utterly untenable without command of the heights from which these shells had been fired, and they immediately sent a heavy force to take possession of them. Stuart at once informed General Lee and received word that Jackson and Longstreet were *en route* to support him; but again the guides proved incompetent, and Longstreet was led six or seven miles out of the way, and Stuart, after resisting as long as he could, was compelled to yield possession of the heights, which were promptly occupied and fortified by an adequate Federal force, and McClellan's army was, for the first time, safe from successful attack.

After having for the third time traced the failure of the plans of the Confederates to the incompetence or to the delinquency of guides,—in the misleading of Holmes and Huger, of Magruder, and now of Longstreet,—it seems proper to remark that the entire region which was the theatre of the Seven Days' battles is, for the most part, covered by heavy pine forests and cypress swamps, and these traversed by many wood roads, or paths rather, undistinguishable the one from the other. The confusing character of the country is well illustrated by the fact that the last time I went there, with a party of survivors of our old battery, with the view, if possible, of identifying certain positions occupied by our guns in the campaign of '64, we had two guides born and reared in the neighborhood and who professed to be perfectly familiar with the country and with the positions we desired to find; and yet these men insisted upon leading us astray, and would have done so, but that my recollection and my instinct of locality were so opposed to their views that I simply refused to be misled. Unassisted and unaccompanied I found the first position sought, the rest of the party, with the guides, wandering around for hours and finally working around to me. But it should be remembered that the generals who were misled by guides, to the disarrangement and defeat of General Lee's perfectly arranged plans, so far at least as I have reason to believe, had never been in the region before.

Yet, once more. "Stuart, glorious Stuart," as Colonel Taylor justly calls him, while his boyish indiscretion in firing into the huddled masses of the enemy from Evelington Heights, before informing General Lee of the situation, was apparently the cause of the loss of another great opportunity —yet it should not be forgotten, in this connection, that the great plan of the Seven Days battles owed its inspiration, or at least its completion and perfection, to the information derived from Stuart's marvelous ride around McClellan's entire army just in advance of Lee's attack, more than to any other source outside the imperial intellect of the Commander-in-Chief himself. Stuart was a splendidly endowed cavalry leader, his only fault being a tendency to indulge too far his fondness for achievements that savored of the startling, the marvelous, and the romantic.

One more general reflection: Whatever effect the Seven Days' battles may have had upon other reputations, Federal or Confederate—and there were upon our side generals whose names stood high upon the roster of our main army when these operations began, but never again appeared upon it after they closed—yet there is one name and fame which these seven days gave to history and to glory, as to which the entire world stands agreed, and all the after chances and changes of the war but expanded the world's verdict. When we contemplate Lee's great plan and the qualities of leadership which these operations revealed in him, we know not which most to admire—the brilliance, the comprehensiveness, or the almost reckless audacity of the scheme and of the man. It is a singular fact, and one which seems to demand explanation, that the prominent impression which Lee invariably seems to make is that of roundness, balance, perfection; and yet unquestionably his leading characteristic as a general is aggressive audacity. Take for example his leaving but 28,000 of 80,000 men between McClellan and Richmond, and with the other 52,000 crossing a generally impassable stream and attacking McClellan's 105,000 in entrenched positions. Mayhap old Jubal Early, who knew Lee and knew war as well as any other man on either side, has the right of it and suggests the true explanation when he says, speaking of this very operation: "Timid minds might regard this as rashness, but it was the very perfection of a profound and daring strategy."

And when we attempt to measure the effect of these Seven Days' battles—when we note that within less than one month from the day he took command of an army with which he had had no previous personal connection, Lee had completely secured its confidence and correctly estimated its capabilities, had conceived and perfected his great plan and every detail essential to its successful execution, had begun to put it into operation and actually delivered his first great blow; when we note further that within a week after that blow was struck Richmond was entirely relieved and within a few weeks more Washington was in serious peril, and the United States Government had called for three hundred thousand more men; when, we say, all this is considered, we may well ask when did the weight of one great Captain's sword, only this and nothing more, cause the scales of war to dip with such a determined, downward sag?

One of the most important features of these seven days of battle was that it was the first prolonged wrestle of the Army of Northern Virginia, the struggle that really gave birth to that army; that gave it experience of its own powers, cohesion, character, confidence in itself and in its great commander—proper estimate of its great opponent, the Army of the Potomac, and its commander. Then, too, these days of continuous battle tested the individual men, and especially the officers of the army, winnowing the chaff from the wheat and getting rid of some high in command who did not catch the essential spirit of the army or assimilate well with it, or bid fair to add anything of value to it; at the same time this week of continuous battle brought to the front men who had in them stuff out of which heroes are made and who were destined to make names and niches for themselves in the pantheon of this immortal army.

Among those in my own branch of the service who came prominently to the front, besides Tom Carter, who never lost the place he made for himself at Seven Pines in the affectionate admiration of the artillery and of the army, were the boy artillerists Pegram and Pelham, both yielding their glorious young lives in the struggle—Pegram at the very end, Pelham but eight months after Malvern Hill. The latter, an Alabamian, was commander of Stuart's horse artillery, devotedly loved and admired by his commanding general, the pride of the cavalry corps, one of the most dashing and brilliant soldiers in the service, though but twenty-two years of age when he fell. He was knighted by Lee himself in official report as "the gallant Pelham."

The other, Pegram, was a more serious and a more powerful man, who came of a family of soldiers who had rendered distinguished service, both in the army and navy, prior to the war; an elder brother, a graduate of West Point and a singularly attractive man, rising to the rank of major-general in the Confederate service, and also losing his life in battle. The younger brother, the artillerist, a student when the war began, enlisted as a private soldier in a battery raised in the City of Richmond, which he commanded when the Seven Days' battles opened, rendering with it signal and distinguished service. Eventually he rose to the rank and command of colonel of artillery, and was recommended for appointment as brigadier-general of infantry, General Lee saying he would find a brigade for him just as soon as he could be spared from the artillery; but meanwhile he fell in battle at Five Forks in the spring of '65, even then hardly more than a stripling in years.

He had always been such a modest, self-contained and almost shrinking youth that his most intimate friends were astonished at his rapid development and promotion; but it was one of those strongly-marked cases where war seemed to be the needed and almost the native air of a young man. He was, in some respects, of the type of Stonewall Jackson, and like him combined the strongest Christian faith and the deepest spirituality with the most intense spirit of fight.

As commander of an artillery battalion he built up a reputation second to none for effective handling of his guns, his favorite method, where practicable, being to rush to close quarters with the enemy and open at the shortest possible range. He admitted that it seemed deadly, but insisted that it saved life in the end. When stricken down he lived long enough to express his views and feelings, briefly but clearly, with regard to both worlds, and there never was a death more soldierly or more Christian.

Another, a very different and very racy character, who was a good deal talked about after and in connection with the fighting around Richmond in '62 was old "Extra Billy," ex-Governor William Smith, of Virginia, whom I mentioned as prominent among the Southern members in the Congress of '59-'60. He was one of the best specimens of the political general, rising ultimately to the rank of major-general; a born politician, twice Governor of the Commonwealth,—once before and once after this date,—already beyond the military age, yet one of the most devoted and enthusiastic soldiers in the service.   As a soldier he was equally distinguished for personal intrepidity and contempt for what he called "tactics" and for educated and trained soldiers, whom he was wont to speak of as "those West P'int fellows."

It is said he used to drill his regiment at Manassas, sitting cross-legged on the top of an old Virginia snake fence, with a blue cotton umbrella over his head and reading the orders from a book.   On one occasion he was roused by the laughing outcry, "Colonel, you've run us bang up against the fence!"   "Well, then, boys," said the old Governor, looking up and nothing daunted; "well, then, of course you'll have to turn around or climb the fence."

In '62 this story was current about him,—though I do not vouch for the truth either of this or of that just related,—that he was ordered to carry a work and to take his command through the abattis in front of it, reserving their fire. The regiment started in, the old Governor intrepidly riding in advance.   The abattis swarmed with sharpshooters and his men were falling all about him, but they followed on heroically.   At last they appealed to him, "Colonel, we can't stand this, these Yankees will kill us all before we get in a shot."   It was all the old hero wanted and he blazed forth: "Of course you can't stand it, boys; it's all this infernal tactics and West P'int tomfoolery.   Damn it, fire! and flush the game!"   And they did, and drove out the sharpshooters and carried the work.

My own dear father is one of the prominent figures in my recollections of that summer about Richmond.   He was fond of horses, an excellent judge of them, and used to ride or drive the very best that could be found.   I say "ride or drive."   He was then between sixty-five and seventy years of age and, though vigorous and enthusiastic, found it very comfortable to drive sometimes; but his selected vehicle was at once the most unclerical and unmilitary that could well be imagined—a regulation skeleton "trotting sulky."   He kept his saddle at our battery and his habit was, when we were not actually fighting or on the move, to return to Richmond at night, coming down in the morning with a big market basket strapped under his sulky full of bread and good things.   His approach was generally heralded by the shouts of the soldiers who followed; when, looking up the road, we would see him, often standing on the shafts, scattering biscuit and reading aloud the latest telegrams.   Hundreds of men would sometimes follow him to our camp, and then he would have prayers with them and make a brief religious address.

Coming in this way one morning he did not find us; the battle was on and we had gone to the front.   As he could not get his saddle, he kept right on in his sulky, hoping to overtake us.   In some way he managed to pass through and get ahead of the second line and went on, actually between the first and second lines of battle, until his further progress was obstructed by a line of works which had been captured by the first line, when he was forced to turn back, amidst a storm of ridicule from the second line:

"That's right, old man; this ain't no place for you, nor for me neither, if I could only git my colonel to think so!"

"Say, mister, won't your buggy carry double?"

"Haven't you got a place for me?"

"Oh, please, sir, take me with you!   I ain't feeling so mighty well this morning.   I'm powerful weak, right now."

Father always followed the Scripture rule of "answering a fool according to his folly," and so he jeered back at them, telling them "good-by," but saying he'd be back in a minute —as he actually was, riding, bareback and blind bridle, and passing right ahead with the troops.   I have heard of following a fox hunt in one of these sulkies, but I venture to say this is the very first time a man ever entered battle in one.

It will at once occur to the reader as remarkable that father was not arrested.   He was, a few days later, at Malvern Hill, by order of Gen. Rans. Wright, of Georgia, and a staff officer, as I recollect, of General Armistead, told me that he was directed to arrest him on one of the earlier battle-fields of the Seven Days, and made the attempt; that up to that time he had regarded himself as a pretty daring rider and scout, but that father, whom he did not then know, led him such a chase as he had never before had, and that he returned to his general and reported that he didn't believe there was any harm in that old fellow, though he was certainly a crank, and if he got killed it would be his own fault; but that, unless positively so ordered, he didn't propose to get a bullet through his brain following that old fool right up to the Yankee skirmish line.

It must be remembered that my father was a Christian minister, devoted to the soldiers, and a sort of chaplain-general among them. He was ready to whisper the consolations of religion in the ear of a dying man, to help the litter bearers, or to carry a wounded man off on his horse. Then, too, he was well known to many of our generals to whom, by the way, he carried a vast amount of information gathered on his daring scouts ahead even of our skirmishers. I myself heard two or three of the most prominent generals say that it was their belief my father had seen more of the fighting of the Seven Days, from start to finish, than any other one man in or out of the army. I was of course deeply anxious about him, but he could not be controlled, and my belief was then, and is now, that the Federal skirmishers often refrained from firing upon him simply because they did not care at the time to expose their position.

Many of our soldiers knew him, especially the Georgians, Virginians and Mississippians. Georgia was his native State. In his early days he had done a great deal of evangelistic work in all parts of it, and many young men and boys in the army had heard their parents speak of him. I remember one evening, after a most impressive sermon to Cobb's or Cummings' brigade, overhearing a lot of soldiers talking at a spring, when one of them, anxious to appear a little more familiarly acquainted with the preacher than the rest, said, "I've heard my mother talk of the old Doctor many a time. I reckon the old fellow's given me many a dose of physic for croup."

An incident occurred, on or near the Nine-Mile road, some time before the week of battle opened which is strongly illustrative at once of my father's faith and of the childlike simplicity of the great bulk of our soldiery. Two companies, I think from South Carolina, were supporting a section of our battery in an advanced and somewhat isolated position. About the middle of the afternoon father drove down from Richmond, and after he had distributed his provisions and talked with us a while, proposed to have prayers, which was readily acceded to. Quite a number of men from the neighboring commands gathered, and just as we knelt and my father began his petitions the batteries across the way sent two or three shells entirely too close to our heads to be comfortable—I presume just by way of determining the object of this concourse.

I confess my faith and devotion were not strong enough to prevent my opening my eyes and glancing around. The scene that met them was almost too much for my reverence and came near being fatal to my decorum. Our Carolina supports, like the rest of us, had knelt and closed their eyes at my father's invocation and, simple-hearted fellows that they were, felt that it would be little less than sacrilege to rise or to open them until the prayer should be completed; and yet their faith was not quite equal to assuring them of God's protection, or at least they felt it would be wise and well to supplement the protection of heaven by the trees and stumps of earth, *if they could find them*, and so they were actually groping for them with arms wide extended but eyes tight closed, and still on their knees.

I hardly know what might have been the effect upon me of this almost impossibly ludicrous scene had I not glanced toward my father. As was his habit in public prayer, he was standing; his tall, majestic figure erect and his worshipful, reverent face upturned to Heaven. Not a nerve trembled, not a note quavered. In a single sentence he committed us all to God's special keeping while he worshiped; and then, evidently, he did worship and supplicate the Divine Being without the slightest further consciousness of the bursting shells, which in a few moments ceased shrieking above or about us, and our little service closed without further interruption. And then it was beautiful to observe how these simple-hearted boys gazed at my father, as if indeed he had been one of the ancient prophets; but I heard some of them say they liked that old preacher mighty well, but they didn't just feel certain whether they wanted him around having prayers so close under the Yankee guns; that he "didn't seem to pay hardly enough attention to them things."

Colonel Brandon, father of my Yale classmate of that name, who was a captain in the regiment, was lieutenant-colonel of the Twenty-first Mississippi. He was a dignified, majestic-looking officer and a rigid disciplinarian, but an old man and very stout and heavy. I do not recollect whether Colonel Humphreys was present at Malvern Hill, but Brandon certainly went in with his regiment when the brigade, as I remember, unsupported, made repeated quixotic efforts to capture the Federal guns massed on the hill. They were exposed to the fire I have already described, and of course suffered bloody repulse. Colonel Brandon had his ankle shattered while the regiment was advancing in the first charge. On the way back his men proposed to carry him with them to the rear, but he refused. He was sitting up and pluckily applying his handkerchief as a tourniquet above the wound, and he simply said: "Tell the Twenty-first they can't get me till they take those guns!"

When the line passed him on the second charge, Brandon put his hat on his sword, held it up and waved it, cheering the regiment on, but in a few moments the bleeding remnant staggered to the rear again, and again they came for their colonel, insisting that they must carry him with them. The old soldier actually drew his revolver, declaring that he would shoot down any man who laid hands upon him, and he repeated his former message: "Tell the Twenty-first they can't get their colonel till they take those guns!"

Again the charge swept by the prostrate old man, who waved his sword and his hat, urging his men up the awful slope; but when again they returned to the rear utterly broken and shattered, the old hero had fainted and the litter bearers bore him off the field.

I saw him in Richmond a few days later. His leg had been amputated below the knee. He was doing wondrous well physically, but was full of deep dissatisfaction, mortification and rage about the battle. I admitted the gross mismanagement and was saying something in extenuation, when the old fellow broke in:

"Oh! it is not mismanagement that hurts me, sir; it is cowardice—the disgraceful cowardice of our officers and men."

I was astounded, and protested that I saw nothing of this, when he broke out again:

"Saw nothing of this, sir? Why, I saw nothing else! There is General ———," mentioning a man I never heard mentioned on any other occasion save with admiration for his courage and devotion. "Why, sir, with my own eyes I saw him perceptibly quicken his pace under fire and that right before the men. And I saw him visibly incline his head, sir, and that right in the presence of the men. He ought to be shot to death for cowardice."

I confess I was utterly confounded. I had myself seen General ——— repeatedly passing and repassing a knoll more fearfully torn by artillery fire perhaps than any other spot of earth I ever looked upon. His men were behind it—he passed over it and *in front* of them. My recollection is that officers were not mounted. Of course he quickened his pace, partly because his presence was required first at one end of the line and then at the other; but the marvel to me was that he lived at all. As to the inclination of his head, all I saw was that instinctive inclination, equally natural under a heavy fire and a heavy rain. When I recalled the scene and the heroic conduct of General ———, I remember saying to myself,

"What is the true standard of courage?"

There were a number of Yale men in the Twenty-first Mississippi, among others two brothers, Jud. and Carey Smith. We used to call Jud. "Indian Smith" at Yale. I think it was at Savage Station, when the Seventeenth and Twenty-first Mississippi were put into the woods at nightfall and directed to lie down, that Carey Smith, the younger brother, putting his hand in his bosom, found it covered with blood, when he withdrew it, and saying: "What does this mean?" instantly died. He had been mortally wounded without knowing when.

Judson Smith went almost deranged; yes, I think altogether deranged. He bore his dead brother out of the woods. His company and regimental officers proposed to send the body to Richmond in an ambulance and urged Judson to go with it. He refused both propositions. He kept the body folded to his bosom, and all through the night his comrades heard Judson kissing Carey and talking to him and petting him, and then sobbing as if his heart would break. Next morning he consented to have his brother's body sent to Richmond, but refused to go himself. When the regiment moved he kissed Carey again and again, and then left him, following the column all day alone, allowing no one to comfort him or even to speak to him. So that night he lay down alone, not accepting the proffered sympathy and ministrations of his friends, and resumed his solitary march in the morning.

That was Malvern Hill day, and when the regiment, on its first charge, stopped ascending that fearful slope of death and turned back, Jud. Smith did not stop. He went right on, never returned and was never seen or heard of again.

The family was one of wealth and position in Mississippi, the father an old man, and having only these two boys. When he heard of the loss of both almost in one day he left home, joined Price's army as a private soldier, and at Iuka did just as his eldest son had done at Malvern Hill, which was the last ever seen or heard of him, and the family became extinct.

Walking over the field of Malvern Hill the morning after the battle, I saw two young Federal soldiers lying dead, side by side, their heads upon the same knapsack and their arms about each other. They were evidently brothers and enough alike to be twins. The whole pathetic story was plainly evident. One had first been wounded, perhaps killed, and when the other was struck he managed to get to his dead or dying brother, placed the knapsack under his head, and then lying down by him and resting his head on the same rude pillow, slipped his dying arms around his brother's body and slept in this embrace.

CHAPTER X

SECOND MANASSAS—SHARPSBURG—FREDERICKSBURG

Not at Second Manassas or Sharpsburg—A Glimpse of Richmond in
the Summer of '62—Col. Willis, of the Twelfth Georgia—Jackson in
the Railroad Cut at Manassas—Sharpsburg the Hardest Fought of
Lee's Battles, Fredericksburg the Easiest Won — The Mississippi
Brigade Entertains a Baby—A Conscript's First Fight—Magnificent Spectacle When Fog Curtain Rose—Aurora Borealis at Close
of the Drama.

I was not with the Army of Northern Virginia from the
time it left Richmond moving north after the Seven Days'
battles until it returned to Virginia after the invasion of
Maryland; thus I missed the campaign against Pope and the
first Maryland campaign, the great battles of second Manassas and Sharpsburg, or Antietam. No soldier can expect
to be present for duty in all the battles of a protracted war—
sickness, wounds, and capture will naturally prevent. But
the fact is, I was that exceptionally fortunate soldier who
never experienced either disabling sickness or wounds or
captivity until the very end of the struggle, and my absence
from the active front is to be accounted for on other grounds.

It will be remembered that at Malvern Hill several of the
guns of our battery, my gun among them, were so roughly
handled by the concentrated fire of the Federal artillery that
we were compelled to send them to Richmond to be recast
and remounted. This could not be done in time to enable
the battery to move with the army when it marched against
Pope. One section was equipped a little later and caught
up in time to take part in the battle of Sharpsburg. But this
was not my section, and the captain would not permit me to
leave with the section first ready. Therefore I saw nothing
of the campaigns against Pope in Virginia and McClellan in
Maryland, and if I am to keep to the general line of reminis-

cence I must simply omit the late summer and early autumn of '62, for of course nothing of general interest occurred while we were hanging about Richmond waiting for a new equipment. We had not yet, to any great extent, equipped our artillery, as we did later, especially in the Manassas and Maryland campaigns, by captures from the armies opposed to us.

I have said nothing worth recording occurred during our stay around Richmond. The statement should be modified so far as to say that one of the noticeable features of the general condition was the heartrending affliction of my friends, almost every family having lost a relative, or some intimate associate, during the week of bloody battle. It had not, however, yet come to pass, as it did later, that black became the recognized dress for woman in Richmond, and that she actually appeared flippant and worldly and unfeeling if she wore any color. In the second Punic war, when Hannibal was investing Rome, the tribune Oppius had a law enacted forbidding women to wear colors during the public distress. But in our great conflict no such enactment was necessary, for the devoted women of our seven-hilled city; dark death had entered every home and his sombre garb was everywhere.

Of course, too, the hospitals were crowded just at this time, and in the homes of citizens many wounded soldiers were cared for; so that it seemed the one fitting province of women, young and old, to serve as nurses and attendants upon the wounded and the dying. I think, too, though I am not sure, that the churches had already begun to give their bells to be moulded into cannon. Certainly, long before the end of the war, the people of Richmond went to church through silent streets, and ceased to hear that heavenliest of all earthly sounds, which runs like a holy refrain through the sweetest poetry and the tenderest memories of English-speaking peoples.

To me these weeks around Richmond meant more than I can express in welding the links that bound me to these dear people. I had dedicated my life to them—I was theirs and they were mine. I felt it; they felt it. Yes, these people were my friends, this city was my home. Our mother and sisters had not yet been able to get South, but the faithful people of my father's former pastoral charge assured me that they stood ready to receive and care for them with open hearts in open homes, and, until they arrived, noble women stood ready, in case my brother or I should need such ministrations, to do, as far as possible, a mother's and a sister's part by us.

While I have of course no personal reminiscence to relate either of the Manassas or the Maryland campaign of '62, yet an account was given me of the very crisis and climax of the former, in its essential character and all its surroundings so striking, that I feel called upon to make record of it. I actually did so, indeed, while a prisoner at Johnson's Island in 1865, and now use the memorandum then made.

One of the most promising of the younger officers of the Army of Northern Virginia in the spring of '64 was Col. Edward Willis, of the Twelfth Georgia Regiment. I saw him but once and under the following circumstances: Our battery passed the winter of '63-'64, not in the great artillery camp on the Central Railroad, but with the advanced line of infantry guarding the middle fords of the Rapidan River. Battalion headquarters were in a pine thicket between Raccoon and Morton's fords. One beautiful day in the early spring I was seated in our headquarters' tent at work on one of the battalion reports, which it was my duty, as adjutant, to make to Artillery Headquarters, when a very striking-looking head intruded itself in the tent door and, in a very nonchalant, familiar tone, the owner of the head asked, "Is Gibbes about?"

We were not very punctilious about such matters in the Confederate service, perhaps not enough so; but the intruder and interlocutor was obviously, I thought, a private soldier and a specially untidy looking one at that—his hat unquestionably "a slouch," his hair long and unkempt, his long overcoat, of whatever original ground color, now by long usage the color of the ground, and ending in a fringe of tatters around the skirt; under it no sign of a coat or of anything save a gray flannel shirt, no badge or insignia of rank anywhere visible, nor even an appropriate place for any, and his badly-worn pants turned up around his very small feet shod in very rough shoes. I say it did stir me a little unpleasantly that just this man should ask, in just these words and just this tone, for Major Wade Hampton Gibbes, of South Carolina, a young West Pointer, who had recently been assigned to duty with us. I might have answered differently had not a second glance revealed a face of such commanding intellect and personal force that I said, "If you will wait a moment, I'll see," and a moment later the very effusive meeting between Gibbes and himself, and Gibbes' introduction, to Colonel Cabell and myself, of "Col. Edward Willis, of the Twelfth Georgia," made me very glad I had answered as I had. They had been at West Point together, I think, when the war broke out. Gibbes seated himself, tailor fashion, at one end of a large box of clothing for one of the batteries, which had not yet been opened, and Willis stretched out on the box and put his head in Gibbes' lap, who began running his fingers through the long, tangled, tawny hair, which hung almost to Willis' shoulders. It would have been greatly to the advantage of the hair if Gibbes had used a comb instead of his fingers.

They began talking of their West Point classmates and comrades. I was going on with my work and not listening closely, yet I could not help being struck with the vigor and the trenchant quality of Willis' characterization of the men. But in a few moments he began telling of Jackson, and then I dropped my pen and hung eagerly on his words. I knew he had been on Jackson's staff and hoped he would tell, as he did, how he came to leave it.

He said that after Second Manassas, perhaps after Sharpsburg, Jackson sent for him and said: "Captain Willis, you have earned your promotion, sir. You may take your choice between continued service on my staff, with the rank of major, and a majority in an infantry regiment."

To which Willis, without hesitation, replied: "I'll take the infantry regiment, General."

A reply which revealed the mettle of the man, as Jackson indicated by saying: "Sorry to lose you, sir; but you've made a soldier's choice; you'll be assigned to duty with the Twelfth Georgia."

Ere long he became colonel of the regiment, and at the time of which I write it was well understood throughout the army that no one commanded a better regiment and no regiment had a better commanding officer than the Twelfth Georgia.

Soon Willis began to talk of the campaign against Pope, which he regarded as Jackson's masterpiece, and as he had been closely with Jackson through it all, I considered what he said of value, as it certainly was of surpassing interest. He first expatiated at some length upon the masterly—I had almost said dastardly—way in which Jackson managed to find out all Pope's plans and purposes, and yet to elude and delude and deceive and defraud him in the most heartless and malignant fashion as to his own movements and designs. Part of the time, while waiting for Lee and Longstreet, Jackson was in extreme peril, dodging between and against the huge Federal Army corps, rushing blindly like avalanches to crush him. On one or two occasions, I think Willis said, he even went so far as to sacrifice his skirmish line, that is, arrange to have them captured by Pope's troops in a particular position, from which even the skirmishers themselves, as well as their captors, would naturally infer that "Old Jack" was marching in a certain direction and about a certain time would be about a certain place, when quite the reverse was the actual truth. In short, it must be admitted that all of Jackson's dealings with Pope, about this time, were disingenuous in the extreme. Someone, not Willis, has said substantially that they embodied a continuous, tortuous, twisted, aggravated, protracted *lie*—over fifty miles long.

But at last, as Willis said, all these tactics of deception were exhausted! Jackson was straight in front, in the famous position in the railroad cut, and Pope's whole army moved upon him. They advanced in imposing array, with several lines of battle—bands playing, flags flying, and their artillery, following the second line, slowly firing as they approached. Just as his dispositions—the best he could make for resisting such an onslaught—were complete, Jackson heard from Longstreet, who promised him aid in two hours. The shock could be delayed, however, only a few moments, and Jackson, feeling the imminence of the crisis, started down his lines to communicate to his troops, worn with fatigue and suspense, his own heaven-born faith and fire and Longstreet's assurance of help. I understood from Willis that he rode along the line with him, and that all he said was:

"Two hours, men, only two hours; in two hours you will have help. You must stand it two hours."

It was the crisis of the campaign, and both sides fully appreciated it. The enemy came right on until within two hundred yards, and then broke into the rush of the charge. The officer commanding the leading centre brigade, and who was riding a powerful coal-black charger, carried the colors in his hand and rested the staff on the toe of his boot. Striking his spurs deep into the flanks of his horse, at the same time reining him in, Willis said he came on, with great plunges, the standard flapping about him and the standard bearer, cap in hand, yelling at his side. The whole line thus gallantly led, rushed upon Jackson's men with the enthusiasm of assured victory.

A hundred yards nearer and the full fire from Jackson's line burst upon them, but from the inclination of the musket barrels it looked as if the gallant fellow on the black horse would be the only man to fall. On the contrary, while many fell and the line wavered, he was miraculously unhurt, and his men rallied and pressed on after him. For a moment it looked as if he would actually leap into the cut upon his foes, but the next moment the great horse reared wildly and fell backward, but his heroic rider jammed the color staff into the earth as he went down, only ten yards from the muzzles of Jackson's muskets. The spell that held them together was broken, the advancing lines halted and wavered throughout their length—a moment more and the whole magnificent array had melted into a mass of fugitives.

Again Jackson rode down his lines: "Half an hour men, only half an hour; can you stand it half an hour?"

And now, as Willis said, it seemed as if some of his men exhaled their very souls to him in shouts, while others, too much exhausted to cheer, took off their hats and gazed at him in adoration as he passed. The enemy, reformed, began again to advance, and Jackson quickened his horse's gait. "They are coming once more, men; you must stand it once more; you must stand it half an hour."

Could they have stood it? We shall never know—for before the mighty wave broke again into the crest and foam of the actual charge, the Texas brigade was in on Jackson's right and Old Pete and Old Jack together swept them in the counter-charge like chaff before the whirlwind.

I have not pretended to give Colonel Willis' exact words, and yet in my memorandum account of his visit to our camp above referred to I incorporated his words as nearly as I could recall them, and I have now conformed very closely to that memorandum. I never listened to more vivid delineation of strategy or of battle. He was thoroughly stirred while uttering it, and its impression upon us may be gathered from Colonel Cabell's words as he and Gibbes and I stood watching Willis as his figure disappeared in the thick pines: "Stiles, there goes the only man I ever saw who, I think, by possibility might make another Jackson!"

In less than a month from that time he was made a brigadier-general, for brilliant service on the field, and the very next day yielded up his glorious young life in battle.

Willis' name is not to be found on the roster of Confederate general officers, but there is no doubt about the facts of his promotion and death. The circumstances are entirely familiar to me and are full of touching and tragic interest. These lists of Confederate officers are very imperfect. My Uncle William and my Cousin Edward, mentioned in these reminiscences, are both entered on the list of field officers, but my name is not mentioned.

While I do not regard discussions as to the purposes and success or failure of campaigns, or the comparative numbers engaged on the two sides, as properly within the general scope of this book, yet I shall occasionally, when the matter is of special interest, or I hope to be able to add something of special value, do violence to these declared views—so I here take the liberty of saying that it is by no means admitted among intelligent Confederate soldiers that the only or the main design of the first Maryland campaign was to stir up revolt in Maryland or to recruit our army by enlistment there. It is not disputed that these may have been among the objects sought to be accomplished, nor that, so far as this is true, the campaign was a failure. The Confederate view of the matter, from a military standpoint, is in brief this:

By our invasion of Maryland we cleared Virginia of enemies, sending them home to defend their own capital and their own borders. We subsisted our army for a time outside our own worn-out territory. We gathered large quantities of badly-needed supplies, to a great extent fitting out our troops with improved firearms, in place of the old smoothbore muskets, and replacing much of our inferior field artillery with improved guns. At Harper's Ferry alone we captured eleven thousand prisoners, seventy-three pieces of artillery, thirteen thousand stand of excellent small arms and immense stores; besides all which, we delayed further immediate invasion of Virginia; indeed, as has been strongly said:

Such had been the moral effect upon the enemy that the Confederate capital was never again seriously endangered until the power of the Confederacy had been so broken in other quarters, and its available territory so reduced in dimensions, that the enemy could concentrate his immense resources against the capital.

One word now as to the numbers engaged at Sharpsburg. This battle has been much misunderstood. It was really the most superb fight the Army of Northern Virginia ever made. This will readily appear when we recall the fact that General McClellan in his official report says that he had actually present for duty on the field that day eighty-seven thousand one hundred and sixty-four (87,164) men of all arms. General Early thinks he had ninety-three thousand one hundred and forty-nine (93,149), while Colonel Taylor says and shows that General Lee had less than thirty-five thousand two hundred and fifty-five (35,255); Early says less than thirty thousand (30,000). Take it even at thirty-five thousand (35,000) and eighty-seven thousand (87,000), and remember that General Lee remained on the field all the day following the battle; that McClellan did not attack him, and states in his testimony before the Committee on the Conduct of the War (Reports, Vol. 2, Part 1, 1862-3, p. 441) as the reason therefor, that:

> The next morning (the 18th) I found that our loss had been so great and that there was so much disorganization in some of the commands that I did not consider it proper to renew the attack that day, especially as I was sure of the arrival that day of two fresh divisions amounting to about 15,000 men.

Two further remarks, and we leave this part of the story of the Army of Northern Virginia, of which I am not able to say *quorum pars fui*. And, first, that General McClellan's part in all this campaign appears to have been greatly to his credit and honor. Summoned by the President and begged to see if he could not, by his personal influence, do something to heal the discords and want of union and cohesion in the Army of the Potomac; then asked to take charge of it again himself; then, with wondrous vigor gathering a composite army and unifying and enheartening it; and lastly, so handling it, on the march and in the field, as to save the Federal capital and to clear Northern soil of invasion.

But one incident must not be forgotten: McClellan was inspired and enabled to march with such unwonted speed, to move with such unerring judgment and to fight with such tremendous vigor and pertinacity by the contents of a little paper which was picked up by a Federal soldier in one of our deserted camps, and which turned out to be a copy sent to one of our division commanders of General Lee's order of battle and of campaign, showing in detail the position and duty assigned to each important command in the army, and of course just how our force was divided. There is no doubt as to the facts. McClellan recites them in his testimony above referred to, p. 440, and speaks of the effect of this order upon his movements. It was well understood among us. As Colonel Taylor says:

The God of battles alone knows what would have occurred but for the singular incident mentioned; it is useless to speculate on this point, but certainly the loss of this battle order constitutes one of the pivots on which turned the event of the war.

Again Culpeper Court House is the appointed trysting place of the army, while waiting fuller development of the plan of General Burnside, the new commander of the Army of the Potomac, and we, the right section, having at last gotten our new equipment of guns, had a delightful march thither through a country full of good things and kind people, in the season of harvest and of fruit. Here, too, we met, with great rejoicing, our comrades of the left section, from whom we had been separated during the Manassas and Maryland campaigns; and from this point were ordered, about the 19th of November, to Fredericksburg, in connection with Longstreet's corps, arriving there on the afternoon of the 21st, marching the last day through one of the steadiest, heaviest, and coldest downpours of autumnal rain I ever experienced. As the Federal batteries of heavy guns on Falmouth and Stafford Heights commanded almost the entire southern bank of the river and particularly the road by which we would naturally enter the town, and as it was specially desired that they should not be apprised of our arrival, we were halted just outside the town and back of the point of a hill, until after nightfall, and then marched to a dark and desolate bivouac, without fire and without food, and frozen to the very soul—the more so as we had of course steamed up while walking. I recall this as one of the most comfortless and trying nights of my life, and yet so sound and tough were we that I do not recall that a single man of us wheezed, or even sneezed, from the exposure.

In a few days, everything appearing to be quiet at the front, we were sent down into Caroline County, along and near the R. F. & P. Railroad, to go into camp for the winter. We selected an ideal position, went vigorously to work and built the very best shelters for our horses and cabins for ourselves that we ever put up anywhere; but hardly had they been completed, tried, pronounced eminently satisfactory and christened "Sleepy Hollow," when orders came for us to return at once to Fredericksburg, and that through a blizzard of most inclement weather. Of course we went and without delay—I cannot say absolutely without grumbling. Indeed the right to grumble is the only civil, political, or social right left to the soldier, and he stands much in his own light if he does not exercise it to the full. We found rather an uncomfortable and forbidding location selected for us outside of Fredericksburg, and we were in a temper too bad to do much for its improvement, so that, as to external conditions, we had rather a hard, comfortless winter; though, even as to these, we perhaps did better than the commands who were ordered to the front later.

The next incident of interest was the bombardment of the old town, but I do not care to enlarge upon this. Really I saw then and see now no justification for it. True the town was occupied by armed men,—Barksdale and his men, our old brigade,—but then the fire did not drive them out; in the nature of things, and especially of the Mississippi brigade, of course it would not, and it did drive out the women and children, many of them. I never saw a more pitiful procession than they made trudging through the deep snow, after the warning was given and as the hour drew near. I saw little children tugging along with their doll babies,—some bigger than they were,—but holding their feet up carefully above the snow, and women so old and feeble that they could carry nothing and could barely hobble themselves. There were women carrying a baby in one arm and its bottle, its clothes, and its covering in the other. Some had a Bible and a tooth brush in one hand, a picked chicken and a bag of flour in the other. Most of them had to cross a creek swollen with winter rains, and deadly cold with winter ice and snow. We took the battery horses down and ferried them over, taking one child in front and two behind and sometimes a woman or a girl on either side with her feet in the stirrups, holding on by our shoulders. Where they were going we could not tell, and I doubt if they could.

I was about to say that the armed men had orders to come out, and would have done so at the proper time. But I am not so sure about this, and certainly can't blame the Federals for not knowing it, when we really couldn't get the plaguey Mississippians to understand it themselves. They were ready to fight anything, from his Satanic Majesty down; but they were a very poor set indeed as to judging when not to fight, or when to stop fighting. Why, there was Colonel Fizer, of the Seventeenth. He was down on the river bank below the town. Of course he must have had retiring orders and ought to have seen that the Federal batteries absolutely dominated our shore; and yet he sent word to General Barksdale that if he would just let the Howitzers come down, with a couple of their guns, he could "drive these people back anyhow." And "Old Barksdale," who was every bit as bad as Fizer, and a little worse, actually sent the order, and our boys actually started. It would have been a practical impossibility to get these two poor little guns anywhere near the river. No two fragments of guns or men would have held together five minutes after they appeared on the plain that stretched out from the foot of the hills to the river and their intentions became known to the batteries on Stafford Heights. Fortunately, our division general, McLaws, and his staff met the guns just before they emerged on the plain, and the general demanded of the officer in charge where we were going and by whose order, and, on being told, instantly countermanded the order and sent us back. It is fair to say for General Barksdale that when our captain galloped rapidly into town and explained the matter to him, he himself withdrew his own order; but General McLaws had already acted. The incident strongly accentuated the necessity for the battalion organization of the artillery, and in our case it was put into immediate effect, I think, just after the battle.

But Fizer was not the only officer of the Mississippi brigade that could not get it into his head, even a little later, that the troops were to abandon the town and retire before the enemy, who had now gotten their pontoons down, and the head of their column landed in the town. The brigade had been hospitably received by the citizens and its blood was up in their defense.

The Twenty-first Mississippi was the last regiment to leave the city. The last detachment was under the command of Lane Brandon, already mentioned as my *quondam* classmate at Yale, and son of old Colonel Brandon, of the Twenty-first, who behaved so heroically at Malvern Hill. In skirmishing with the head of the Federal column—led, I think, by the Twentieth Massachusetts—Brandon captured a few prisoners and learned that the advance company was commanded by Abbott, who had been his chum at Harvard Law School when the war began.

He lost his head completely. He refused to retire before Abbott. He fought him fiercely and was actually driving him back. In this he was violating orders and breaking our plan of battle. He was put under arrest and his subaltern brought the command out of town.

Buck Denman,—our old friend Buck, of Leesburg and Fort Johnston fame,—a Mississippi bear hunter and a superb specimen of manhood, was color sergeant of the Twenty-first and a member of Brandon's company. He was tall and straight, broad-shouldered and deep-chested, had an eye like an eagle and a voice like a bull of Bashan, and was full of pluck and power as a panther. He was rough as a bear in manner, but withal a noble, tender-hearted fellow, and a splendid soldier.

The enemy, finding the way now clear, were coming up the street, full company front, with flags flying and bands playing, while the great shells from the siege guns were bursting over their heads and dashing their hurtling fragments after our retreating skirmishers.

Buck was behind the corner of a house taking sight for a last shot. Just as his fingers trembled on the trigger, a little three-year-old, fair-haired, baby girl toddled out of an alley, accompanied by a Newfoundland dog, and gave chase to a big shell that was rolling lazily along the pavement, she clapping her little hands and the dog snapping and barking furiously at the shell.

Buck's hand dropped from the trigger. He dashed it across his eyes to dispel the mist and make sure he hadn't passed over the river and wasn't seeing his own baby girl in a vision. No, there is the baby, amid the hell of shot and shell, and here come the enemy. A moment and he has grounded his gun, dashed out into the storm, swept his great right arm around the baby, gained cover again, and, baby clasped to his breast and musket trailed in his left hand, is trotting after the boys up to Marye's Heights.

And there behind that historic stone wall, and in the lines hard by, all those hours and days of terror was that baby kept, her fierce nurses taking turns patting her, while the storm of battle raged and shrieked, and at night wrestling with each other for the boon and benediction of her quiet breathing under their blankets. Never was baby so cared for. They scoured the country side for milk, and conjured up their best skill to prepare dainty viands for her little ladyship.

When the struggle was over and the enemy had withdrawn to his strongholds across the river, and Barksdale was ordered to reoccupy the town, the Twenty-first Mississippi, having held the post of danger in the rear, was given the place of honor in the van and led the column. There was a long halt, the brigade and regimental staff hurrying to and fro. The regimental colors could not be found.

Denman stood about the middle of the regiment, baby in arms. Suddenly he sprang to the front. Swinging her aloft above his head, her little garments fluttering like the folds of a banner, he shouted, "Forward, Twenty-first, here are your colors!" and without further order, off started the brigade toward the town, yelling as only Barksdale's men could yell. They were passing through a street fearfully shattered by the enemy's fire, and were shouting their very souls out—but let Buck himself describe the last scene in the drama:

"I was holding the baby high, Adjutant, with both arms, when above all the racket I heard a woman's scream. The next thing I knew I was covered with calico and she fainted on my breast. I caught her before she fell, and laying her down gently, put her baby on her bosom. She was most the prettiest thing I ever looked at, and her eyes were shut; and —and—I hope God'll forgive me, but I kissed her just once."

Fredericksburg was the simplest and easiest won battle of the war. The Federal batteries on Falmouth and Stafford Heights across the river absolutely dominated the town and our bank of the river and the flats on our side; but our troops were back on the hills, which we had fortified somewhat, and which we could have held against the world. It is believed that less than twenty thousand of our men, about one-fourth of those present for duty, were actually engaged. Our loss was comparatively light, the Federal loss very heavy, especially in the attack upon Marye's Heights and the famous stone wall, in front of which dead men were lying thicker than I ever saw them on any other field. I attempted to count them, but found it impossible. I could have walked considerable distances in front of this wall, stepping only on dead men, and it was with difficulty that I so guided my horse as to avoid trampling upon them. Burnside saw, or his corps commanders showed him, his mistake, and he refused to renew the attack, as we were hoping that he would. There is, or perhaps I should say there was, a feeling that we should have ourselves made attack upon him, and that General Jackson favored it. Colonel Taylor, General Early, and other authorities scout any such idea. I do not feel that anything would be gained by reopening the discussion.

Tennyson is in error when he says, in "Locksley Hall," that "Woman is the lesser man." She is the greater man. A good woman is better than a good man, a bad woman is worse; a brave woman is braver than any man ever was. During the bombardment I was sent into Fredericksburg with a message for General Barksdale. As I was riding down the street that led to his headquarters it appeared to be so fearfully swept by artillery fire that I started to ride across it, with a view of finding some safer way of getting to my destination, when, happening to glance beyond that point, I saw walking quietly and unconcernedly along the same street I was on, and approaching General Barksdale's headquarters from the opposite direction, a lone woman. She apparently found the projectiles which were screaming and exploding in the air, and striking and crashing through the houses, and tearing up the streets, very interesting—stepping a little aside to inspect a great, gaping hole one had just gouged out in the sidewalk, then turning her head to note a fearful explosion in the air. I felt as if it really would not do to avoid a fire which was merely interesting, and not at all appalling, to a woman; so I stiffened my spinal column as well as I could and rode straight down the street toward headquarters and the self-possessed lady; and having reached the house I rode around back of it to put my horse where he would at least be safer than in front. As I returned on foot to the front the lady had gone up on the porch and was knocking at the door. One of the staff came to hearken, and on seeing a lady, held up his hands, exclaiming in amazement: "What on earth, madam, are you doing here? Do go to some safe place if you can find one." She smiled and said, with some little tartness: "Young gentleman, you seem to be a little excited. Won't you please say to General Barksdale that a lady at the door wishes to see him." The young man assured her General Barksdale could not possibly see her just now; but she persisted. "General Barksdale is a Southern gentleman, sir, and will not refuse to see a lady who has called upon him." Seeing that he could not otherwise get rid of her, the General did come to the door, but actually wringing his hands in excitement and annoyance. "For God's sake, madam, go and seek some place of safety. I'll send a member of my staff to help you find one." She again smiled gently,—while old Barksdale fumed and almost swore,—and then she said quietly: "General Barksdale, my cow has just been killed in my stable by a shell. She is very fat and I don't want the Yankees to get her. If you will send some one down to butcher her, you are welcome to the meat."

Years afterwards I delivered a Confederate memorial address at Fredericksburg, and when I told this incident noticed increasing interest and something very like amusement among the audience, who had ceased to look at me, but all eyes were turned in one direction, and just as I finished the story and my eyes followed theirs—there before me sat this very lady, apparently not a day older, and the entire audience rose and gave her three deafening cheers.

One of the marked features of the battle was that when we lay down in our blankets on the night of the 12th we could see nothing, but could plainly hear Burnside's immense force getting into position, and when we rose on the morning of the 13th a dense fog overhung the entire flat in our front, shutting out all vision. Once or twice we did see men, our own skirmishers, moving about, as the blind man in the Scriptures saw when partially healed—"Men as trees walking." I remember that when a Federal cavalry officer lost his bearings in the fog and came too near our lines we heard every command and every movement, till suddenly two or three of the horsemen loomed up in the mist in dim outline, magnified to the size of haystacks. A moment more and they ran into the Texas brigade at the foot of the hill in our front, and a volley emptied many a saddle, their gallant leader's among them.

A little later a light breeze sprang up. There was a swaying movement of the thick vapor and then, all at once, it rolled up like the stage curtain of a theatre, and there, spread out in the wide plain beneath, was the most magnificent martial spectacle that can be imagined—a splendidly-equipped army of at least one hundred thousand men, in battle array. General Burnside testified that he had that number on our side of the river. For a moment we forgot the terrible business ahead of us in the majesty and glory of the sight.

We were stationed on what was afterwards known as "Lee's Hill," an elevation centrally located between the right and left flanks of our line, and jutting out at quite a commanding height into and above the plain. For these reasons General Lee made it, for the most part, his field headquarters during the fight. Portions of the city and of Marye's Heights were not visible, at least not thoroughly so; but every other part of the field was, clear away down, or nearly down, to Hamilton's Crossing. From it we witnessed the break in our lines on the right, where the Federals came in over a piece of marshy ground, supposed to be impassable, between Lane's North Carolina and Archer's Tennessee brigade. The entire attack, from its inception to its unexpected success, was as clearly defined as a movement on a chessboard, and I confess that tears started to and even from my eyes; but a moment later a great outburst of fire a little back of the line of battle indicated that the intruders had been gallantly met by our second line, or our reserves, and in a few moments out they rushed, the victors yelling at their heels. My uncle, William Henry Stiles, colonel of the Sixtieth Georgia, and who, in the absence of the general, was in command of Lawton's brigade in the battle, told me an amusing story of this particular fight.

When his brigade, with others, was ordered to stem this irruption, drive out the intruders and reestablish—or rather, for the first time properly extend and connect—our lines, his men were double-quicking to the point of peril and he running from one end to the other of his brigade line to see that all parts were kept properly "dressed up," when he observed one of the conscripts who had lately been sent to his regiment—a large, fine-looking fellow—drop out and crouch behind a tree. My uncle, a tall, wiry, muscular man, was accustomed to carry a long, heavy sword, and having it at the time in his hand, as he passed he struck the fellow a sound whack across his shoulders with the flat of the weapon, simultaneously saying, "Up there, you coward!" To his astonishment the man dropped his musket, clasped his hands and keeled over backwards, devoutly ejaculating, "Lord, receive my spirit!"

Uncle William said the entire dénouement was so unexpected and grotesque and his haste so imperative, that he scarcely knew how he managed to do it, but he did turn and deliver a violent kick upon the fellow's ribs, at the same time shouting, "Get up, sir! the Lord wouldn't receive the spirit of such an infernal coward;" whereupon, to his further amazement, the man sprang up in the most joyful fashion, fairly shouting, "Ain't I killed? The Lord be praised!" and grabbing his musket he sailed in like a hero, as he ever afterwards was. The narrator added that he firmly believed that, but for the kick, his conscript would have completed the thing and died in good order.

On our part of the line I witnessed a scene not quite so humorous as this, but strongly characteristic. I saw a tall

Texan bring up the hill, as prisoners, some fifteen or twenty low, stolid Germans,—Bavarians I think they were, —no one of whom could speak a word of English. He must have been a foot taller than any of them, as he stood leaning on his long rifle and looking down upon them with a very peculiar expression. I asked him where he got them and he replied in the most matter-of-fact way, "Well, me and my comrade surrounded 'em; but he got killed, poor fellow!" He really looked as if he could have surrounded the entire lot alone.

Not often have I come in contact with relations more beautiful than existed in some cases between young Southern masters in the service and their slave attendants. These latter belonged for the most part to one of two classes: either they were mature and faithful men, to whose care the lad's parents had committed him, or else they were the special chums and playmates of their young master's boyhood days, who had perhaps already attended and waited upon him in college.

My first cousin, eldest son of the uncle above mentioned, and who was a captain in his regiment, was seriously wounded late in the evening of the battle, but the casualty was not generally known, probably because the surgeons finding him on the field, after a hurried examination, pronounced his wound necessarily and speedily mortal, and added: "We are sorry to leave you, Captain, but we and the litter bearers have all we can attend to." To which he replied: "Certainly, gentlemen, go on and attend to the men; but you are mistaken about me. I haven't the least idea of dying."

They left him; the litter bearers of course did not report his case, and probably neither his father nor any member of his company was aware of his having been wounded. But there was one faithful soul to whom he was more than all the rest of the regiment. If he continued "missing" the world was empty to him, and so, in cold and darkness and sadness, he searched every foot of ground the regiment had fought over, till at last he found him. Then he wandered about until he got from the bodies of dead men blankets enough to make a soft, warm bed, and carefully lifted him on to it, and covered him snugly. He then managed to start a fire and get water for him, and finally, most important of all, got from the body of a dead Federal officer a small flask of brandy and stimulated him carefully.

About daylight the doctors came by again and, surprised to find him alive, made a more careful examination and found that the ball had passed entirely through his body from right to left, just between the upper and lower vital regions; but they added that he would have died of cold and exposure had it not been for the faithful love that refused to be satisfied until it had found and provided for him. That was the night of the 13th of December. On the 25th, I think it was, he walked up to the third story of a house in Richmond to see my mother, who had meantime gotten through from the North.

The battle closed, as it began, with a marked, and this time a beautiful, natural phenomenon. It was very cold and very clear, and the aurora borealis of the night of December 13th, 1862, surpassed in splendor any like exhibition I ever saw. Of course we enthusiastic young fellows felt that the heavens were hanging out banners and streamers and setting off fireworks in honor of our victory.

Our friends, the enemy, seemed in no hurry to leave our neighborhood, though they did not seem to long for another close grapple, and as we appeared equally indifferent to any closer acquaintance with them, General Burnside and his army, on the night of December 15th, apparently insulted, retired to their own side of the river and began to get ready for Christmas.

CHAPTER XI

Revival in Barksdále's Brigade at Fredericksburg—A Model Chaplain—
Personal Conferences with Comrades—A Prayer Between the Lines
—A Percussion Shell at Gettysburg.

No account of my experience as a Confederate soldier would be complete if it failed to refer to the religious life of the army. This was an element of importance in all our armies, from the outset to the end, and was recognized and fostered as such by our leading generals, many of whom attended the religious services held among the men of their commands, some of them taking loving direction of these services.

I remember on one occasion, when my father was preaching to Tom Cobb's brigade, on the lines about Richmond in '62, that the service was interrupted by sharp firing in front and the command marched off into the woods. It proved a false alarm, however; the troops soon returned and the service was resumed. But the men were preoccupied, nervous, and widely scattered, and everything dragged, until the general, rising, begged my father to wait a moment, and called out: "Men, get up close together here in front, till your shoulders meet. You can't make a fire if the sticks don't touch." They "closed up" and the meeting proceeded with great power.

Volumes have been written on this general theme by chaplains and others, and I have already made brief incidental reference to it; but more than this is required. Not that I propose to condense into this chapter every fact or incident within my knowledge illustrative of this phase of life in the Confederate armies. On the contrary, I shall, in the main, throughout this book, allow the religious element to mingle with others that gave character to our soldier life, and to crop out here and there, as it actually did in our every-day experiences; for with a Confederate soldier, especially, religion was not at all a mere Sunday matter, to be put on and off with his Sunday clothes, even if he had any such.

But as the revival at Fredericksburg in the winter of '62-'63 concerned especially the infantry brigade with which I was longest and most closely associated I may be pardoned for giving a brief sketch of what was probably the most marked religious movement in our war and, as I believe, rarely paralleled anywhere or at any time.

The religious interest among Barksdale's men began about the time of, or soon after, the battle of Fredericksburg, which was about the middle of December, '62, and continued with unabated fervor up to and through the battle of Chancellorsville and even to Gettysburg. In addition to the labors of the regimental chaplains, the ablest and most distinguished ministers in Virginia, of all denominations, delighted to come up and speak to the men. My father, who was nearly seventy years old, came over from Jackson's corps late in February and remained for many weeks. The fraternal spirit of the Christian workers is thus portrayed in a letter by Rev. William J. Hoge, D. D., of the Presbyterian Church, written from Fredericksburg in the spring of 1863. Says Dr. Hoge:

A rich blessing had been poured upon the zealous labors of the Rev. Mr. Owen, Methodist chaplain in Barksdale's Brigade. The Rev. Dr. Burrows, of the Baptist church, Richmond, had just arrived, expecting to labor with him for some days. As I was to stay but one night, Dr. Burrows courteously insisted on my preaching. So we had a Presbyterian sermon, introduced by Baptist services, under the direction of a Methodist chaplain, in an Episcopal church! Was not that a beautiful solution of the vexed problem of Christian union?

The Baptist church had been so injured during the bombardment that it could not be used. The meetings were first held in the Presbyterian church and then in the Methodist, and finally were transferred to the Episcopal church, St.

George's, which was the largest in the city, and accommodated, I should say, packed as it invariably was, from a thousand to twelve hundred men. I have never seen such eagerness to hear the Word of God, nor greater simplicity, directness and earnestness in religious services. Long before the hour appointed the men would begin to gather, intent on getting into the church and securing a seat. Thereafter every moment was occupied with some act of worship of uncommon intensity and power. The singing, in which everyone joined, was hearty and impressive; the prayers, offered generally by the men themselves, were soul-moving "cries unto God;" the preacher was sometimes a distinguished divine from Richmond, sometimes one of the army chaplains, sometimes a private soldier from the ranks, but whoever he might be, he preached the gospel and the gospel only. The following is an extract from a letter written by my father just after he reached Fredericksburg:

After my arrival we held three meetings a day—a morning and afternoon prayer-meeting and a preaching service at night. We could scarcely ask of delightful religious interest more than we received. Our sanctuary has been crowded, lower floor and gallery. Loud, animated singing always hailed our approach to the house of God; and a closely packed audience of men, amongst whom you might have searched in vain for one white hair, were leaning upon the voice of the preacher as if God himself had called them together to hear of life and death eternal. At every call for the anxious, the entire altar, the front six seats of the five blocks of pews surrounding the pulpit, and all the spaces thereabouts ever so closely packed, could scarcely accommodate the supplicants.

To this graphic picture may I add a few touches. There was a soldier in a red blanket overcoat who had a voice like the sound of many waters, and who almost invariably sat or stood on the pulpit steps and led the singing. I remember, too, the many marks of cannon balls upon and in and through the building, and that it added to the thrill of the services to realize that we were gathered under the frowning batteries upon Stafford Heights. And while I greatly enjoyed the many powerful sermons we heard from distinguished ministers, yet I was still more impressed by the simple song and prayer and experience meetings of the men, which were generally held for at least an hour before the regular service began.

Many of the "talks" delivered by the private soldiers in these preparatory services were thrilling beyond expression. Let me attempt to reproduce two or three of these, promising that if I cannot be sure of the precise words employed by the speakers, I at least will not fail to reproduce the substance and the spirit of their addresses:

I remember that one of these private soldiers, in illustrating and enforcing the folly of living in this world as if we were to live in it forever, asked his comrades what they would think of the good sense or even the sanity of one of their number who should to-morrow morning send to Richmond for an elegant wrapper, velvet smoking cap and slippers, and when they came, throwing away his blanket and stout shoes and clothes, should insist upon arraying himself in "these butterfly things" in the face of the fact that the next moment the long roll might turn him out into the deep snow or the guns of the enemy batter down his cantonment over his head.

Another, speaking of the trivial things to which a man gives his heart and for which he may lose his soul, speculated with the finest fancy as to what it was, and how very a trifle it may have been, that turned the heart and the gaze of Lot's wife back toward Sodom and turned her breathing body into a dead pillar of salt.

And still another—a great, broad-shouldered, double-jointed son of Anak, with a head like the Farnese Jove and a face and frame indicative of tremendous power, alike of character and of muscle—delivered himself of his "experience" in one of the most graphic and moving talks I ever listened to. He said in substance:

"Brethren, I want you to know what a merciful, forgiving being the Lord is, and to do that I've got to tell you what a mean-spirited liar I am. You remember that tight place the brigade got into, down yonder at ———, and you know the life I lived up to that day. Well, as soon as ever

the Minies began a-singing and the shell a-bursting around
me, I up and told the Lord that I was sorry and ashamed
of myself, and if He'd cover my head this time we'd settle
the thing as soon as I got out.   Then I got to fighting and
forgot all about it, and never thought of my promise no
more at all till we got into that other place, up yonder at
————; you remember it, 'tighter than the first one.   Then,
when the bullets begun a hissing like rain and the shell was
fairly tearing the woods to pieces, my broken promise come
back to me.   Brethren, my coward heart stopped beating
and I pretty night fainted.   I tried to pray and at first I
couldn't; but I just said, 'Look here, Lord, if You will look,
I feel I have lied to you and that you won't believe me again,
and may be you oughtn't to; but I don't want to go to hell,
and I'm serious and honest this time, and if You do hear
me now, we'll meet just as soon as I get out safe, and we
certainly will settle things.'

"Well, brethren, He did all I asked of Him, the Lord did;
and what did I do?   Brethren, I'm ashamed to say it, but I
lied again, and never thought one thing about it at all till
one day we was shoved into the very worst place any of us
ever was in.   Hell gaped for me, and here come the two
lies I had told and sat right down upon my heart and my
tongue.   Of course I couldn't pray, but at last I managed to
say, Lord! Lord!   I deserve it all if I do go there, right
now, and I can't pray and I won't lie any more.   You can
do as You please, Lord; but if You do——.   But, no, I
won't lie any more, and I won't promise, for fear I should
lie.   It's all in your hands, Lord—hell or mercy.   I've got no
time to talk any more about it.   I've got to go to killing
Yankees.   But, oh Lord! oh Lord!—no, I daresn't, I
daresn't; for I won't lie any more; I won't go down there
with a fresh lie on my lips; but, oh Lord! oh Lord!'

"And so it was, brethren, all through that dreadful day;
fighting, fighting, and not daring to pray.

"But, brethren, He did it, He did it; and the moment the
thing was over I wouldn't give myself time to lie again, so I
just took out and ran as hard as ever I could into the deep,
dark woods, where God and me was alone together, and I

threw my musket down on the ground and I went right down myself, too, on my knees, and cried out, 'Thank you, Lord; thank you, Lord! but I'm not going to get up off my knees until everything's settled between us;' and neither I didn't, brethren. The Lord never held it over me at all, and we settled it right there."

It is said that more than five hundred men professed conversion in these Fredericksburg meetings, and this statement is based upon careful figures made by the regimental chaplains, and particularly by Rev. William Owen, who really began these meetings, and was practically in charge of them. Some of the chaplains were very uncommon men. My father, who was in the ministry more than fifty years and had a very wide experience with men, expressed the highest estimate of them.

Easily the most marked man among them, however, was the Rev. William Benton Owen, chaplain of the Seventeenth Mississippi Regiment. My recollection is that he had been a private soldier and was commissioned chaplain, because he was already doing the work of one—yes, of half a dozen —without the commission. Of all the men I ever knew, I think he was the most consecrated, the most unselfish, and the most energetic, and that he accomplished more that was really worthy of grateful recognition and commendation than any other man I ever knew, of his ability. By this I do not mean to imply that his ability was small, but simply that I do not include in this statement a few men I have known, of extraordinary abilities and opportunities.

"Brother William," as we used to call him, was also a man of the sweetest, loveliest spirit, but of the most unflinching courage as well. After he became chaplain he never felt it right or fitting that he should attempt to kill or wound a man, so he never fired another shot, yet he was seldom back of the actual line of battle. It may give some faint idea of his exalted Christian heroism to say that his regular habit was to take charge of the litter-bearers in battle, and first to see to the removal of the wounded, Federal as well as Confederate, when the former fell into our hands; and then to attend to the burial of the dead of both sides, when we held the field and the enemy did not ask leave to bury their own dead.

It will be remembered by Federal soldiers that the American Tract or Bible Society published Testaments with the United States flag on the fly leaf, and, on the folds of the banner, the printed words, "If I should fall, send this to ————," space being left for his home address, which each soldier was supposed to write in the appropriate place. Dear Brother William could not always burden himself with all these Testaments taken from the dead soldiers' pockets; but because that was not possible, he used to carry a little blank book in which he would copy the home addresses of the dead soldiers and would afterwards write to their friends, telling them where they were buried, and, if possible, how their bodies might be identified.

After one of the bloody repulses of the enemy at Spottsylvania in 1864, Brother William was, as usual, out in front of our works, utterly unconscious of his own heroism or his own peril. He had removed the wounded of both sides and taken note of our dead, and was making his memoranda of the home addresses of the Federal dead, when a Minie ball struck his left elbow, shattering it dreadfully. He was at once carried to the field hospital, and some of Barksdale's (now Humphreys') men sent word down the line to me. As soon as our guns were disengaged I galloped to the hospital to see him; but when I arrived he was under the knife, his elbow being in process of resection, and, of course, was unconscious. My recollection is that I saw him but for a moment only. Much as I would have given for even so little as one word from him, I could not possibly wait, but was obliged to return to my post.

I never saw him again. As usual, after one of these death grapples of '64, Grant slipped off to his left and we to our right, this time too far for me to get back. In a few days we heard that Mr. Owen was in Richmond and then that he had been sent home, and our hopes grew bright that he would ultimately recover. But no; he was never really a strong man; indeed he was one of the few small and slight men I remember in the entire brigade, and, besides, he was worn and wasted with his ceaseless labors. He never really rallied, but in a short time sank and passed away. Few servants of God and man as noble and consecrated, as useful and beloved, as William Owen have lived in this world or left it for Heaven.

I have referred incidentally to two special friends of mine in the company,—whom we will now identify as Allan and Billy,—and in a later chapter will refer again to the sincerity and candor of the intercourse, especially the religious intercourse, of soldiers with each other. If now I can, by a touch here and there, reveal something of what passed between me and each of these noble boys as they were led into the higher life, I will have done more than I could do in any other way to put before you the every-day religious life of the army.

Both my friends were younger than I, both were high, moral men, but neither was a christian; Allan and I were law students when the war interrupted our studies—he at the University of Virginia, I at Columbia College, New York. It was he who, having been previously a pronounced Union man, left the University before breakfast the morning President Lincoln's call for troops was published and joined a military company in Richmond before going to his father's house. Billy was the guide who met us at the train the day we joined the battery, and conducted us to the Howitzer camp. We were all in the same detachment, that is, attached to the same gun, so I readily could and actually did pass much of my waking life first with one and then with the other, and I generally laid down by one or the other at night. Our religious conferences were seldom all three together, for the other two differed in nature and did not have the same temptations or difficulties to overcome. I began earnest effort with both of them as far back as Leesburg, and when I was promoted and left the battery, just after Chancellorsville, both had become Christians.

It may seem almost grotesque in such a connection to remark that one of the most difficult things for a soldier to do is to keep his person and his scant clothing reasonably clean, and that one of the large memories of my soldier life is a record of "divers washings." Yet I cannot recall ever having bathed or washed, while with the company, with any one other than my two dear friends, and it is singular how vividly I do recall standing waist deep in a pool or stream of water with Billy or with Allan, each of us scrubbing away at his only shirt, or at one of his two shirts, as the case might be, meanwhile earnestly discussing some aspect of the one great matter.

Both my dear friends were exceptionally strong men intellectually, but Billy had the simpler nature, with less tendency to self-analysis and introspection, stronger physical life and higher animal spirits; so that with him it was a clear and a clearly-confessed case of light-hearted content and happiness as he was, and consequent light-hearted indifference to any great change. But he was growing more thoughtful, more tender, more perfect in his moral life.

He was wounded seriously at Malvern Hill and threatened with the loss of an eye, and was at home in the country with his mother and sisters for some months. Meanwhile his father died, and he began to realize that if he lived through the war he would have a great burden to carry with his "seven women," as he afterwards called them when nobly bearing them on his great shoulders. "Seven women taking hold of the skirt of one man, and that the skirt of a round-about jacket," as Billy used to say. He returned to us just before Chancellorsville to find the great revival at Fredericksburg in progress and a general condition of thoughtfulness throughout the army, including our battery. He attended some of these wonderful services and we were together as much as possible. I felt the greatest yearning and the strongest hope for him.

Suddenly Chancellorsville burst upon us, and as Hooker's really great plan was disclosed we all felt that the next few days were indeed big with fate. Hooker had crossed an immense force at the upper fords of the Rappahannock and Sedgwick was crossing in front of Fredericksburg. All of us were deeply stirred; and when night fell and our lines began to grow still, I proposed to Billy that we should walk out to the point of the hill overlooking the wide river bottom and hear, if we could not see, the Federal army getting into position. We did so, and no previous hour of our lives had ever proved as impressive as that which followed. We passed beyond our pickets and continued to walk until we got where the murmur of our lines could no longer be heard, while every movement of Sedgewick's great host was plainly audible. We heard the commands of the officers, the tramp of the men, the rumble of the artillery carriages, the shouts and curses of the drivers. We thought of the great meetings in Fredericksburg violently brought to a close, and of the great audience of worshipers to-night manning the lines with us. We thought of the morrow and then of our dear ones praying for us, while I found my arms gradually embracing my friend and drawing him closer to my bosom; and then, taking off our hats, we prayed,—oh, so quietly, yet so earnestly!—committing us and ours to God's merciful keeping, for the night, for the morrow, forever. I do not remember that we spoke after the prayer ceased, but I felt a new answering pressure in Billy's arms which now closely enfolded me, and the sense of a new brotherhood between us. We walked silently back to the guns, but with a new strength, a deep trust and peace in our souls, and we laid down with our arms about each other and slept as quietly as little children—as indeed we were, God's dear soldier children, who had felt His gentle assurance that all was and would be well.

The facts relating to Allan's conversion and death are so remarkable that I would scarcely dare record them were it not that I have before me a written memorandum of them prepared while I was a prisoner at Johnson's Lsland in the spring of 1865. Allan was, as before intimated, rather prone to introspection, but his mental processes were so definite and his verbal expression of them so clear that one experienced no difficulty in understanding him and always felt assured that he thoroughly understood himself.

A few days before Billy's return, Allan and I were washing our clothes, and I, as usual, talking, when he abruptly and almost impatiently interrupted me, saying substantially that, while I evidently thought I was speaking sensibly and appositely, yet what I was saying had in fact no sort of application to his case.

"No doubt," said he, "it is enough if a man believe on the Lord Jesus Christ; but this direction is given to one who has, in all sincerity and earnestness, asked, 'What must I do to be saved?' Now I feel that I have never sincerely and seriously asked that question, and I am not asking it now. The fact is, the whole current of my being sets toward the fulfilment of my earthly purpose; though just now the immediate pursuit of it is kept in abeyance by the war. It is not worth while to attempt to deceive myself or you; what I really desire and am absorbed in, my dear Bob, is not eternal life, but the life which now is. Now then, what should, what can a man do, who is in my condition? Tell me what you really think; and speak quietly and practically, so there will be no mistaking your meaning."

I knew he was honest and hoped he was more earnest than he realized at the moment, so I begged for light and guidance before answering, and then I said:

"Allan, do you intellectually and firmly believe the New Testament records and the main outline of the Christian system; and if you do, have you any feeling at all connected with them and their bearing upon your life?"

"Yes," he said, "my intellectual belief is definite and decided, and I probably, yes, certainly, have *some* desire to accept the truth in the fuller, Christian sense."

"Then," said I, "your present duty is clear and it is to pray to God to help you to accept in this fuller sense. Tell Him of your full intellectual faith and your feeble heart faith. Utter sincerely that prayer of prayers for a man in such a world and such a life as this, 'Lord, I believe, help Thou mine unbelief!' Do this sincerely, and I feel satisfied the heart or soul part of your faith will grow."

He protested that the best prayer he could offer would be but half-hearted and an insult to God. I combatted this idea, contending that it would be a greater neglect and insult not to attempt to pray at all, and he finally promised he would try. When I next saw him alone I think we were on the march for Chancellorsville. He was evidently unhappy, and when I asked him if he had prayed, he said he had not, that he had been upon his knees, but could not pray, and added that his nature must be more paralyzed and things even worse with him than he had supposed. I saw that another Teacher and Physician had taken the case out of my hand. He rather clung to me, but I thought best to leave him with his new Teacher, and I did.

Two of our comrades were killed and horribly mangled by solid shot or whole shell in our Chancellorsville fights, and we buried one of them at night in a thicket. Returning there after the burying party had withdrawn, I saw a man on his knees at the graveside. It was Allan, and at my approach he rose and advanced to meet me, saying:

"Bob, I am a mystery to myself. I don't see how I am to go up to the gun in to-morrow's fight and face temporal and eternal death; and yet I presume I shall be able to do my duty."

I said decidedly:

"You have no business, Allan, and no need to face eternal death. That is not before you, unless you will have it so."

We said a few words to each other, a few more to God, went back and joined the sad circle around the camp fire a short while, and then laid down together. I think I told him about Billy, and then we slept.

The next day, after evening roll call, we each put an arm around the other's waist and walked off into the woods, and as soon as we got out of earshot of others I began:

"Well, Allan, to go back where we left off—"

He put his other hand in mine and I felt a thrill as he did so, while, with the sweetest smile, he said:

"No, Bob, I don't think we will go back there. I've gotten beyond that point, and I don't like going back. I have found the Lord Jesus Christ, or, rather, He has found me and taken hold of me."

It was the largest, the most thrilling moment of my life. Never before had I been conscious of such overpowering spiritual joy. We were for the moment two disembodied human souls alone with God. The earth with its trappings had disappeared.

It was my last word with him. It must have been the next day that I received my first promotion and left for Richmond, for Beers was killed at Chancellorsville and I buried him at Richmond. When I returned to the army it was to Early's division of the Second Corps. True, we did not begin the advance into Pennsylvania for almost a full month after Chancellorsville, and what became of this month to me I cannot say, except that I went where I was ordered, and do not recall meeting the Howitzers again until after Gettysburg.

On his way to his last battle this splendid youth wrote to his family a brief note, in which he said:

"In the hurry of the march I have little time for thought, but whenever my eternal interests do occur to me, I feel entire assurance of full and free pardon through Jesus Christ, and if called upon to die this moment I think I could do so cheerfully."

These were the last words he ever wrote.

After Gettysburg I rode over to the old battery and they told me this story. On the last day, worn with that tremendous fight, two of our guns had taken up their last position. All thought the struggle over. Allan had just seen a friend on the staff who promised to, and did, send word home of his safety at the close of the battle. Suddenly a terrific fire burst thundering, flashing, crashing upon them and No. 1, while ramming home the shot, had the sponge-staff shattered in his hands. No. 1 was Billy; Allan was gunner, and stooped to unkey the other sponge. A frightful explosion, the piece is dismounted and most of the detachment hurled violently to the earth!

The sergeant, a quite, phlegmatic man, looked about him in horror. The lieutenant, running up, demanded:

"Why don't you change that wheel?"

"I haven't men enough left, sir; we've used up the supernumeraries."

"Where's Allan?"

"There he is, sir!"—pointing to a mangled mass which no one had the nerve to approach. There lay our noble comrade, each several limb thrice broken, the body gashed with wounds, the top of the skull blown off and the brain actually fallen out upon the ground in two bloody, palpitating lobes. A percussion shell had struck the rim of the wheel while he bent behind it unkeying the rammer.

His chariot and horses of fire had caught him up into Heaven.

CHAPTER XII

In the four or five months between Fredericksburg and
Chancellorsville, that is to say, between the middle of December, '62, and the first of May, '63, several things occurred of special interest to me personally, as well as several
others of more general and public significance. It is not
possible now to relate these events in their exact sequence,
nor even to be confident that every incident referred to as
belonging to this period actually happened between the dates
mentioned; but neither of these considerations is important.

To my next younger brother, Randolph, and myself the
one event of transcendent interest about this time was the
long-deferred arrival in Richmond of our mother and sisters, whom we had left behind in New Haven in the spring
of '61. Neither of us had heretofore asked anything in the
nature of a furlough, or leave of absence, feeling that our
comrades who, by such leave, would be enabled to see father
and mother, sisters and home, should be entitled to the pref-
erence; and now, when it became known that our dear people
were in Richmond, everyone stood back for us and urged
our claims. Not only did the captain approve our application, but the first lieutenant offered me his thoroughbred
horse, "Rebel," by the aid of whose fleet limbs it was

thought I might be able to get around to the necessary headquarters in a day, and also, perhaps, have a chance to say a
word in behalf of my brother and myself, instead of waiting the slow process and the somewhat uncertain result of
the papers working their own way through "the regular
channels." My recollection is that all this happened about
Christmas time, so that the goodness of our comrades in
standing back for us was the more praiseworthy.

I did succeed in making "the grand rounds" in a day, but
might not have done so but for the combined intelligence and
stubborness of little Rebel. It was almost dark when I left
the last headquarters I had to visit, and started for camp,
which was a long distance off, and the latter part of the
way almost a labyrinth of undistinguishable army tracks.
The road was yet, however, distinct, and my horse not at all
fatigued and making good speed; but just as I was felici-
tating myself that all was working well, the road turned
sharply to the left, to avoid an apparently impassable
swamp, but the little horse absolutely refused to turn with it,
insisting upon going directly forward into the swamp.

I fought him for ten or fifteen minutes to no purpose. He
only balked and wheeled and reared and plunged, until
finally, utterly worn out, I gave him his head and he took
and kept his course, as the crow flies, into and through the
swamp, over and past fence and ditch, on through brush and
brake and briar and thicket, I making no effort to guide or
control him; indeed, after a short time, utterly unable even
to see where he was going and only attempting to lie as
close as possible to his back and as far as possible to protect
my face and eyes. I never took another such ride, before or
since, and had no idea when or where it would end, until at
last—yet in an incredibly short time—the little fellow pushed his determined front through the fringe of low pines that
protected our battery horse shelters and—we were at home.
I was bruised and scratched, tired and cold, wet and hungry,
but I made the plucky little horse comfortable before doing
anything for myself, and next morning satisfied myself that
he had never before been over the tract of country we had
traversed together, and that it was a clear case of unerring

instinct for locality and direction. I had all the required en-
dorsements, and that very day "Randy" and I took the train
for Richmond, the two happiest boys among all Marse
Robert's ragged thousands.

When it is recalled that it had been nearly two years since
we left our mother and sisters in the North; that during all
this time we had only irregular, illegal, and very infrequent
communication with them, and consequently had now all
the vivid experiences of two such years to interchange, the
intense interest and bliss of these furlough days in Richmond
may be faintly imagined. My memory is not absolutely
clear, but I am almost positive that Mrs. Beers and her little
girls had come on with our mother and sisters and that Beers
had also gotten a furlough to meet them and was in Richmond with us. If so, it was the last time I ever saw the
noble fellow alive. It will be remembered he fell at Chancellorsville.

One matter of very great importance which took shape
between Fredericksburg and Chancellorsville was the organization of our (Cabell's) battalion of artillery. It was
made up of four batteries—ours, the First Company, Richmond Howitzers, of Virginia; Manly's Battery, of North
Carolina; the Troupe Artillery and Frazier's Battery, of
Georgia; and it included, at different times, from sixteen to
eighteen guns, mostly brass Napoleons. Its commanding
officer was Col. H. C. Cabell, a member of the historic and
illustrious Virginia family of that name and a man every
way worthy of his lineage.

For eighteen months of the hottest part of the war I was
the adjutant of Colonel Cabell, fighting by his side by day
and sleeping by his side by night, eating and drinking often
out of the same tin cup, lying upon the same oil cloth and
covered with the same blanket—side by side, heart to heart,
soul to soul. If ever I knew a man through and through, I
knew him; and a cleaner, sweeter, more loyal soul I never
knew. His essential characteristics were pure and unselfish
nature, tender and affectionate heart, gentle and unfailing
courtesy, single-hearted and devoted patriotism, quiet but
indomitable courage. I never knew him to fail to be at the

point of peril along the front of his battalion, nor there nor anywhere to fail to measure up to the full standard of a battalion commander's duty and responsibility.   I never knew him to shrink from any hardship or any duty or any sacrifice for the cause to which we had devoted our lives.   I never knew him to fail to treat a private soldier with a consideration which was grateful to him, and yet never knew this courtesy to interfere with the maintenance of discipline.   I never knew him to wound intentionally the feelings of a human being, or fail to repair the wrong if committed inadvertently.   He was a man of intellect and culture, as well as character; as a friend ever faithful, as a companion always agreeable, as an officer enjoying the unqualified confidence and approval of his superiors, and the universal respect and affection of his subordinates.

I am well aware that all this should have resulted in even more, but he who never did injustice to others never did full justice to himself.   He lacked self-assertion and aggression; to some extent, too, he lacked the manner and bearing of a soldier, and he never maneuvered for position for himself or his battalion.

He was not, however, lacking in proper soldierly ambition.   He already enjoyed distinguished position; for the officer who attains and reputably maintains the rank of full colonel of artillery fills a position of great honor and responsibility.   But he was much pleased to learn late in the war that certain of his friends, as they announced themselves, were planning to secure for him the exceptional rank of brigadier-general of artillery.   He was interested and gratified until he accidentally discovered that it was involved in the plan that he should be retired to the permanent defenses of Richmond, and another officer should take his battalion in the field.   When this feature was developed, for once he flamed into ungovernable rage.   It was the only time I ever heard him swear.   "Stiles," said he, "what do these people take me for?   Have I given men any reason to consider me a damned sneak and coward and fool?"

I cannot forbear a trifling incident, revealing in a flash the simplicity and beauty of his nature and of our relations and intercourse. It occurred at the left base of the Bloody Angle at Spottsylvania in 1864, where one or two of his batteries had been ordered to take the place of some of our artillery which had been captured, and to stay the rout. The guns were in column back of the lines, awaiting our return, we having ridden into that gloomy pit of defeat and demoralization to determine exactly where they should be placed. As we came out, before riding back to bring up the guns, we dismounted in a place of comparative security, just to stretch our limbs and unbend a moment from the awful tension. Leaving his horse, Colonel Cabell walked up to me, color mounting his face and tears filling his eyes, and threw his arms about me, saying in a voice husky with feeling exactly these words: "Stiles, if you should dare to get killed, I'd never forgive you."

Such was the commanding officer of our battalion. Either at the organization or soon after, Major S. P. Hamilton, of South Carolina, was assigned to duty with the command, and at a later period Major W. H. Gibbes, of the same State, was with us for a few weeks or months. I am not certain as to the date of my first service with the battalion as adjutant. Some of my comrades insist that it was from the inception; but I am sure this is not true, unless, as is possible, I may have been detailed by Colonel Cabell to aid temporarily in arranging matters and getting the new organization in working order. I could not have been regularly even "acting adjutant," for I held no commission until after Chancellorsville, a battle in which we were fought as a battalion, though in two divisions, while I distinctly remember I fought as a private soldier, in the old battery, in my usual position at my own gun.

Soon after the battle of Gettysburg, whether on the Virginia or Maryland side of the river I do not now remember, Colonel Cabell met me and asked what I was doing, and learning that I was at the time a sort of free lance, with one of the artillery battalions of the Second Corps, urged me to get the informal permission of General Early, with whose headquarters I kept up some sort of connection, and go back with him to the First Corps and act as adjutant of his battalion, which I did; he promising to get a regular order assigning me to this duty. Upon reflection, I think the first order of detail for duty at his headquarters, by Colonel Cabell himself, prior to Chancellorsville, as above suggested, is very probable, as I do not otherwise see how the Colonel would have known me or had reason to suppose I would be satisfactory to him in the position.

Among matters worthy of note occurring prior to Chancellorsville, it may not be out of place to mention the very active commerce or interchange of commodities, carried on by tiny sailing vessels, between the north and south banks of the Rappahannock River, at and below Fredericksburg, both before and after that battle. The communication was almost constant and the vessels many of them really beautiful little craft, with shapely hulls, nicely painted; elaborate rigging, trim sails, closed decks, and perfect working steering apparatus. The cargoes, besides the newspapers of the two sides, usually consisted on our side of tobacco and on the Federal side of coffee and sugar, yet the trade was by no means confined to these articles, and on a sunny, pleasant day the waters were fairly dotted with the fairy fleet. Many a weary hour of picket duty was thus relieved and lightened, and most of the officers seemed to wink at the infraction of military law, if such it was. A few rigidly interdicted it, but it never really ceased.

Another institutional amusement of the army in the winter of '62-3, which tended greatly to relieve the almost unendurable tedium of camp life, was the snow-ball battle. These contests were unique in many respects. In the first place here was sport, or friendly combat, on the grandest scale, perhaps, known in modern times. Entire brigades lined up against each other for the fight. And not the masses of men only, but the organized military bodies—the line and field officers, the bands and the banners, the generals and their staffs, mounted as for genuine battle. There was the formal demand for the surrender of the camp, and the refusal, the charge, and the repulse; the front, the flank, the rear attack. And there was intense earnestness in the struggle—sometimes limbs were broken and eyes, at least temporarily, put out, and the camp equipment of the vanquished was regarded as fair booty to the victors.

I recall a visit paid in company with my father, not long after the battle of Fredericksburg, to the camp of my uncle mentioned in a former chapter as having been in command of Lawton's brigade in that fight. He was still in command of it. My father asked the cause of several very heavy bruises on his face. I never saw my uncle more deeply embarrassed, as he related, blushing like a girl, what he called his "preposterous experience" in leading his brigade the day before in a snow battle with Hoke's, which lasted several hours—and as the really laughable picture was developed, its strong coloring heightened by my uncle's embarrassed blushes, I never saw my father more heartily amused. It seemed that my uncle at one point in the conflict had been dragged from his horse and captured by Hoke's men, but later had been recaptured by his own command, and on both occasions had been pretty roughly handled. One would have supposed these veteran troops had seen too much of the real thing to seek amusement in playing at battle.

I had now been in the army for nearly two years and was still a private soldier, yet quite content as such. My mental attitude in this regard was perhaps rather unusual. I had originally volunteered exclusively from sense of duty, regarding the war, so far as it affected me personally, as an interruption to my personal purposes and ambitions in connection with the law; but I was never one of those who considered the conflict to be a matter of sixty or ninety days or a year, and soon came to look upon it as of indefinite duration and likely to prove an absorbing business to me for a long time to come. Gradually I became interested in military life and began to contemplate it as perhaps my life work, and from this time my interest in it grew apace. Still I had thought little of promotion except in the aspect of making myself deserving of it. True, General Hill had, at quite an early period, said something of a commission, but none had come, and I had continued to look upon the position, even of a corporal, as requiring a certain amount of military aptitude, not to say talent and training, which I was not confident I had.

But this morbid and unpractical view of things was giving way before the stubborn fact, established by observation and experience, that I every day saw men in position far above me, obviously my inferiors in every qualification and requisite for rank and command; nor could I be blind to the further fact that my commanding officers regarded me with rather special confidence and approval. Gradually I came to entertain the idea that I might some day be offered promotion and perhaps should not feel called upon to reject it, though I could never contemplate any effort on my part to secure it.

While I was in this state of mind, some little time before the opening of the Chancellorsville campaign, I received a communication from the Engineer Bureau in Richmond containing an appointment to a second lieutenancy in "Engineer Troops," a new corps about to be organized in the Army of Northern Virginia. There was no explanation accompanying the paper, and I did not recognize as familiar any name connected with it, and after due reflection concluded that the communication had been sent me by mistake and was intended for my cousin, Robert Mackay Stiles, who was an engineer, as I understood, then serving in the far South in some appropriate capacity. I supposed his services were desired in organizing the new corps, and I actually returned the paper, with the above suggestion, and therewith dismissed the matter from my mind. Meanwhile there occurred one of the most noteworthy experiences of my life.

The very day, I think it was, of what might be termed "our spring opening" of '63, and probably before we made the first move looking toward Chancellorsville, I was busy about some duty in the battery, when I heard the captain's voice calling me sharply, and as I approached his quarters noticed a courier just leaving. The captain informed me that General Jackson had sent an order for me to report immediately at his headquarters. When my first surprise subsided I told Captain McCarthy, what I was then confident was the case, that the message was doubtless from my father, who loved to work in the Second Corps, and spent much time at the General's quarters; but the captain protested that the order was from "Old Jack" himself, that he could not imagine what he wanted with me; he hoped not to have me shot for some violation of military law. "However," said he, "you had better take one of the sergeant's horses and go and find out for yourself"—which I proceeded at once to do; but had not gotten beyond the confines of camp before I heard the captain calling again, the utterance of my name this time alternating with shouts and peals of laughter. On riding up I found him reading, for the second time, an autograph note from General Jackson, addressed to Captain Mc-Carthy, and to the following effect: that if we had not already received orders to move we would receive them in a few moments; that Robert Stiles must not report to him until further orders; that he didn't want any *"untried man"* about him when about to move.

The relations of our captain to the better soldiers in the battery were peculiar and enjoyable. On duty he was our commanding officer, off duty our intimate friend. I used to call him "the intelligent young Irishman," and to tell the following story in explanation: Just before the Howitzers left Richmond, in the spring of '61, General Magruder called upon Major Randolph to send him a suitable man for a courier, adding, "intelligent young Irishman preferred"—and McCarthy was sent as "filling the bill." The captain had long been "laying for me," as the saying is, and now he had his revenge—"Old Jack" had conferred upon me orthodox Presbyterian baptism as "the untried man," and so far as the captain was concerned, certainly the name "stuck."

What would he and I have given, two or three days later, to recall the action of the next few moments. I distinctly remember the general appearance of General Jackson's note. It was written in pencil on a small half sheet of bluish paper, evidently torn from a letter, and I remember, too, how Captain McCarthy—laughing still—tore it up, when he had read it out three or four times, and how the fragments floated adown the air. I told Mrs. Jackson of the circumstance not long after the war, and she pronounced the contents of the note, and particularly the last clause, to be strongly illustrative of the directness and concentration which rendered her husband oblivious of everything but the one idea at any one time having possession of him.

A few days later, but after Jackson's death, my father gave me what I may term the obverse, or face side, of this incident. He was at Jackson's headquarters when the General, as it were in a tone of inquiry, said:

"Doctor, I understand you have a son in the army?"

"Yes, General," my father answered, "I have three of them."

"One is like you, isn't he?"

"No, sir; I don't know that either of them is specially like me."

Then, somewhat impatiently:

"Well, your oldest son is named Robert, isn't he?"

"Yes, Bob is my eldest son."

"From what I have heard of him, I think I should like to have him with me."

"Well, sir, I would be delighted to have him come."

"But it isn't for you to say, Doctor; he ought to be allowed to decide for himself. Besides, both of you should consider that the probability of his being killed will be greatly increased. I am liable to make mistakes in my orders and to send a man into danger that might be avoided by going around some longer and less perilous route. But he must not stop to consider this. He must take his life in his hand and carry my orders as I send them."

"Yes, sir; I think I understand, and I am sure Bob will carry your orders *as you send them.* His life is in God's hands. Longer or shorter, I would like to have him spend it with you, and I am sure that would be his choice, too."

"But, Doctor, you have no right to decide for him. Tell him all I have told you, and let him decide for himself."

"But, General, I do decide and have decided, for Bob and for myself. He will be delighted to come to you."

"Very well, sir. In my opinion you have no right to make this decision, but if you insist upon taking the responsibility, I'll send for your son."

And he did, with the result already given.

He was not as sure of me as my dear father was; to Jackson, certainly, I was "the untried man." I have often thought what might have been if I had gone to him that day. Of course my blood would have been up, and the chances are very great that I would have fallen that fateful night in the Chancellorsville Wilderness, when the wondrous captain did make one of those mistakes to which he said he was "liable," and which then cost, not a little life like mine, but that great life of his, upon which destiny and history hung.

Among the pet names with which our constant lover, the Army of the Potomac, was wont to soften and sweeten its early spring wooings of us was "Damned sassafras-tea-drinking rebels." If a trifle vigorous and not even a trifle euphonious, it was yet certainly appropriate and suggestive, for the first steady spring sunshine, that dried out the roads and caused the sassafras buds to swell, sent the first tremors of returning life darting through the coils of the great serpentine armies which had lain torpid in the winter's cold, until suddenly the one or the other monster glided, hissing from its den, and delivered its stroke. To our friends, the enemy, the only relation between the swelling of the sassafras buds and the spring-burst of battle was chronological; but with us the sassafras amounted almost to a sub-commissariat—we chewed it, we drank it, we smelled it, and it was ever at hand without the trouble or expense of transport.

All through the latter part of April, '63, even more than the normal premonitory spring shudderings were noted throughout the great winter camps and quarters of the Federal army corps across the river, and very soon the marvelous army telegraph was in full operation. Every surviving veteran of either side will understand what I mean. It was really little less than miraculous the way in which information—often astonishingly correct—as to what had happened or was about to happen, was transmitted along the lines of the army. Partial explanations readily occur, but I have yet to meet the first intelligent and observant soldier of the Army of Northern Virginia who is not ready to admit that, in some instances, the rapid transmission of news and the detailed accuracy of forecast that sifted through the army were at the time, and remain to-day, inexplicable.

Of course we knew of the resignation or removal of Burnside and the appointment of Hooker as his successor, late in January, and we had seen, too, the remarkable order of the latter, issued upon assuming command, in which he declared that: "In equipment, intelligence, and valor, the enemy is our inferior. Let us never hesitate to give him battle whenever we can find him." From this order, as well as from his military history, with which we were familiar, we "knew our man." We knew also the atmosphere that surrounded his appointment, but I for one never saw, until long after the war, the remarkable letter of Mr. Lincoln to his appointee, which not only revives and bears out my recollection of the spirit of the times, but fills me with amazement that a self-respectful officer could have accepted an appointment confirmed or accompanied by such a letter:

EXECUTIVE MANSION,
WASHINGTON, D. C.,
January 26, 1863.

MAJOR-GENERAL HOOKER:

General:—I have placed you at the head of the Army of the Potomac. Of course I have done this upon what appears to me to be sufficient reasons. And yet I think it best for you to know that there are some things in regard to which I am not quite satisfied with you. I believe you to be a brave and skilful soldier, which, of course, I like. I also believe you do not mix politics with your profession, in which you are right. You have confidence in yourself, which is a valuable, if not an indispensable quality. You are ambitious, which, within reasonable bounds, does good rather than harm. But I think that during General Burnside's command of the army you have taken counsel of your ambition and thwarted him as much as you could, in which you did a great wrong both to the country and to a meritorious and honorable brother officer. I have heard in such a way as to believe it of your recently saying that both the army and the Government needed a dictator. Of course it was not for this, but in spite of it, that I have given you the command. Only those generals who gain successes can set up as dictators. What I now ask of you is military success, and I will risk the dictatorship. The Government will support you to the utmost of its ability, which is neither more nor less than it has done and will do for all commanders. I much fear the spirit you have aided to infuse into the army, of criticising their commander and withholding confidence from him, will now turn upon you. I shall assist you as far as I can to put it down. Neither you nor Napoleon, if he were alive again, could get any good out of an army while such a spirit prevails in it. And now, beware of rashness! beware of rashness! but with energy and sleepless vigilance, go forward and give us victories.   Yours very truly,

A. LINCOLN.

One of the ablest discussions of Chancellorsville from the Confederate side is to be found in an address delivered by Gen. Fitzhugh Lee before the Virginia Division of the Army of Northern Virginia, on the 24th of October, 1879. In that address the author says of this battle that, "It brings before the military student as high a type of an offensive battle as ever adorned the pages of history." Col. Walter Taylor says: "Of all the battles fought by the Army of Northern Virginia, that of Chancellorsville stands first as illustrating the consummate audacity and military skill of commanders and the valor and determination of the men." It is probable that the general consensus of opinion among the surviving officers and soldiers of the Confederacy concurs in these estimates. My own conception of the matter was at the time, and has ever since been, that the brilliant genius and audacious courage of Lee and Jackson shone so conspicuously throughout these operations, partly because the plan of their adversary was truly great—far superior to anything that had theretofore been projected against Lee and his staunch soldiers.

The battle is of such exceptional interest, and at the same time savors so much of the marvelous, that I ask pardon for making a lengthy quotation from Colonel Taylor's book, premising that it was twelve miles or more from Deep Run, below Fredericksburg, where Sedgwick and Early opposed each other, to Chancellorsville, the position selected by Hooker as the base of his main operations and where he had concentrated the bulk of his army. On pages 83-5 of his "Four Years with General Lee," Colonel Taylor says:

General Lee, with fifty-seven thousand troops of all arms, intrenched along the line of hills south of the Rappahannock, near Fredericksburg, was confronted by General Hooker, with the Army of the Potomac, one hundred and thirty-two thousand strong, occupying the bluffs on the opposite side of the river.

On the 29th of April the Federal commander essayed to put into execution an admirably conceived plan of operations, from which he doubtless concluded that he could compel either the evacuation by General Lee of his strongly fortified position, or else his utter discomfiture, when unexpectedly and vigorously assailed upon his left flank and rear by the "finest army on the planet"—really more than twice the size of his own.

A formidable force, under General Sedgwick, was thrown across the river below Frederickburg, and made demonstrations of an intention to assail the Confederate front. Meanwhile, with great celerity and secrecy, General Hooker, with the bulk of his army, crossed at the upper fords, and in an able manner and wonderfully short time had concentrated four of his seven army corps, numbering fifty-six thousand men, at Chancellorsville, about ten miles west of Fredericksburg. His purpose was now fully developed to General Lee, who, instead of waiting its further prosecution, immediately determined on the movement the least expected by his opponent. He neither proceeded to make strong his left against attack from the direction of Chancellorsville, nor did he move southward so as to put his army between that of General Hooker and the Confederate capital; but leaving General Early with about nine thousand men to take care of General Sedgwick, he moved with the remainder of his army, numbering forty-eight thousand men, toward Chancellorsville. As soon as the advance of the enemy was encountered, it was attacked with vigor, and very soon the Federal army was on the defensive in its apparently impregnable position. It was not the part of wisdom to attempt to storm the stronghold; but Sedgwick would certainly soon be at work in the rear, and Early, with his inadequate force, could not do more than delay and hamper him. It was, therefore, imperatively necessary to strike—to strike boldly, effectively and at once. There could be no delay. Meanwhile two more army corps had joined General Hooker, who had now about Chancellorsville ninety-one thousand men—six corps, except one division of the second corps (Couch's) which had been left with Sedgwick at Fredericksburg. It was a critical position for the Confederate commander, but his confidence in his trusted lieutenant and brave men was such that he did not long hesitate. Encouraged by the counsel and confidence of General Jackson, he determined still further to divide his army; and while he, with the divisions of Anderson and McLaws, less than fourteen thousand men, should hold the enemy in his front, he would hurl Jackson upon his flank and rear and crush and crumble him as between the upper and nether millstone. The very boldness of the movement contributed much to insure its success.

This battle illustrates most admirably the peculiar talent and individual excellence of Lee and Jackson. For quickness of perception, boldness in planning and skill in directing, Lee had no superior; for celerity in his movements, audacity in the execution of bold designs and impetuosity in attacking, Jackson had not his peer.

About the 28th of April dispatches by the army or grapevine telegraph began to come in very rapidly, and that, too, minutely and correctly revealing the situation. We were at the time in camp a little back of the main fortified line. That evening, I think it was, we received orders to be ready to move at a moment's notice. Very early next morning we heard firing in the direction of Fredericksburg. It was very foggy, and we could see nothing, but understood that a heavy force of the enemy was crossing to our side. They remained all day concealed under the river bank, but at night—I think the night of the 29th—deployed out into position in the great plain. Meanwhile our battery had been ordered to the same position it had occupied in the battle of Fredericksburg, and all during that day Hooker's plan of operations was becoming more and more clearly developed, and with Sedgwick in our front and Hooker in overwhelming force in the rear of our left flank, we deeply felt its power.

The discussion waxed hot as to what Marse Robert would do. Until he decided, none of us knew what was best, yet the counter plot was intensely absorbing, and when at last—I think it was the night of the 30th—orders came for us to limber up and move out by the little road by which we had come in, and which ran at right angles between the lines and the main road running parallel to the river, the interest was intense, and the dry betting ran high as to whether, when we struck the main road, it would be "head of column to the right" or to "the left." If the latter, then we would know Marse Robert had concluded that it was the part of wisdom to put his army between Sedgwick and Richmond and to maneuver all the attacking columns of his enemies to his front. In that case we might exhale a deep, full breath; for a little while, at least, the extreme tension would be off. But if the horses' heads turned to the right, then we knew well that it was to be the closest and deadliest grapple we had ever experienced. I cannot remember which I thought the wiser alternative or what part I took in the dis-

cussion; but I do distinctly recall that when the first gun
struck the main road and the heads of the leaders swung
around *to the right,* I drew in my breath and set my teeth,
calling upon what was best and strongest in my entire being
to brace me for the struggle.

I think it was a day or so before we finally left the Fredericksburg lines that there occurred one of the most remarkable minor incidents I witnessed from the beginning to the
end of the war. We had lifted the ammunition chest out
of the hole, back of and beneath the little work we had
been occupying, and had replaced it upon the gun carriage
and limbered up the piece. A group of about a dozen men,
not all belonging to our battery, were standing upon the
earth-work gazing across the river bottom to the Stafford
side, when a little puff of white smoke indicated that the
gentlemen on the other side had determined to try their long-
range guns. The shell flew a little too high, but directly above
us and too close to be comfortable. Before quite reaching us,
however, it began to wobble and turn over, indicating that
the projectile or propulsive force was well nigh exhausted.
My recollection is that we could see the shell distinctly. An
infantryman jumped from the work into the hole just va-
cated by the limber chest. The shell exploded just after it
passed us, and the base came hurtling back and actually
dashed out the brains of that man, the only man who had
not stood his ground. Several other shots were fired, but
not a man flinched and not another man was injured.

I was reminded of a story of the Emperor Napoleon, who
in visiting his picket line with the corporal of the guard
came to a position which commanded just the view he wanted of the enemy's lines, but was exposed to a galling and dangerous fire from their sharpshooters. The little corporal
was standing, absorbed as was his wont when analyzing a
battle-field, head sunk between his shoulders, hands behind
his back and limbs far apart. He turned to speak to the corporal of the guard, and just as he did so a ball passed between the Emperor's legs and killed the corporal, crouching
behind him for protection. Two soldiers stooped to pick
up the body, but the Emperor hissed out, "Behold the just
fate of the coward. Let the carrion rot."

CHAPTER XIII

CHANCELLORSVILLE

On the March—The Light Division Passes Our Guns—Marse Robert
Passes the Light Division—The Two Little Dogs of the Battalion
—Two of Our Guns Take Chancellorsville in Reverse—Interview
with General McLaws—Entire Regiment from New Haven, Conn.,
Captured—Brother William and Marse Robert—Sedgwick—Hooker
—His Battle Orders—His Compliment to Lee's Army—Lee's Order
Announcing Jackson's Death.

I recall but one or two features of the march to Chancellorsville. We were with McLaws' division, and of the
14,000 (Anderson's and McLaws' commands) with which
General Lee undertook to hold, and did hold, the front of
Hooker's 92,000, while Jackson, with the balance of our
forces, swung around his right flank and rear.

Two of our batteries, the Howitzers and Manly's, left
Fredericksburg at midnight, April 30th, 1863, and early on
the morning of May 1st were drawn up in column on the
side of the Old Turnpike, head toward Chancellorsville, to
allow the "Light Division," as Gen. A. P. Hill's command
was called, to pass. Jackson, as we understood, was somewhere ahead, and Hill's superb troops seemed to be resolved that he should not be compelled to wait even a moment for them. They were in light marching order, and I
thought I had never seen anything equal to the swinging,
silent stride with which they fairly devoured the ground.
The men were magnified in the morning mist which overhung the low flat-lands they were traversing, and at the same
time imparted a ghostly indistinctness of outline, which
added to the impressiveness of the scene. All was silent as
the grave, save the muffled and almost synchronous tread of
the thousands of feet in the soft road, and the low clatter or
jingle of accoutrements.

There was a sudden outburst in the rear of tumultuous shoutings, which rapidly swept toward us, and very soon General Lee, with a full staff, galloped to the front, passing between us and the Light Division, which, however, had now halted and stacked arms across the road from our guns. I cannot recall a moment of higher enthusiasm during the four years of the war. The troops were transported with the wildest excitement and the General also appeared to be unusually impressed. I cannot say that it was his habit, but I distinctly remember that on this occasion he lifted his hat, taking it by the crown with his right hand and holding it suspended above his majestic head as far as we could see him. I remember, too, how the men greeted him, shouting, "What a head, what a head! See that glorious head! God bless it, God bless it!"

In a short time the Light Division got under way again, resuming its swaying, swinging, panther-like step, others of Jackson's command following them. When the last of his troops had passed, we resumed our march and continued it until we finally reached the position assigned us, with McLaws' division, which formed a part of the thin Confederate line covering Hooker's front, and a most peculiar position it was. It was an old house site in a small clearing, but the main building had been burned or destroyed, apparently years ago, while one or two outbuildings were standing. Our guns came into battery in an old pansy bed, which before we left was spattered with splotches of intenser color. We could see absolutely nothing of the enemy, nor of any other part of our own lines; indeed the entire region was a gloomy thicket and our infantry line so stretched and attenuated that the men were scarcely in sight even of each other. It was currently, and I have every reason to believe correctly, reported, that in inspecting the line of his division, General McLaws found one of his brigades actually faced to the rear.

Although the enemy was not in sight from our position, nor we from theirs, yet we interchanged occasionally a considerable fire, which resulted on our side in a few sad and ghastly casualties; but we have already spoken of these and may speak of them again in another connection. For the present, let us turn to something of a less painful nature.

There were two little dogs in the battalion which afforded not only a good deal of amusement, but also a field for some interesting observation and discrimination. Both were small, the Troupe Artillery dog, the larger of the two, about the size of a small coon without a tail, which he in general resembled. He was dark, stone gray on his back, inclining (somewhat more than a coon) to tan or fawn color underneath. He had also rough, coarse hair; short, stout legs, and, as implied, little or no tail. He had entered the service early, joining the battery during the unfortunate campaign in Western Virginia, and was named after the commanding general, "Robert Lee." He was very plucky in a personal difficulty, but I blush to say, an abject coward in battle. The Howitzer dog, whom we christened "Stonewall Jackson," came to us a mere puppy in the summer of 1862, after the battles around Richmond, and while we were waiting for the re-equipment of the battery. He was a Welsh fice, very small, but beautifully formed, gleaming white in color, with a few spots of jet black, his hair fine and short, and lying close and smooth. He did not carry guns enough, metaphorically speaking, to amount to much in a canine encounter, but he was a born warrior, a perfect hero in battle. When our guns were in action he was always careering wildly about them, and in any pause of their hoarse thunders the shrill treble of his tiny bark was always to be heard.

In the battle of Chancellorsville, while we were occupying the position above described, I had occasion to go down the little declivity in rear of the gun to the caissons. I had just left the battery firing actively and Stonewall even more than usually excited, when my eye chanced to light upon poor little Bob Lee sneaking to the rear, in fright absolutely pitiable. It may serve as an excuse for him that he had gotten separated from his company, which had been left behind at Fredericksburg with Early. To my astonishment, he made for a large tree, back of which and as close in and under as possible he crept, and crouched and squatted, very much as a demoralized man might have done. The action and the purpose were unmistakable. I do not know that I could have believed it if I had not seen it with my own eyes, but there was no room for doubt. One might not feel generously and sympathetically inclined toward a man under such circumstances, but it is pleasant to be able to say that little Bob's prudent precautions accomplished their object. As I have always understood, he passed safely through the war and followed the men of his battery to Georgia.

Stonewall was a remarkable little animal. It was surprising that he was not lost or killed in action, especially when we had to change our position rapidly under fire, which was very often. Under such circumstances, whoever happened to be nearest the little fellow, if by a frantic dive he could manage to get him in time, would lift the lid of a limber chest, drop him in an empty partition, and clap the lid down again before the gun dashed off with the rest; but as soon as it came into battery in the new position, No. 6, before getting at his fuses, would first lift the little warrior from his dark, close quarters and drop him on the ground, where, in a twinkling, he would recover his balance, resume his part in the fight and keep it up until, in another move, he was again imprisoned *in transitu,* either in an ammunition chest or under someone's arm.

He was an intelligent, companionable little chap, and the boys taught him some uncommon tricks. His special master, teacher, patron and friend was dear old "Van,"—chief of the second detachment,—who could do anything from shoeing a horse to making a clock out of pine bark, and must of necessity be always doing something, even if it were but training a puppy. Van taught Stonewall to attend roll-call, and to sit up on his haunches, next to him, on the advanced rank of non-commissioned officers, and he made a little pipe for him, which Stonewall would hold firmly in his mouth when Van had once inserted it between his teeth. Then when the orderly sergeant, before beginning the roll, called "Pipes out!" Van would stoop and slip Stonewall's pipe from his mouth to his left paw, which would then instantly drop to his side with the other, and the little corporal would stand, or sit, stiffly and staunchly in the position of a soldier, eyes front, until the company was dismissed.

Stonewall was stolen from us several times by Harry Hayes' brigade, his Louisiana Creoles having the ungovernable passion of the French soldier for pets. At last the cunning thieves succeeded in hiding him, and we lost him finally, to the deep regret, not to say grief, of every man in the battery.

After fighting for some hours in a very indecisive and unsatisfactory fashion, in the unsatisfactory position above described, two of our pieces, my gun one of them, were advanced by a neighborhood road, several hundred yards to the right and front and to the top of a hill from which we could see the entire formation of the Federal lines about Chancellorsville. Who discovered this position I never knew, but it was one of the most remarkable, perhaps the most remarkable, I ever saw. It was on the left flank and rear of the Federal lines about Chancellorsville house, and not more than a thousand or twelve hundred yards distant from our guns. The Federal artillery was as regularly and accurately stationed as if on parade or at drill—guns in front and in action, the motions of the cannoneers at the manual of the piece being distinctly recognizable, except when the smoke of the successive discharges momentarily shut them off; limbers the required distance in rear of guns, caissons in rear of limbers, drivers sitting bolt upright on their horses, and three heavy, black lines of infantry lying down back of the artillery.

I never before felt such a rising of my heart into my throat as I did while lying just behind the crest of the ridge, gazing intently upon this scene and aiding the gunners of the two pieces in making careful estimate of the distance. We were unwilling to waste a shot, knowing that, in the very nature of things, such an opportunity would not be long vouchsafed us. In the pauses or subsidences of the cannonade we could hear the clear, high-pitched, thrilling, dauntless yell of our charging infantry, and we felt what our fire, if well directed, might mean to those gallant fellows. We had already unlimbered and moved the guns forward by hand, so that their muzzles just failed to project over the brow of the hill. We went back to the limbers, took out two shells and cut the fuses accurately in accordance with our estimate of the distance, loaded and ran both pieces forward again until they just cleared the crest of the ridge; then, running down the screws and elevating the muzzles appropriately to the distance, every man in the detachment fell into place, the primers were inserted in the vents and both lanyards pulled simultaneously. The ear detected but one discharge, and the two shells flew screaming and bursting together in the very midst of the mass of Federal artillery, exploding certainly one, and, as it seemed, two, ammunition chests or caissons.

The blow was utterly unexpected, the effect overwhelming, and we gave them no time to recover, but kept throwing in *shell* as rapidly as the guns could be loaded and discharged, until the entire hillside seemed to be cleared for the time of both artillery and infantry. Suddenly we heard the regular huzzas of Federal infantry very close to us, apparently at the foot of the hill on which we stood, but concealed by the scrub forest. No pickets had been thrown out in our front so far as we knew; there was no infantry support with us; minie balls began to drop in very briskly; the hillside we had cleared filled up again, and it was deemed prudent for us to retire.

Strange it is, but I have not the slightest recollection as to what artillery officer was in charge of us, but I do remember that in retiring to our former position we passed very close to Gen. Lafayette McLaws, commanding the division to which generally, as on this occasion, we were attached. I was more deeply stirred than I had ever before been, and have some indistinct recollection of urging one or two of our artillery officers that the eight guns we had with us should be advanced to the position our two guns had just left, accompanied by infantry support.

The suggestion was not approved by them, and I went to General McLaws with it. He received me without the slightest reproof for my impertinence, but said we had done our work with two rifles, and that from what he knew of the ground the distance must be too great for smooth-bore guns. I assured him that he was misinformed, and that I knew what I was talking about, as I had helped to estimate the distance and cut the fuses. I do not now exactly recall what the distance was, but I am positive now, as I was then, that it was within range of our shortest-ranged guns, and I insisted that with our eight guns in action on that hill (the other eight had been left at Fredericksburg with Early) we could fairly blow up Chancellorsville. While I was saying this Major Goggin, adjutant-general of the division, and a fine soldier, rode up and confirmed all I had said. I have an indistinct recollection that we boosted the general, who was short and stout, to the top of an old tobacco barn, but his view was very little extended even from that vantage ground. Nevertheless, he came to our opinion and sent the order for all our eight guns to advance to the position indicated, supported by Semmes' brigade.

I was almost delirious with joy, and ran back to the guns, anticipating a scene of destruction and of triumph such as no one of us had ever before witnessed. But just as the two batteries were drawn out in column on the road we learned that our troops had carried the enemy's works, that he had abandoned the position we were to have shelled, and our opportunity was gone. Semmes, however, went right on, and by a skilful movement and a short, sharp fight, cut off and captured a Federal force which seemed to have been sent forward with the view of capturing our two rifled guns. A little later he marched his prisoners into the clearing we had occupied, and it turned out that he had an entire regiment, I think of "hundred-day men," from New Haven, Conn.

General Lee, convinced that there was, for the present at least, no more dangerous fight in Hooker, had ridden through to General McLaws' position to talk with him about turning back to help Early take care of Sedgwick. He and McLaws were conferring, I think, at the moment on horseback. My enthusiasm had spent itself, or rather had oozed out with our disappointment, and I was walking down the front of the captured regiment, kept, however, at proper distance by the guard which had been placed over them. I had heard where the prisoners hailed from and was carefully scanning their faces, recognizing many of them. At last a little fellow who had been in my Sunday-school class in New Haven recognized me. How he happened to do this is a mystery, as there was not a trace of my former self visible, except my height and my muscular figure. I had lost my hat, my hair was close-shingled, skin tanned red brown; I had on only flannel shirt, pants, belt and shoes; shirt front wide open, sleeves rolled up, clothes and skin spattered black with powder water from the sponge—indeed I was, all in all, about as desperate-looking a ruffian as could well be found or imagined. But when this little chap, through all this disguise and transformation, recognized me and called out my name, there was a simultaneous shout of "Bob Stiles" from many throats. General Lee called me to him and asked whether I really knew "those people,"— the peculiar phrase which he employed habitually in speaking of the Northern people or the Federal soldiery,—and upon my telling him that I did, he ordered the guard to pass me in the lines, telling me to find out what I could and let him know. He also offered to do anything in his power for any prisoner whose circumstances I might think required his intervention, and in this way I arranged a special exchange for a young man named Sheldon, whom I had known at Yale or at a preparatory school in New Haven. I also gathered considerable information, which I gave to the commanding general.

A short time after this, I cannot say exactly how long, but that same evening and before we started back after Sedgwick, General McLaws called me to him and said I ought not to be in the ranks; that I was right about that movement of all our guns to that advanced position, and this showed I had a gift for handling artillery; that he would send for a commission as captain and have me assigned to the command of a certain Georgia battery which he mentioned; that it was true this battery had a way of getting its captains killed and wounded, but that bad luck like that didn't last forever, and that it was time the luck was turning with this battery. I thanked him heartily, but told him that I had not discovered the commanding position he referred to and didn't know who was entitled to the credit of pointing it out; that I had simply reported what we had seen and done—other men no less than I; that as to the battery he had mentioned, while I thought I could sincerely say that the fate of its former captains would not deter me, yet I presumed there were officers in this battery who deserved and would expect promotion, and if so I would not be willing to cut them out of their proper dues; and besides, I much questioned whether I was really competent to be put at once in command of a battery in the field. He seemed to be a little disappointed at what he evidently thought my lack of proper ambition, but said he would talk with me further about it, and I left him, making a great effort not to show how profoundly moved I was. Here, for the third time within a week, was promotion offered and a door opened before me; for while I had returned the commission in the engineer troops, yet I could not be sure it was not intended for me, especially as it began to appear as if there was a general consensus that I should be promoted.

Shortly after I left General McLaws, he and General Lee resumed their conference, and, just as they did so, there occurred an incident which beautifully revealed the equipoise of General Lee's character and the charm of his manner.

If any of the minor characters mentioned in these reminiscences has a distinct personality every way worthy of approval and of remembrance, it is "Brother William," the consecrated, courageous chaplain of the Seventeenth Mississippi, or rather of Barksdale's brigade—the real hero of the great revival at Fredericksburg. He, of course, had remained behind there, with his brigade, under the general command of Early, to watch Sedgwick.

I was standing in the shade of a tree, near our guns, which had been ordered to draw out on the road, head of column to the rear, that is, toward Fredericksburg,—an order and movement which we all well understood,—when my attention was called to a horseman coming at full speed from the direction in which we were heading, and as he drew near I saw it was "Brother William," and that he was greatly excited. My recollection is that he did not have a saddle, but was riding upon a blanket or cloth of some kind, and that his horse was reeking with sweat and panting from exertion. When his eye fell upon General Lee he made directly for him, and I followed as fast as I could. He dashed to the very feet of the commanding general, indeed, almost upon him, and gasping for breath, his eyes starting from their sockets, began to tell of dire disaster at Fredericksburg—Sedgwick had smashed Early and was rapidly coming on in our rear.

I have never seen anything more majestically calm than General Lee was; I felt painfully the contrast between him and dear little Brother William. Something very like a grave, sweet smile began to express itself on the General's face, but he checked it, and raising his left hand gently, as if to protect himself, he interrupted the excited speaker, checking and controlling him instantly, at the same time saying very quietly:

"I thank you very much, but both you and your horse are fatigued and overheated. Take him to that shady tree yonder and you and he blow and rest a little. I'm talking to General McLaws just now. I'll call you as soon as we are through."

I said Brother William was at once dominated and controlled, and he was—but not quite satisfied. He began a mild protest: "But, General!" but he did not persist in it— he simply could not. He had already dismounted, and he started back with me to the tree, leading his horse.

Unfortunately, I had none of General Lee's power over him, and he began to pour out to me his recital of disaster and prediction of ruin. All was lost below, Sedgwick had stormed the heights and seized the town, the brigade had been cut off, and, he feared, captured; Early had been beaten and pushed roughly aside, and at least 30,000 victorious troops were rapidly pressing on in our rear. Substantially, he alone was left to tell the tale, and had fortunately been able to secure this horse on which to come to tell it. If not already too late, it very soon would be, to do anything even to moderate the calamity.

In vain I suggested that General Lee could not be ignorant of all this; that his scouts had, doubtless, given him information; that General Early certainly would have found means to communicate with him; that Lee had beaten Hooker and his calm and self-reliant bearing clearly indicated that he felt himself to be master of the entire situation. But Brother William would not be comforted or reassured. General Lee had not been upon the spot and could not know; he had been and did know. The very calmness of the general showed he did not appreciate the gravity of the situation. While we were thus debating the matter, General Lee finished with McLaws, who at once started his division on the back track to reinforce Early and help him take care of Sedgwick—and, true to his promise, Marse Robert now called for Brother William, and, as he approached, greeted him with a smile, saying:

"Now what were you telling us about Major Sedgwick?"

Brother William again told his tale of woe—this time with somewhat diminished intensity and less lurid coloring. When he had finished the general thanked him, saying again:

"I am very much obliged to you; the major is a nice gentleman; I don't think he would hurt us very badly, but we are going to see about him at once. I have just sent General McLaws to make a special call upon him."

I did not, at the time, quite appreciate the marked peculiarity of General Lee's allusion to Sedgwick, but, as I now understand, the latter had been a major in the old service, of the regiment of which Lee was colonel, and they had been somewhat intimate friends.

There is a decided difference of opinion, and that among both Federal and Confederate authorities, as to whether or not Sedgwick heartily and vigorously supported and co-operated with Hooker's plans in this campaign. Both Hooker and Warren reflect seriously upon him for failure to do so, and Early and Fitzhugh Lee, on the Confederate side, take a like view. The two latter estimate Sedgwick's force at thirty thousand troops, while Early had only some ten thousand to oppose him. Fitz says in substance that Sedgwick's attacks were desultory, nerveless, and easily repulsed, even by our very inferior force, until the extreme weakness of our lines was discovered under flag of truce granted him to take care of his wounded. Then he attacked with more determination and captured Marye's Heights and several pieces of artillery, but even then did not push his advantage with vigor. Barksdale seems to have been for the time separated from Early, and it was at this juncture that Mr. Owen procured the horse and galloped to Chancellorsville with his blood-curdling tale of disaster. A staff officer of General Early had, however, preceded him, as we afterwards learned.

It was currently reported at the time that the whole of the Mississippi brigade would have been captured, as part of it was, had not the giant musketeer of the Twenty-first Regiment clubbed his gun and rushed bare-headed down the hill upon the Federal troops who were climbing it. At this fearful apparition they broke and ran, and in the gap and confusion thus occasioned a large part of the brigade made its escape.

After McLaws joined forces with Early, Sedgwick, though still outnumbering his foes, became the hunted rather than the hunter, and seems to have counted himself happy, under cover of the friendly darkness, to make his escape across the river.

It is fair to say that some military critics take a different view of Sedgwick's operations, and it may well be, after all, that Hooker's lieutenant has suffered in general estimation mainly by reason of his being brought, under the circumstances, into comparison with Lee's matchless second and his absolutely perfect appreciation, support, and execution of the plans of his great chief in this the most brilliant of his battles.

Hooker's own part in these operations would seem to have been more creditable, but his great weakness was a tendency to boasting. There was a striking contrast between the records he made for himself in his order book and in the field. When, on the 26th of January, 1863, he took command of the Army of the Potomac, his first act was to christen it in the memorable, high-sounding phrase—"The Finest Army on the Planet." On the same day, in General Order No. 1, he emphasized the inferiority of its enemy, and added: "Let us never hesitate to give him battle whenever we can find him." After just three months of waiting he did find him, right across the river where he had all the time been, and moved upon him. Then, after three days of really skilful maneuvering, on the 30th of April, as he took up his position at Chancellorsville, he issued his General Order No. 47, congratulating his army that now, "Our enemy must ingloriously fly, or come out from behind his defenses and give us battle on our own ground, where certain destruction awaits him." The rash enemy chose the latter alternative, but objected strongly to the predicted result of "certain destruction." And lastly, on the 6th day of May, after he had abandoned his famous and almost impregnable position, and retired across the river in the dark, as Sedgwick had already done, he published his General Order No. 49, of which he asked, but apparently never got, President Lincoln's opinion—in which "The Major-General Commanding tenders to the army his congratulations on its achievements of the last seven days * * *," and adds: "The events of the last week may swell with pride the heart of every officer and soldier in this army."

All these, however, are but the blasts of the war trumpet, and are calculated to blind us to the admirable character of Hooker's general plan and his creditable maneuvers in the attempted execution of it. In parting with him I cannot refrain from saying that no soldier of the Army of Northern Virginia can fail to kindle toward him, at least a little, upon reading his testimony before the Committee on the Conduct of the War, in which he gives the following curious and tortuous, yet, upon the whole, manly explanation of the defeat and failure of "The Finest Army on the Planet:"

Our artillery had always been superior to that of the rebels, as was also our infantry, except in discipline; and that, for reasons not necessary to mention, never did equal Lee's army. With a rank and file vastly inferior to our own, intellectually and physically, that army has, by discipline alone, acquired a character for steadiness and efficiency unsurpassed, in my judgment, in ancient or modern times. We have not been able to rival it, nor has there been any near approximation to it in the other rebel armies.

It is strange that I cannot recall when I first heard of Jackson's being wounded, nor even of the overwhelming calamity of his death. There is an impression on my mind that I saw his body lying in state in the Capitol at Richmond; but upon reflection I am inclined to think this is an error and that I am confounding impressions derived from reading the detailed accounts in the daily press with the actual sight of the eye. The only reliable data I have, bearing upon the time of this visit to Richmond, is Beers' burial there, at which I certainly was present. He fell on the 3rd of May and was buried on the field. It was warm weather and his re-interment at Richmond could not have been many days later. Jackson did not die until the 10th of May, and I could not have witnessed the funeral obsequies in Richmond unless I remained there longer than I now think I did.

Under these circumstances, there being nothing of value I can add in the way of personal reminiscence, nothing would be gained by my repeating the familiar story of that week of fearful suspense or the heroic recital of the last interchange of confidence, admiration, and affection between the great leader and his peerless lieutenant. Suffice it to say, there are few passages in human story as lofty, as tender, or in every way as creditable to human nature. The following is the order which General Lee issued to his army announcing the death of Jackson:

HEADQUARTERS ARMY OF NORTHERN VIRGINIA.

General Order No. 61.

With deep regret the commanding general announces the death of Lieutenant-General T. J. Jackson, who expired on the 10th instant, at quarter past three P. M.

The daring, skill, and energy of this great and good soldier, by the decree of an All-wise Providence, are now lost to us. But while we mourn his death, we feel that his spirit still lives, and will inspire the whole army with his indomitable courage and unshaken confidence in God as our hope and strength. Let his name be a watch-word to his corps who have followed him to victory on so many fields. Let his officers and soldiers emulate his invincible determination to do everything in the defense of our loved Country.

R. E. LEE, *General.*

Meanwhile the commission in engineer troops had been returned to me, accompanied by directions to report at Richmond for orders. This seemed to settle the question. Evidently I could not wait for the chance of the reopening of the appointment on Jackson's staff, or for the captaincy in artillery of which General McLaws had spoken, either of which I should have greatly preferred to the engineer appointment. I had informed the Bureau when I returned the commission that I was not an engineer and, with this knowledge, the appointment had been confirmed. Besides, either before or when I reported in Richmond, I found that I owed my appointment to a lady; that Mrs. Gilmer, the wife of General Gilmer, the head of the Engineer Bureau of our service, had told her husband that she wished to nominate one officer when he made his appointments in engineer troops, and had nominated me, without any previous personal acquaintance, basing her action upon what she had heard of me from others and particularly from my father, and out of regard for him.

Under these circumstances, to decline the appointment was out of the question. So I tore myself away from my dear comrades, my own brother among them, and reported at Richmond for my orders, as directed.

CHAPTER XIV

FROM THE RAPPAHANNOCK TO THE POTOMAC

The Engineer Troops—Jubal Early—His Ability and Devotion—His
Caustic Tongue—Lee a Master of the "Offensive Defensive"—His
Army Organized into Three Corps—He Turns Northward and
Maneuvers Hooker Out of His Position on the Rappahannock—The
Battle of Winchester—Fine Work—Large Captures—Scenes and
Incidents of the Battle.

It is singular that I cannot recall with distinctness anything that occurred during this visit to Richmond, save
the burial of poor Beers; and as to that I remember only
what I have related. I do not recall much enthusiasm or
elation of spirit about my promotion; indeed I felt little, for
it severed the strong ties that bound me to my old comrades;
it removed me from a branch of the service which I loved
and in which I felt competent to do efficient work, and transferred me to another for which I possessed neither taste nor
training.

My orders were to report to Major-General Early, in the
field, and in connection with the other officers of my company to organize a company of engineer troops from men
to be furnished us from his division. I do not remember
where General Early was, but somewhere in the northern
or central portion of the State, and I reported promptly at
his headquarters, meeting there for the first time Captain
Williamson, the commanding officer of our prospective company, who proved to be a gentleman of character, a competent engineer and thorough soldier, though, unfortunately,
somewhat deaf. I do not think he heard all that was said
by the general during our conference, or that he observed
him quite as closely as I did.

After the conference was over I saw Captain Williamson
privately and asked him how much aid and co-operation he

expected from the general in getting up his company. He said he hardly knew, and asked my views, which were quite decided and decidedly expressed—to the effect that General Early had no idea of losing a musket from his division if he could avoid it; that he would aid us just so far as he was compelled to do so and no further; that our orders were somewhat defective, or at least not framed to meet such a case; that I did not mean to imply that the general was not right in the position he had taken, but that right or wrong he had clearly taken it; and as he was evidently a man of uncommon intelligence and determination, I felt satisfied he would carry his point.

In the course of two or three days the situation became clearly defined, the general taking little or no pains to conceal it, and I had another talk with Captain Williamson, who felt that nothing more could be done just now in the way of organizing the company, adding that General Early had asked him, for the present, to act as engineer officer on his staff. He had made no such suggestion or request in my case, and Captain Williamson seemed to feel badly on my account; but I begged him to think no more about it, assuring him that I had sense enough to see that any such action in my case was out of the question, as I was not an engineer. I omitted to say that my orders entitled me to a horse to be furnished and fed, as I remember, by the quartermaster of the division, and the general was very kind and prompt in seeing that these requirements were complied with; but I saw clearly that I was neither needed nor desired on the division staff and that, if I remained, the best I could expect would be the position and duty of a sort of upper courier, which I was not willing to assume.

I therefore went directly to General Early and had a full talk with him. I did most of the talking, but he heartily acquiesced, and when I was through I felt sure we thoroughly understood each other, and I thought he liked me. I told him I saw clearly that, for the present, no company of engineer troops was to be organized from his division; that indeed I rather thought the division pioneer corps, under command of Lieutenant, or Sergeant, Flood, was all the engineer company he cared to have. Flood was a New Orleans stevedore, a rough but very efficient man, who, among his many admirable qualifications, possessed this highly acceptable one, that he had no sort of objection to Old Jube's airing his choice vocabulary of profane rhetoric about him, or his work, or his men whenever he might happen to need relief in that direction.

I said further to the general that I thought the pioneer corps might perhaps be regarded as the nucleus of the future company of engineer troops, and while I had no idea of meddling with Flood's work, which he was vastly better qualified to manage than I was, yet I could help him about his requisitions, reports, etc.; but that as we were evidently going into an active and aggressive campaign I thought I would, in action, fight in some battery of Col. Hilary Jones' Battalion, if he thought he could make use of me—standing ready, however, at all times to report back to Division Headquarters for staff duty or for anything I could at any time do for the general.

This arrangement seemed to be entirely satisfactory to General Early, as it was also to Colonel Jones, in one or other of whose batteries—usually with the Charlottesville Artillery, a corps that reminded me somewhat of our old battery—I fought, whenever they were engaged, throughout the campaign, notably at Winchester and Gettysburg; sometimes in charge of one or more pieces, and again fighting as a private soldier at a gun, or in any position where they were weakest and most needed help. I said the arrangement seemed to be entirely satisfactory to General Early, and yet in connection with it there occurred a series of awkward and amusing incidents which admirably illustrate some of the general's strongly-marked traits.

Soon after Gettysburg my brother and I passed and missed each other, I riding over to the First Corps to learn what had befallen my friends of the old battery, while he came over to Early's division of the Second to inquire for me. His description of the old general was so characteristic and vivid that to this day I am prone to imagine that I saw and heard instead of my brother. He said the sun was shining after the rain, and at Early's headquarters he saw a man rather above middle age, heavily built, with stooping shoulders, a splendid head and a full gray-brown beard, sitting in his shirt sleeves on a camp stool, with one leg thrown over the other, his hands and apparently his every thought employed in combing out and smoothing a somewhat bedraggled black ostrich feather. My brother had no idea who this figure was, but he passed beyond him to inquire of some less absorbed person as to my welfare and whereabouts. The person addressed, probably some courier, did not happen to know anything of me, and the feather dresser piped in a whining, querulous voice:

"Who are you looking for—Stiles? I can't tell you where he is, but I can tell you where he ain't. He ain't with the division pioneer corps, where he belongs; I reckon your best chance to find him would be lying around with some battery."

When my brother told me this, as he did when we next met, I was at once irritated and amused. It was after I had, with General Early's approval, gone back to the old battalion to serve as its adjutant, under Colonel Cabell. I did not happen to meet the general for some time, and meanwhile fortune had smiled upon me in many ways. I was located to my entire satisfaction, had a fine horse, was better dressed and equipped every way, and was feeling generally satisfied, independent, and happy. We had gotten back to the sacred soil of Old Virginia, and, under Clark's Mountain, riding alone, I overtook and passed the general accompanied by only a single courier. My horse had the better action and movement, and I merely saluted as I rode rapidly by. I had gotten perhaps a hundred yards or more ahead, when the general called after me:

"Hold on, Stiles;" and as he drew near, "you're a little offish this morning."

"No, General, I think not."

"Well, what the devil's the matter?"

"Nothing in the world, sir, except that I didn't suppose you'd care for the company of a man of whom the best you could say was that you felt sure he wasn't where he ought to be."

Old Jube cocked his head and cut his eyes around at me with an expression of the intensest enjoyment, and in that inimitable voice drawled out:

"Stiles, you are an infernal fool. Why, man, I meant what I said of you as a compliment. The main use I had for a pioneer corps was to bury dead Yankees and horses, and you never seemed to fancy that kind of business. You preferred to take a hand at the guns and prepare 'em to be buried, and I thought a damned sight more of you for it."

It is useless to say that this sledge-hammer stroke broke the ice; indeed the ice disappeared and I was thawed out completely. From that day the grand old fellow was one of the best friends I had in the army, and our friendship continued to the day of his death. I don't know that I was ever more touched than when—long years afterwards, at one of the meetings of the "Virginia Division of the Army of Northern Virginia," in introducing me as one of the speakers—he told this story, making use of the identical phraseology above recorded, as nearly as I can recall it.

It may be well to say that a full regiment of engineer troops was ultimately organized, though the men were not drawn from the troops in the field, as at first provided— General Lee agreeing with his division generals that this should not be done. The corps rendered very efficient service. It was under the command of Col. T. M. R. Talcott, a member of General Lee's staff, and a thoroughly educated, experienced, and able engineer, in whom the general felt as much confidence as in any officer of his rank in the army. Strange to say, I never served a day with the regiment, though holding a commission in it, and I had the honor of being, for a year or more, a bone of contention between the engineer troops and the artillery. Colonel Talcott would every now and then report my absence from duty and ask that I be ordered back to my post with his regiment, and this application being referred to Colonel Cabell, he would answer that it would be highly detrimental to the service to remove me, just at this time, from my position as acting adjutant of his battalion. As these papers had to pass through army headquarters, and in some instances even to and from the Adjutant-General's Office in Richmond, months would sometimes elapse before the grand rounds were completed. One feature of the case very aggravating to the officers of the engineer troops was that on one occasion, I presume through inadvertence, I was actually advanced one grade in engineer troops for meritorious service in artillery. At last, however, I was again promoted, this time in artillery, which terminated the irritating, yet amusing, paper war.

Some time after the close of the struggle, at a social gathering in Richmond, I observed a gentleman staring and pointing at me in a very peculiar manner, who, on being introduced, grasped my hand and burst into an uncontrollable fit of laughter. Upon recovering his composure he said that if our meeting had occurred a few years earlier his feeling, and possibly his action, might have been different; that he was one of the officers of the engineer regiment over whose heads I had unceremoniously and irregularly vaulted, they having served faithfully with the regiment and I having never even reported to it. He further said that my name had been repeatedly read out at dress parade of the regiment as "absent from duty," when the officers would speculate as to how soon I would be lassooed and dragged in; but as the capture was constantly delayed and I ultimately made good my escape, my fellow-officers in engineer troops had changed their minds about me and concluded I was a strategist of a high order and deserving of high position and command. I may add that my personal relations with Colonel Talcott since the war have been of a close and intimate character, and that he is to-day one of my best friends.

After the death of Jackson, Early was undoubtedly one of the strongest and ablest of Lee's lieutenants. He was not perhaps the brilliant and dashing soldier that A. P. Hill was, nor a superb, magnetic leader like Gordon, and possibly he could not deliver quite as majestic a blow in actual battle as Longstreet; but his loyal devotion, his hardy courage, his native intellect, his mental training, his sagacity, his resource, his self-reliant, self-directing strength, were all very great, and the commanding general reposed the utmost confidence in him. This he indicated by selecting him so frequently for independent command, and to fill the most critical, difficult, and I had almost said hopeless, positions, in the execution of his own great plans; as for example, when he left him at Fredericksburg with nine thousand men to neutralize Sedgwick with thirty thousand. Later, he sent him to the Valley, with a very inadequate force, to occupy and embarrass the enemy and to prevent overwhelming concentration against the Confederate capital, where his operations indicated the highest ability.

Early was in some respects a bundle of inconsistencies and contradictions; of religion and irreligion, of reverence and profanity. I have heard my father speak of the General's deep interest in religious work among the men of his division, and his readiness to do everything in his power to facilitate it. I do not think I ever knew one human soul to look up to another with a feeling nearer akin to worship than that with which Early regarded Lee and Jackson, not alone as great soldiers, but as great Christians also; and yet he was the only man who was ever known to swear in General Lee's presence. The general used to reprove him gently, yet at the same time to express his special affection for him, by calling him "My bad old man."

Old Jube struck the popular fancy in two respects only— his intense unionism before President Lincoln's proclamation calling for troops and his intense Southernism afterwards, and his caustic, biting tongue. He was a sort of privileged character in the army and was saucy to everybody, but many of his brightest utterances will not bear publication because of the sting in them. One of this general character, which, however, had no real bitterness in it, is too good not to be told.

The Hon. Jere Morton was in the Secession Convention with Early, as extreme a Secessionist as Early was Unionist, and very fond of talking about "our rights in the territories." Morton was not in the army, and was probably above fighting age. His handsome estate, "Morton Hall," was upon the outskirts of the great battle-fields of Central Virginia, and on one occasion Mr. Morton narrowly escaped capture there, and was obliged to mount a horse and fly. It so happened that Early commanded the vanguard of the Confederate forces advancing to meet the enemy. Riding at the head of his column, and seeing Morton coming in hot haste, digging his spurs into his horse's flanks, Early playfully threw a line of troops across the road to intercept his progress, at the same time calling out to him, "Hold on, Morton! Are you going for our rights in the Territories?"

One evening, during General Jackson's life-time, after a hard day's march, General Early received, soon after coming to camp, substantially the following note:

HEADQUARTERS 2d CORPS, A. NO. — VA.

To GEN. JUBAL A. EARLY, Commanding Division:

GENERAL—Gen. Jackson's compliments to Gen. Early, and he would like to be informed why he saw so many stragglers in rear of your division to-day.

Respectfully,

A. G. PENDLETON, *A. A. G. 2d Corps.*

To which Old Jube promptly dictated and sent the following reply:

HEADQUARTERS EARLY'S DIVISION, A. NO. — VA.

To COL. A. G. PENDLETON, *A. A. G. 2d Corps:*

COLONEL—General Early's compliments to General Jackson, and he takes pleasure in informing him that he saw so many stragglers in rear of my division to-day, probably because he rode in rear of my division.

Respectfully,

JUBAL A. EARLY, *Commanding Division.*

There was not another officer in the Army of Northern Virginia who would have dared to send such an impertinent note to Jackson, nor another, save Stuart, whose impertinence in sending it would have been met with a laugh.

After the war, its memories were Early's religion; his mission, to vindicate the truth of history with regard to it. So long as the old hero was alive in his hill city of Virginia, no man ever took up his pen to write a line about the great conflict without the fear of Jubal Early before his eyes.

As already stated, it is not within the scope of this book to discuss the causes or the objects of the war, or who was responsible for it; therefore, when I say that upon the side of the Confederates it was a war of defense I am enunciating a military and not a moral proposition. I mean simply that the Confederacy had not the requisite resources, that its leaders had no purpose or expectation of carrying on a war of aggression or conquest, and that our invasions of Northern soil were intended merely as subsidiary parts of our general scheme of defense; that is, as diversions, as derangements of the general scheme of Federal invasion.

General Lee was a soldier who thoroughly appreciated the value of an offensive defensive. He never allowed his adversary quietly to mature and uninterruptedly to adhere to and carry out his own plan of campaign. Although conducting a defensive struggle, he was yet generally the attacking party. It was so in the Seven Days' battles with McClellan, so in the Manassas campaign with Pope and the Maryland campaign that followed. It was so at Chancellorsville. And even in 1864, after the resources and fighting strength of the Confederacy had been so fearfully reduced, when Grant entered the Wilderness, Lee immediately pressed in after him and closed with him in a death grapple in the very heart of the jungle.

But perhaps the most perfect instance and illustration of this characteristic feature of Lee's strategy and tactics, and of the real significance of his two invasions of Northern territory, is what occurred after Chancellorsville. When Hooker retired across the Rappahannock and reoccupied his former position it would manifestly have been little short of madness for Lee to attack him there, especially deprived as he was of Jackson, his offensive right arm; yet he did not sit down, as a less courageous and resourceful leader would have done, gloating over his victory, conceding the initiative to Hooker, and awaiting developments. On the contrary, he proceeded to maneuver his adversary out of a position from which he could not drive him, and to force him to abandon all idea of further aggressive campaign in Virginia for that year.

Early in June, with his army reorganized into three corps, the First under Longstreet, embracing the divisions of Mc-Laws, Picket, and Hood; the Second under Ewell, embrac-ing Early, Rodes, and Jackson; and the Third under A. P. Hill, Anderson, Heth, and Pender,—all the corps command-ers being lieutenant-generals,—Lee drew away from the line of the Rappahannock, leaving Hill, however, for a short time, to watch Hooker, proceeded northward, by way of Culpeper and the Valley of Virginia,—the Second Corps in advance,—crossed the Shenandoah near Front Royal about June 12th, and, near Winchester, routed and captured a large part of the force which, under Milroy, was holding the Lower Valley. Hill followed Ewell, Longstreet's corps hov-ering yet a while east of the mountains, to cover their opera-tions.

It was about this time that President Lincoln and General Hooker had their famous serpentine telegraphic correspond-ence:

"Where is the Rebel army?"

"The advance is at the fords of the Potomac and the rear at Culpeper Court House."

"If the head of the animal is at the fords of the Potomac and the tail at Culpeper Court House, it must be very thin somewhere. Why don't you strike it?"

This battle of Winchester—there were many conflicts in and around that devoted old town—was one of the most per-fect pieces of work the Army of Northern Virginia ever did. Possibly the plan seemed so admirably clear and defi-nite and to move with the precision and decision of a prob-lem in mathematics, because, for the first time, as a mounted officer and in an unusually free and independent position, I personally watched every movement. I may add that the execution of the plan was committed largely to Old Jube, who certainly wrought it out and fought it out beautifully.

The town of Winchester and the surrounding country were dominated by a strong closed earthwork, heavily armed and manned, which it would have been madness to assault, yet folly to neglect; and this work, on the only side which seemed to offer anything like a practicable approach, was protected and itself dominated by an outwork which it was absolutely necessary to carry before the inner and more powerful work could be reduced. Our scouts and engineers had done their work thoroughly and our column was conducted by a long detour, in every foot of which we were concealed from observation from either work by forests and the configuration of the ground; until at last we found ourselves in a position which had been attained with difficulty, but which perfectly commanded the outwork. The infantry now lay down to rest and recover breath, while the men of Hilary Jones' battalion of artillery shoved their guns forward by hand up to and just back of a rock fence which ran along the crest of a ridge, under cover of which we had approached, and then loaded them. They next removed a few of the stones in front of the muzzle of each gun, taking great care to remain concealed while doing this; and when everything was ready and everyone warned to do his part on the instant, the guns were discharged simultaneously upon the outwork and a rapid fire kept up upon it, while the infantry rose, and, with the wild rebel yell bursting from their lips, rushed forward in the charge. The surprise was complete, the distance not great, and the effect overwhelming. The outwork was abandoned almost without a struggle, its defenders retiring to the main fortification, and our infantry again lying down for rest and protection and to wait for us, while our guns galloped forward to the captured work, some occupying and firing from it, and others passing to the right and front to a level field hard by, from which we had the main work beautifully in range.

But this work had us in range not less beautifully, indeed even more perfectly, and played havoc with us for a short time. My recollection is that I was acting as No. 6 at one of the limbers, and that I several times instinctively clapped down the lid of the ammunition chest as the shell seemed to burst immediately over it. We were at a loss to account for the preternaturally accurate aim of the guns and cutting of the fuses, until someone chanced to observe the practice target of the fort standing between the gun at which I was serving and the one next to it, when, of course, we shifted our position in a twinkling, dashing up still closer to the fort and finding, to our relief, that here the shells passed for the most part over our heads.

On one of the two occasions in which our guns passed to the right and front of the recumbent infantry I observed our old friend Extra Billy Smith, on the front line of his brigade, standing erect, with his arms folded, his horse's bridle rein over one shoulder and his blue cotton umbrella under the other, he and his horse the only two figures I saw standing in all the long line. The heroic old man was as cool as a cucumber and as smiling as a basket of chips, and he was actually bowing to the artillerymen—as with hair flying and eyes flashing they passed on a run—with that same manly, hearty greeting which had, for more than a generation, proved irresistible on the hustings in the Old Dominion. It was an unparalleled scene—unparalleled as an exhibition of courage, of personal force, and of the force of habit. I noted the expression on the face of each artilleryman as he recognized and responded to the old Governor's salute, and felt—there's one vote sure for Extra Billy as long as that gallant cannoneer lives. The old hero was at this time Governor-elect of the Commonwealth of Virginia.

I cannot determine exactly when, but I received a very singular, and what threatened to be a very serious, injury during one of the moves our guns made after becoming engaged—I rather incline to think it must have been the first time we shifted position. At all events, I had, for some reason, given up my horse to someone and was fighting on foot in some position with one of the guns of the Charlottesville battery, when the orders were given, "Cease firing, limber to the front, cannoneers mount!" I sprang upon a limber chest upon which there were already the full complement of three men, all faced, of course, to the front. I faced to the rear, and bracing my back against the back of the middle man, attempted to hold my position with my feet resting on the "lunette plate"—a flat piece of iron fitted over the end of the trail of the gun, ending in a heavy ring, which was slipped over the "pintle hook" on the front axle, thus coupling the gun to the limber. We started at a run and were galloping under fire through a grove, by a wood road the track of which was full of limestone rocks projecting more or less above the ground. It was very difficult to keep my footing, as I had on a pair of stiff and slick-soled English shoes, the nails in which had worn perfectly smooth.

Suddenly, at full run, we struck a large rock. The jar was terrific, and all the men were thrown off, but the others, having firm footing, described arcs which landed them on the turf at the side of the road. My feet, however, slipped, and I went down between the front and rear wheels and directly under the gun. The concussion was so tremendous that I supposed the limber chest had exploded, and distinctly remember thinking to myself, "Then this is the way it feels to be blown up, is it? Well, I'll try anyhow to save my arms and legs in case I shouldn't be killed," and with a violent effort I did manage to get them out of the track of the hind wheels, one of which, however, ran directly, or rather, diagonally, across the small of my back on a flat limestone rock.

My comrades picked themselves up, all right though slightly shocked. They thought me dead, but dragged me out of the track of the other guns, and left me lying on the grass under a tree. In a short time I came to myself, and, on taking a hurried inventory, found that though very badly jarred and bruised, yet no bones seemed to be broken, and concluded I would try to hobble on into the fight, which I did, lying down that night in a pouring rain and sleeping in a puddle—I presume about as good treatment as could have been prescribed. Next day I was carried into Winchester, and after two or three days' rest rode on after the army. The mark of the gun wheel remained on my back for a year or more, but I never experienced any serious pain or inconvenience from the injury. I attribute my escape, in part at least, to my unusually full muscular development at the time.

Upon one of our shiftings of position in the battle I was on foot, abreast of one of the guns of the Charlottesville battery, and following close after John Hunter, sergeant of that piece, who was riding his little chestnut mare, "Madge," when a thirty-pounder Parrott shell passed through her body, just back of the legs of the rider, exploding as it emerged, and spattering me profusely with the blood of the poor animal. Little Madge was not even jarred—any experienced artillerist will understand this. She "never knew what hit her," but sank gently down; while Hunter did not get even so much as a decent "shaking up," not a very easy thing to administer to him, I frankly admit. When his feet touched the ground—they were not far from it even while Madge stood up on all fours—he simply disengaged them from the stirrups, turned around, glanced a moment at the bloody horror, and said: "Well, poor little Madge!"

True, there was nothing more to be said, but all the same there was not another man of my acquaintance who would not have said more.

The sergeant still lives. His yea is still yea and his nay, nay. He is a shining example of that admirable class of men and philosophers who never say anything superfluous or give strained or exaggerated expression to anything; yet his heart, as everyone knows, is not only in the right place, but the very rightest kind of a heart. He is one of my best friends and the husband of one of Billy's "seven women."

During our next change of position, or it may have been during the same move, I witnessed a scene of horror and of agony so extreme that I would not describe it were it not that a knowledge of the widest swings of the pendulum of war, through the entire orbit of human experiences and emotions, is needed for adequate appreciation of the life of the soldier.

The entire battalion, Hilary Jones', was moving in column, the Charlottesville battery, in which I was serving, following immediately after Garber's. The farm road we were using led between two heavy old-fashioned gate posts. My recollection is that they were of stone and that there was no gate and no fence on either side of the posts, but the ground outside of and near the posts was somewhat rough and steep. One of Garber's men, belonging to his rear gun, attempted to run abreast of the piece between the gate posts, presumably to avoid the rough ground outside. There was not room enough for him to pass, and the wheel crowding him against the post, the washer hook caught and tore open his abdomen, dragging the poor wretch along by his intestines, which were literally pulled from his body in a long, gory ribbon.

At one of the last positions we took in the fight—it may have been the very last—there passed before me one of those scenes which give a flash-light revelation of the incomparable greatness of war and the sublime self-abnegation of the true soldier. The fire of the Federal guns was very deadly and demoralizing, and the captain of the battery next on our right, I think the Louisiana Guard Artillery, came up the hill between his battery and ours to steady his men. He was a fine horseman, finely mounted, and might well have served as a model for an equestrian statue as he rode out between the smoking muzzles, and, rising in his stirrups, cheered on his gunners. At that moment a shell tore away his bridle arm high up near the shoulder. Instantly he caught the reins with his right hand and swung his horse's head sharply to the left, thus concealing his wounded side from his men, saying as he did so, "Keep it up, boys; I'll be back in a moment!" As he started down the hill I saw him reel in the saddle, and even before he reached the limbers the noble fellow fell from his horse—dead.

We were actively engaged, as I remember, until almost or quite dark; but as soon as the fire slackened I lay down, very sore from the severe bruising and crushing I had received, and of course in no condition for close or accurate observation, so I do not know when it was discovered that the garrison were abandoning the fort and preparing to retreat, or what steps were taken to intercept them. They were intercepted, however; our operations resulting, as General Lee reported, "in the expulsion of the enemy from the Valley, the capture of four thousand prisoners, with a corresponding number of small arms; twenty-eight pieces of superior artillery, including those taken by General Rodes and General Hayes; about three hundred wagons and as many horses, together with a quantity of ordnance, commissary, and quartermaster's stores."

The remnant of Milroy's forces took refuge behind the fortifications of Harper's Ferry; but as the reduction of that place had proved a very disturbing element in General Lee's plans for the Maryland campaign of the preceding year, we gave it the go-by this time; Lieutenant-General Ewell with his three divisions, still in the van, crossing the Potomac in the latter part of June, rapidly traversing Maryland and advancing into Pennsylvania.

CHAPTER XV

Impressing Horses the Only Plundering Lee's Army Did—A Remarkable Interview with An Old Lady in a Pennsylvania Town—She Expects to Meet Stonewall Jackson in Heaven—Two Pennsylvania Boys Make Friends with the Rebels —"Extra Billy" Leads the Confederate Column into York, His Brigade Band Playing "Yankee Doodle," and Makes a Speech on the Public Green—"Old Jube" Breaks Up the Meeting—"Dick" Ewell and the Burghers of Carlisle.

I do not remember where I overtook Ewell's corps, but think I entered Pennsylvania with them. General Lee had issued stringent orders against plundering and, certainly in the main, the men carefully observed these orders. I was constantly told by the inhabitants that they suffered less from our troops than from their own, and that if compelled to have either, they preferred having "the rebels" camped upon their lands. I saw no plundering whatever, except that once or twice I did see branches laden with fruit broken from cherry trees.

Of course, it goes without saying, that the quartermasters, especially of artillery battalions, were, confessedly and of malice aforethought, horse thieves. It was, perhaps, adding insult to injury to offer to pay for the horses, as we did, in Confederate money; yet occasionally the owners took it, as "better than nothing"—how better it would be difficult to say. I felt sorry for the farmers, some of whom actually concealed their horses in their dwelling houses, or, rather, attempted to conceal them, for we became veritable sleuth-hounds in running down a horse, and were up to all the tricks and dodges devised to throw us off the track.

After all, we gained very little by our horse stealing. The impressed animals were, for the most part, great, clumsy, flabby Percherons or Conestogas, which required more than twice the feed our compact, hard-muscled little Virginia horses required, and yet could not do half the work they did, nor stand half the hardship and exposure. It was pitiable, later, to see these great brutes suffer when compelled to dash off at full gallop with a gun, after pasturing on dry broom sedge and eating a quarter of a feed of weevil-eaten corn. They seemed to pine for the slow draft and full feed of their Pennsylvania homes.

To me this campaign of invasion was of somewhat peculiar interest. Not only did I have a wide general acquaintance with the North, but two or three of my Yale classmates were from the very section of country we were traversing, and I therefore felt somewhat acquainted and connected with the people and the region. I was struck, too, with the resemblance, both of the country and its inhabitants, to the Valley of Virginia. I noted the same two great stocks and races as making up the population,—the Dutch and the Scotch-Irish,—and to a great extent they had laid out their smaller towns and arranged their buildings, orchards, wells, —everything, in short,—upon their farms, very much after the familiar Valley pattern.

One bright day toward the end of June, our column was passing through the main street of such a town, when, being very thirsty, I rode up to the front fence of a house which, with its yard and surroundings, might have been set down in the main street of any one of a half-dozen Valley of Virginia towns without being in any respect out of place, and asked an elderly lady sitting in the porch if I might get a drink of water from the well. She courteously gave permission and I entered the yard, got a delicious drink of water, thanked her, and was in the act of leaving, when the old lady—who looked like the typical Valley gran'ma—very pleasantly asked if I wouldn't take a seat and rest a little. I thanked her, stepped up on the porch and sat down, and we soon got into a friendly and pleasant conversation, in the course of which she asked me of myself, family, and surroundings, and seemed much interested to know that I had a sister in New Haven, Conn. She gladly consented to mail a letter for me, and had a table, pen, ink, paper and stamps brought that I might write it. This letter was faithfully mailed by the old lady, and was the only communication my sister received from me for a year or more.

As I finished writing a young married woman, evidently the daughter of my kindly hostess, came to the door, saying that her little son, naming him, was missing. In a few moments they brought the child, a boy of five or six years, to the front porch, pale and trembling violently. They had found him between the mattress and feather bed in an upstairs room, where he had hidden for fear of the rebels, of whose ferocious cruelty, blood-curdling tales had been told him. In a few moments he was in my lap, and we were the best of friends.

Just as he was beginning to warm into his nest his mother announced that she had not seen anything of her elder son for some time, when, on the instant, a bright boy of ten or twelve summers burst into the gate, breathless with excitement, and gasped out, "Mother, mother! may I go to camp with the rebels? They are the nicest men I ever saw in my life. They are going to camp right out here in the woods, and they are going to have a dance, too!"

Harry Hayes' Louisiana brigade was passing at the moment, and in the open gate stood the lad's companion, waiting for him—a bowing, smiling, grimacing, shoulder-shrugging Frenchman, who promised, in rather broken English, that he would take the best possible care of him. The mother hesitated, but a glance at her youngest, whose arm had now stolen around my neck, decided her, and off went her eldest with his Creole comrade; and if the brigade did have the dance, then the lad saw what was really worth seeing, for if there was anything Hayes' Creoles did and loved to do better than to fight, it was to dance; and their camp stag dances, sandwiched in between a big march and a big battle, were said to be the most "utterly utter" performances in the way of faun-like pranks, that grown and sane men ever indulged in.

Before I left the old lady asked me if I had ever seen Stonewall Jackson, and upon my responding that I had, she said quietly, but with the deepest feeling, that she expected to see him soon, for if anyone had ever left this earth who had gone straight to Heaven it was he.

This was almost too much, and I said to her, "Madam, who on earth are you and where did you come from?" She said she was born in the Valley of Virginia and had been brought to this country when a girl. I could not forbear kissing her hand as I departed, and told her I felt sure she would get There, and I hoped we would meet in that blessed country where there would be no more wars nor separations between God's dear children.

By this time the reader has doubtless learned that things were not likely to be dull when our old friend "Extra Billy" was about; that in fact there was apt to be "music in the air" whenever he was in charge. On the occasion below described, the old Governor seemed to be rather specially concerned about the musical part of the performance.

We were about entering the beautiful Pennsylvania town of York, General Smith's brigade in the lead. Under these conditions, feeling sure there was likely to be a breeze stirring about the head of the column, I rode forward so as to be near the General and not to miss the fun. As we approached the population seemed to be very generally in the streets, and I saw at a glance that the old Governor had blood in his eye. Turning to Fred, his aide,—who was also his son, and about the strongest marked case of second edition I ever saw,—he told him to "Go back and look up those tooting fellows," as he called the brigade band, "and tell them first to be sure their drums and horns are all right, and then to come up here to the front and march into town tooting 'Yankee Doodle' in their very best style."

Fred was off in a jiffy, and soon here came the band, their instruments looking bright and smart and glistening in the June sunlight—playing, however, not "Yankee Doodle," but "Dixie," the musicians appearing to think it important to be entirely impartial in rendering these national airs, and therefore giving us "Dixie" by way of prelude to "Yankee Doodle."

When they got to the head of the column, and struck up "Yankee Doodle," and the Governor, riding alone and bareheaded in front of his staff, began bowing and saluting first one side and then the other, and especially every pretty girl he saw, with that manly, hearty smile which no man or woman ever doubted or resisted—the Yorkers seemed at first astounded, then pleased, and finally, by the time we reached the public square, they had reached the point of ebullition, and broke into enthusiastic cheers as they crowded about the head of the column, actually embarrassing its progress, till the old Governor,—the "Governor-General," we might call him,—nothing loth, acceded to the half suggestion and called a halt, his brigade stacking arms, and constituting, if not formally organizing, themselves and the people of York into a political meeting.

It was a rare scene—the vanguard of an invading army and the invaded and hostile population hobnobbing on the public green in an enthusiastic public gathering. The general did not dismount, but from the saddle he made a rattling, humorous speech, which both the Pennsylvanians and his own brigade applauded to the echo. He said substantially:

"My friends, how do you like this way of coming back into the Union? I hope you like it; I have been in favor of it for a good while. But don't misunderstand us. We are not here with any hostile intent—unless the conduct of your side shall render hostilities unavoidable. You can see for yourselves we are not conducting ourselves like enemies to-day. We are not burning your houses or butchering your children. On the contrary, we are behaving ourselves like Christian gentlemen, as we are.

"You see, it was getting a little warm down our way. We needed a summer outing and thought we would take it at the North, instead of patronizing the Virginia springs, as we generally do. We are sorry, and apologize that we are not in better guise for a visit of courtesy, but we regret to say our trunks haven't gotten up yet; we were in such a hurry to see you that we could not wait for them. You must really excuse us.

"What we all need, on both sides, is to mingle more with each other, so that we shall learn to know and appreciate each other. Now here's my brigade—I wish you knew them as I do. They are such a hospitable, whole-hearted, fascinating lot of gentlemen. Why, just think of it—of course this part of Pennsylvania is ours to-day; we've got it, we hold it, we can destroy it, or do what we please with it. Yet we sincerely and heartily invite you to stay. You are quite welcome to remain here and to make yourselves entirely at home—so long as you behave yourselves pleasantly and agreeably as you are doing now. Are we not a fine set of fellows? You must admit that we are."

At this point my attention was called to a volley of very heated profanity poured forth in a piping, querulous treble, coming up from the rear, and being mounted and located where I commanded a view of the road, I saw that the second brigade in column, which had been some distance in the rear, had caught up, and was now held up by our public meeting, which filled and obstructed the entire street, and that Old Jube, who had ridden forward to ascertain the cause of the dead-lock, was fairly blistering the air about him and making furious but for the time futile efforts to get at Extra Billy, who in plain sight, and not far off, yet blissfully unconscious of the presence of the major-general and of his agreeable observations and comments, was still holding forth with great fluency and acceptability.

The jam was solid and impervious. As D. H. Hill's report phrased it, "Not a dog, no, not even a sneaking exempt, could have made his way through"—and at first and for some time, Old Jube couldn't do it, and no one would help him. But at last officers and men were compelled to recognize the division commander, and he made his way so far that, by leaning forward, a long stretch, and a frantic grab, he managed to catch General Smith by the back of his coat collar. Even Jube did not dare curse the old general in an offensive way, but he did jerk him back and around pretty vigorously and half screamed:

"General Smith, what the devil are you about! stopping the head of this column in this cursed town?"

With unruffled composure the old fellow replied:

"Having a little fun, General, which is good for all of us, and at the same time teaching these people something that will be good for them and won't do us any harm."

Suffice it to say the matter was amicably arranged and the brigade and its unique commander moved on, leaving the honest burghers of York wondering what manner of men we were. I should add that General Early had the greatest regard and admiration for General Smith, which indeed he could not well avoid, in view of his intense patriotic devotion and his other sterling and heroic qualities. I have seldom heard him speak of any other officer or soldier in the service, save of course Lee and Jackson, in such exalted terms as of the old "Governor-General."

May I be pardoned for relating one more incident of our Pennsylvania trip, and that not strictly a reminiscence; that is, I was not present and did not myself hear the conversation I propose to relate. During the latter part of the war I enjoyed the privilege and pleasure of intimate personal acquaintance with Lieutenant-General Ewell, but at this time I knew him only as every soldier in the army knew him. Some of his salient peculiarities, as well as the peculiar character of some of our intercourse with the people of Pennsylvania, are well brought out in the following story, which I have every reason to regard as authentic.

The General was, I think, at Carlisle, though I am not quite certain of the place, when the burghers of the town, or rather a deputed committee of solid citizens, called at headquarters to interview him with reference to several matters. Amongst other things they said there was a certain mill, the product of which was used largely by the poorer people of the place, who were suffering and likely to suffer more, because of the mill's not running, and they asked whether he had any objection to its being run.

"Why, no," said Old Dick; "certainly not. It isn't my mill; what have I got to do with it anyhow? But stop, maybe this is what you want—if any of my people should interfere with your use of your mill, you come and tell me. Will that do, and is that all?"

They thanked him profusely and the spokesman said:

"No, General, that isn't quite all. We are Lutherans and we've got a church."

"Glad to hear it."

"Well, can we open it next Sunday?"

"What? What do you mean? It isn't my church. Certainly, open it, if you want to. I'll attend it myself if I am here."

"O, thank you, General! we hoped you wouldn't object."

"Object? What do you mean, anyway? What's the matter? What do you want? Out with it. I'll do anything I can for you, but I've got nothing to do with your mills or your churches. I'm not going to interfere with them, but I haven't time to stay here all the evening talking nonsense like this."

"But, General, we hope you won't be mad with us. We are Lutherans and we have a church service. Can we use it next Sunday?"

"Look here, I'm tired of this thing! What have I got to do with your mill, your church, or your service? Speak quick and speak plain, or leave at once!"

"Well, then, General, we hope you won't get mad. In our service we pray—we pray for—we pray for the President of the United States. May we use our service? Can we pray for him?"

"Who do you mean, Lincoln? Certainly, pray for him; pray as much as ever you can—I don't know anybody that stands more in need of prayer!"

CHAPTER XVI

GETTYSBURG

Lee Without His Cavalry—The Battle, When and Where Fought, An Accident—The Army of Northern Virginia in Splendid Condition— Gordon on Black Auster—A Fistic Encounter at the Crisis of the Great Battle—"Limber to the Rear"—A Great Disappointment—A Desperate Ride—Dead Enemies More to Be Dreaded Than Living Ones—The Dutch Woman's Ankles.

Gettysburg, generally regarded as the pivotal battle of our great civil war, has been more studied and discussed than any other, and much unpleasant feeling between prominent actors in the drama on the Confederate side and their adherents and partisans has been brought out in the discussion. The writer has his own opinions upon most or all of the disputed points; but, while resting upon grounds satisfactory to himself, these opinions are not based upon such a thorough study of the battle as would alone justify the effort to influence the views of others, if indeed such an effort could be regarded as properly within the scope of such a work as this.

As usual with great battles, it was not the plan or purpose of either side to fight this one when and where it was fought. Meade, who had succeeded Hooker, had selected a position on Pipe Clay Creek, where he would have concentrated his army—but for the capture of President Dayis' message to General Lee, revealing the fact that he feared to uncover Richmond by detaching Beauregard to threaten Washington as Lee had advised—and Lee had ordered the concentration of his army at Cashtown; but there was this great difference between the circumstances of the two armies. The battle was brought on by the advance of the Federal cavalry, in the discharge of its legitimate work of developing our forces and positions and gathering information for the Federal commander. The Confederate leader, on the other hand, was, in great measure, without his cavalry; no information whatever had been received by him, since crossing the Potomac, of or from General Stuart or his troopers. His army was, therefore, in the condition of a blind man surrounded by enemies endowed with vision and making full use of it.

It is fair to Stuart to say that it had been left to his discretion when and where he should cross the river—whether east of the mountains, or in the track of the infantry at the mouth of the Valley; but Colonel Taylor says: "He was expected to maintain communication with the main column, and especially directed to keep the commanding general informed of the movements of the Federal army." Did his one besetting weakness betray him again? Was he too much absorbed and infatuated with the fun of seeing how near his eastern sweep could approach the fortifications of Washington, or how far his bursting shell could terrorize the Federal capital?

On the eve of Gettysburg the Army of Northern Virginia, with the exception of the cavalry, was well in hand and in the finest possible plight. Of course its equipment was not perfect, though better, I think, than I remember to have seen it at any other time, while the physical condition and the spirit of the men could not have been finer. The way in which the army took the death of Jackson was a striking test of its high mettle. I do not recall having talked with a man who seemed to be depressed by it, while the common soldiers spoke of it in wondrous fashion. They seemed to have imbibed, to a great extent, the spirit of Lee's order announcing Jackson's death. They said they felt that his spirit was with us and would be throughout the campaign. It seemed to be their idea that God would let his warrior soul leave for a time the tamer bliss of Heaven that it might revel once more in the fierce joy of battle.

The Third Corps, A. P. Hill's, the last to leave the line of the Rappahannock, was the first to become engaged in the great fight.

On the 29th of June, Hill, who was at Fayetteville, between Chambersburg and Gettysburg, under general orders to co-operate with Ewell in menacing the communication of Harrisburg with Philadelphia, sent Heth's division to Cashtown, following it on the 30th with Pender's, and on the 1st of July with Anderson's division. On the 1st, Heth sent forward Pettygrew's brigade toward Gettysburg, where it encountered a considerable Federal force, how considerable Pettygrew could not determine; but it consisted in part at least of cavalry, and this information was at once sent, through Heth and Hill, to the commanding general, who directed Heth to ascertain if possible what force was at Gettysburg, and if he found infantry to report at once, but not to force an engagement. He did find infantry, a large body of it, and finding himself unable to draw away from it, soon became hotly engaged. The sound of artillery hurried Hill to the front and he put in Pender's division in support of Heth. Anderson did not get up in time to take part in this fight.

But the Second Corps, Ewell's, to which I was attached, or rather two divisions of it, Early's and Rodes', which were already en route for Cashtown, hearing at Middletown that Hill was concentrating at Gettysburg, turned toward that point, and Rodes, who was in the advance, gathering from the cannonading that a sharp engagement was in progress, hurried forward and made his dispositions for battle. But before he could form his lines so as to most effectively aid Hill's two divisions, he found fresh Federal troops deploying in his own front and soon became engaged with these. Meanwhile, our division (Early's) was subjected to one of the most straining of the experiences of the soldier—approaching a field of battle, invisible as yet, and played upon by the cadence and the swell of the fire. I well recall the scene as, about three o'clock in the afternoon, our column left the road and deployed out into line upon an elevated plateau, from which we had a full view of the field and of the drawn battle trembling in the balance in our front.

Every experienced soldier, particularly if he is a man of sensitive nature and pictorial memory, will appreciate my saying that two strongly contrasted figures are almost

equally prominent in my recollections of this scene. One is
Old Jube, as with consuming earnestness he connected his
right with Rodes' left and gave the order to advance—his
glossy black ostrich feather, in beautiful condition, seeming
to glisten and gleam and tremble upon the wide brim of his
gray-brown felt hat, like a thing of life; and the other, a
dwarfish, dumpy little fellow, of the division pioneer corps,
who at this moment came running up to his command, just
as I was leaving it to take my place with the artillery, carrying under each arm a great, round, Dutch loaf of bread
about the size of a cart wheel, giving him, upon a side view,
such as I had of him, the appearance of rolling in on wheels.

Early's attack was one of great impetuosity, especially that
of Gordon's brigade, and while, even after his two brigades
—Hayes' and Gordon's—entered the fight, the preponderance
in numbers was still with the Federal side, yet they broke
almost immediately in front of Early; whereupon our entire
line— the two divisions of our corps and the two of Hill's—
made a simultaneous advance, and the whole Federal force,
consisting of the First and Eleventh Corps, of three divisions
each, and Buford's cavalry, gave way in utter rout. The
Charlottesville battery followed immediately in rear of Gordon, and I was in charge of one of their pieces. We drove
the enemy pell-mell over rolling wheat fields, through a
grove, across a creek, up a little slope and into the town itself. The pursuit was so close and hot that, though my gun
came into battery several times, yet I could not get in a shot.

Gordon was the most glorious and inspiring thing I ever
looked upon. He was riding a beautiful coal-black stallion,
captured at Winchester, that had belonged to one of the Federal generals in Milroy's army—a majestic animal, * whose
"neck was clothed with thunder." From his grand joy in

---

*In *Scribner's* for June, 1903, General Gordon mentions this horse,
describing him very much as I have done. He adds that he only rode
him in one battle; that he behaved well at first under artillery fire, but
later, encountering a fierce fire of musketry, he turned tail and bolted
to the rear a hundred yards or more.

I am glad I did not witness this disgraceful fall. Nothing could have
been more superb than his bearing so long as he was under my eye. /

battle, he must have been a direct descendant of Job's horse, or Bucephalus, or Black Auster. I never saw a horse's neck so arched, his eye so fierce, his nostril so dilated. He followed in a trot, close upon the heels of the battle line, his head right in among the slanting barrels and bayonets, the reins loose upon his neck, his rider standing in his stirrups, bareheaded, hat in hand, arms extended, and, in a voice like a trumpet, exhorting his men. It was superb; absolutely thrilling. I recall feeling that I would not give so much as a dime to insure the independence of the Confederacy.

The loss of the enemy was terrific. General Butterfield, chief of staff of the Federal army, testifying before the Committee on the Conduct of the War, puts the total Federal force engaged in this fight at twenty-two to twenty-four thousand, and Swinton estimates their loss at "near ten thousand men." Our loss, at least in Gordon's brigade, was slight. I distinctly remember, in a momentary pause, calling out to Gordon, "General, where are your dead men?" and his reply: "I haven't got any, sir; the Almighty has covered my men with His shield and buckler!" Later in the war General Ewell said to me that he believed Gordon's brigade that evening put *hors de combat* a greater number of the enemy in proportion to its own numbers than any other command on either side ever did, from the beginning to the end of the war; but he added that he would not be misunderstood as awarding this gallant brigade credit in like proportion, because it simply turned the scale of a theretofore evenly-balanced battle.

I cannot forbear telling how, a few months later, this heroic scene was brought again vividly to my mind.

Happening to be in Richmond for a few hours, I went down to a train to aid in getting off some wounded men, and was helping to ease down from a box-car a Georgia soldier very badly shot. With some difficulty we managed to get him on a litter and then to lower him to the platform, without a jar; when, as he was resting a moment, I asked the universal soldier question, "What command do you belong to?" His pained and pallid face lit up with a glow of pride as he answered: "I belong to Gordon's old brigade, Cap'n. Did you ever see the Gin'ral in battle? He's most the prettiest thing you ever did see on a field of fight. It'ud put fight into a whipped chicken just to look at him."

My gun had come again into battery in the outskirts of the town. No enemy was in sight in our front; but in anticipation of a sudden rush I had the piece loaded and several rounds of canister taken from the ammunition chest and put down hard by the gaping muzzle, ready to sweep the street in case they should turn upon us. At this moment little George Greer, a chubby boy of sixteen, rode on by further into the town. George was General Early's clerk and a favorite with Old Jube, just because more fond of riding courier for him and of driving spurs into the flanks of a horse than of driving pen across paper. I shouted a caution to him as he passed, but on he went, disappearing in the smoke and dust ahead. In a few moments a cloud of blue coats appeared in the street in front of us, coming on, too, at a run. I was about to order the detachment to open fire, when beyond and back of the men in blue I noticed little Greer, leaning forward over the neck of his horse, towering above the Federals, who were on foot; and with violent gesticulations and in tones not the gentlest, ordering the "blue devils" to "double quick to the rear of that piece," which they did in the shortest time imaginable. There must have been over fifty of them.

I am aware this statement sounds incredible, but the men had thrown away their arms and were cowering in abject terror in the streets and alleys. Upon no other occasion did I see any large body of troops, on either side, so completely routed and demoralized as were the two Federal corps who were beaten at Gettysburg the evening of July 1st.

And this one reminds me of other incidents of those tremendous moments when our fate hung in the balance.

There was an Irishman named Burgoyne in the Ninth Louisiana,—Harry Hayes' brigade,—a typical son of the Emerald Isle, over six feet high in his stockings (when he had any), broad-shouldered and muscular, slightly bow-leg-

ged, and springy as a cat; as full of fire and fight and fun as
he could hold; indeed, often a little fuller than he could hold,
and never having been known to get his fill of noise and
scrimmage. Whenever the Ninth supported Hilary Jones,
if the musketry fire slackened while the artillery was in action, Burgoyne would slip over to the nearest gun and take
someone's place at the piece.

Seeing us unlimber in the street, as above related, he
had come over now for this purpose, seized the sponge-staff
and rammed home the charge, and was giving vent to his
enthusiasm in screams and bounds that would have done
credit to a catamount.

Standing on the other side of the gun, with his arms
folded, was a Federal Irishman, a prisoner just captured—
a man even taller than Burgoyne and somewhat heavier in
frame, altogether a magnificent fellow. Catching Burgoyne's brogue, he broke out—

"Hey, ye spalpane! say, what are yez doing in the Ribil
army?"

Quick as a flash, Burgoyne retorted:

"Be-dad, ain't an Irishman a freeman? Haven't I as
good right to fight for the Ribs as ye have to fight for the
—— Yanks?"

"O, yes!" sang out the Federal Irishman, "I know ye,
now you've turned your ougly mug to me. I had the plizure
of kicking yez out from behind Marye's wall, that time
Sedgwick lammed yer brigade out o' there!"

"Yer a —— liar," shouted our Pat, "and I'll jist knock
yer teeth down yer ougly throat for that same lie," and suiting the action to the word, he vaulted lightly over the gun,
and before we had time to realize the extreme absurdity of
the thing, the two had squared off against each other in the
most approved style and the first blow had passed, for the
Federal Irishman was as good grit as ours.

Just as the two giants were about to rush to close quarters, but before any blood had been drawn in the round, I
noticed that the right fist of the Federal gladiator was gory,
and the next movement revealed the stumps of two shattered fingers, which he was about to drive full into Burgoyne's face.

"Hold!" I cried; "your man's wounded!" On the instant Burgoyne's fists fell.

"You're a trump, Pat; give me your well hand," said he. "We'll fight this out some other time. I didn't see ye were hurt."

Just as this intensest climax of the great battle was happily avoided, a member of General Early's staff—I thought it was Major Daniel, but he says not—galloped by, and shouted, "Lieutenant, limber to the rear!"

"*To the front,* you mean, Major!"

"No," came the answer, *to the rear!*"

"All right, boys," said I, "I reckon the town's barricaded, and we'll just pass round it to the front."

But, no. *Back, back,* we went, for perhaps a mile or more, and took position on a hill from which, next morning, we gazed upon the earthworks which had sprung up in the night on Cemetery Ridge, and the tide, which taken at the flood might have led on to overwhelming victory and even to independence, had ebbed away forever. So it looked to me then, and nothing I have read or heard since has altered the impressions of that moment.

It is my nature to be reverential toward rightful authority and not to question the wisdom of its decisions; but on this occasion I chafed and rebelled until it almost made me ill. I was well nigh frenzied by what appeared to me to be the folly, the absolute fatuity of delay. One point must be cleared up. It has been suggested that General Lee himself was responsible; that, coming late upon the field, he forbade the advance which his lieutenant would have made. Mr. Swinton goes so far as to say unqualifiedly that "Ewell was even advancing a line against Culp's Hill when Lee reached the field and stayed the movement." Nothing could be less like Lee and nothing further from the truth. Colonel Taylor makes this full and explicit statement:

General Lee witnessed the flight of the Federals through Gettysburg and up the hills beyond. He then directed me to go to General Ewell and say to him that, from the position which he occupied, he could see the enemy retreating over those hills, without organization and in great confusion; that it was only necessary to press "those people" in order to secure possession of the heights, and that, if possible, he wished him to do this. In obedience to these instructions I proceeded immediately to General Ewell and delivered the order of General Lee; and after receiving from him some message for the commanding general in regard to the prisoners captured, returned to the latter and reported that his order had been delivered.

At this time I admired General Ewell as a soldier; later I loved him as a man, and he treated me with more informal and affectionate kindness than any other of our leading generals ever did. But the truth must be told, and Ewell was the last man on earth to object to this. Colonel Taylor speaks of the discretion General Lee always accorded to his lieutenants. In the exercise of this discretion, Ewell probably decided it best not to press his advantage on the evening of July 1st. Why, we do not know; at least I do not recall any statement from him on the subject, and his lips are now sealed. I ask no judgment against him, but only that General Lee's skirts should be cleared of responsibility for the failure to go right on that evening and occupy the heights.

It is also undeniably true, that Lee desired and purposed to renew the attack, in full force, at daylight next morning, the morning of July 2d, but was again thwarted by lack of prompt and vigorous co-operation among his generals. This book being in the main a record of personal reminiscence, I do not care to go into the details of these various and desultory movements and failures to move, until some time, I think early in the afternoon of the second, when I was brought again in personal touch with the matter and ultimately into one of the most tremendous experiences of my life.

As I remember, about the time mentioned, two of Early's brigades, Gordon's being one, were sent off to watch the York road and a suspicious-looking body of troops which had appeared and disappeared in that direction, say two miles to the left, and which threatened the left flank and rear of Edward Johnson's division, which was our extreme left, and under orders to take part in a general advance against the enemy. Gordon was in command of this little army of observation, and as I was mounted and relished the idea of a scout and the prospect of adventure, I joined the expedition.

When we reached our objective we readily satisfied ourselves that no danger boded from this direction, and that the troops we had regarded with suspicion were not hostile. We did not come into absolute contact with them,—we could not wait for that,—but my recollection is that they proved to be the advance of Stuart's cavalry, which had just come up, and were really doing just what we had come to do, that is, guarding our left flank and rear.

After making this discovery, the point was to get word to Johnson at the earliest possible moment, that he could press on, feeling no uneasiness about his flanks. Not a member of Gordon's staff was with him—all were off on various errands. Captain Mitchell came up at the moment, but both he and his horse were exhausted, utterly unfit for such a ride as this. The General called for volunteers, mounted officers, to take the message—two, I think; one to go around a longer and safer way, but one to cut right across, or rather, as his course would be after the first quarter of a mile, directly in the teeth of the artillery fire, which was sweeping the approaches to the Federal position from our left.

I offered to take this latter ride and do my best to get word to General Johnson promptly. The General thanked me, and off I dashed, braced, as I thought, for anything, yet little dreaming what the ride would really be.

For the first few hundred yards, as above suggested, the configuration of the ground was such that the fire was entirely cut off—not so much as even one stray shell whistled above my head. But in a few moments, as I rose a hill and my course veered to the left, I struck a well-defined ærial current, a meteoric stream, of projectiles and explosions, and I felt my little horse shudder and squat under me, and then he made one frantic effort to turn and fly. I pulled him fiercely back against the iron torrent until he breasted it squarely and then, seeming to realize the requirements of the position, he elongated and flattened himself as much as possible, while I lay as close to him as I could, and we fairly devoured the way.

One of the horrors of the thing, during a large part of the ride, was that I could see almost every shell that passed, as they were coming straight toward me, and their propulsive force was pretty well exhausted. As I approached the points at which the fire was directed, while I could not see so large a proportion of the shells, and this strain was of course diminished, yet the number of projectiles and explosions increased—until at last there was absolutely no separation between the reports, but the air was rent by one continuous shriek of shell and roar of explosion, and torn with countless myriads of hurtling fragments.

When a man is undergoing an experience like this he does not think—his entire conscious being is concentrated upon the one point of endurance. But unconsciously, inadvertently, he may receive powerful impressions and bear away with him vivid and unfading mental photographs.

I have borne with me ever since, in my recollections of this ride, three pictures. The first is a silhouette of my little horse and me as we sped on our perilous way. I put him first because he did it, I only endured. After his first shy he never shrank or swerved again, but held to his course straight and swift as a greyhound; nay, as an arrow flies. He seemed to be possessed, whether intelligently or instinctively, of the double purpose of making himself small and getting there. His figure was that of a running hare—low to the ground, with her ears laid flat and every limb stretched; while I was nothing but the smallest possible projection above his back and along his flanks.

I am not satisfied whether this is purely a mental and inferential picture, or whether, as I incline to think, my eye, in an involuntary sidelong glance, caught our shadow as we flew. But of this I am satisfied—that, in all the years since, the battle of Gettysburg has never obtruded itself upon my mental vision that this strange figure, of horse and man blent together into one by the terrible tension, has not been the frontispiece.

The next picture is of Latimer's Battalion, which, with splendid pluck but little judgment, had engaged in a most unequal artillery duel with the Federal batteries massed upon Cemetery Ridge and Culp's Hill. Never, before or after, did I see fifteen or twenty guns in such a condition of wreck and destruction as this battalion was. It had been hurled backward, as it were, by the very weight and impact of metal from the position it had occupied on the crest of a little ridge, into a saucer-shaped depression behind it; and such a scene as it presented—guns dismounted and disabled, carriages splintered and crushed, ammunition chests exploded, limbers upset, wounded horses plunging and kicking, dashing out the brains of men tangled in the harness; while cannoneers with pistols were crawling around through the wreck shooting the struggling horses to save the lives of the wounded men.

I said the little horse did not again swerve from his course. He was compelled to do so at this point, as it was impracticable to ride through the battalion, which lay directly in our track; but we had a full view of it as we followed the higher ground from which it had been driven.

The third and last picture connected with my desperate ride is of the finish and of the doughty division commander in whose behalf I had taken it. He was sometimes called "Alleghany Johnson" and "Fence-Rail Johnson," because of his having been wounded at the battle of Alleghany, and, in consequence, walking with a very perceptible limp and aiding the process with a staff about as long as a rail and almost as thick as the club of Giant Despair. He was a heavy, thick-set man, and when I saw him was on foot and hobbling along with the help of this gigantic walking-cane. It was toward the gloaming and I did not see him very distinctly, but remember that when I gasped out the message I bore from Gordon, he simply growled back, "Very well, sir"—and, my responsibility discharged, I dropped from the saddle to the ground, the last thing I remember being my little horse standing over me, his sides heaving and panting and his head drooping and sinking until his muzzle almost touched my body. How long I lay and he stood there, or where we went after we recovered breath and motion, I have not the faintest recollection.

Johnson's attack was made not long before dark, but it was not vigorously supported, except by two of Early's brigades, and it failed to accomplish any important result.

I was not in any way personally connected with the main operations of the next day, July 3d, the last day of the great battle. That was a matter primarily of Longstreet's corps, a part of Hill's acting as support to his attack. I shall, therefore, not enter into the hotly-debated question of responsibility for the failure of the Confederate assault, nor indulge in any heroics over its gallantry.

Nor shall I discuss the question which side is entitled to claim the victory. It is clear that the Confederates retired first from the field, but they did not do so until the 5th of July, the rear guard leaving late on that day, and even then they were not pursued. General Sickles, before the Committee on the Conduct of the War, testified that the reason the Confederates were not followed up was a difference of opinion among the Federal generals whether their army should not retreat; that "it was by no means clear, in the judgment of the corps commanders, or of the general in command, whether they had won or not."

There is but one other scene of the battle-field which I care to mention, and that only for a reason already touched upon in a like connection, namely, to give to those who had no actual experience of war some approximate conception of the variety and extravagance of horrors which the soldier is called upon, from time to time, to undergo.

On the 4th of July, in readjusting and straightening our lines, the guns of Hilary Jones' battalion were put in position on a part of the field which Hill's corps had fought over on the 1st, and upon which the pioneer corps and burying parties had not been able to complete their work; so that the dead bodies of men and horses had lain there putrefying under the summer sun for three days. The sights and smells that assailed us were simply indescribable—corpses swollen to twice their original size, some of them actually burst asunder with the pressure of foul gases and vapors. I recall one feature never before noted, the shocking distension and protrusion of the eyeballs of dead men and dead horses. Several human or unhuman corpses sat upright against a fence, with arms extended in the air and faces hideous with something very like a fixed leer, as if taking a fiendish pleasure in showing us what we essentially were and might at any moment become. The odors were nauseating, and so deadly that in a short time we all sickened and were lying with our mouths close to the ground, most of us vomiting profusely. We protested against the cruelty and folly of keeping men in such a position. Of course to fight in it was utterly out of the question, and we were soon moved away; but for the rest of that day and late into the night the fearful odors I had inhaled remained with me and made me loathe myself as if an already rotting corpse.

While a prisoner at Johnson's Island, in the spring of '65, I became much interested in one of my fellow-prisoners, a Major McDaniel, of Georgia. He did not at first strike one as an impressive man. Indeed, if I recollect rightly, he had somewhat of an impediment in his speech and was not inclined to talk much; but there was a peculiar pith and point and weight in what he did say, and those who knew him best seemed to regard him as a man of mark and to treat him with the greatest respect. The impression he made upon me was of simplicity and directness, good sense and good character, dignity, gravity, decorum. They told me this surprising story of him:

He was seriously wounded at Gettysburg, and, of course, in the hospital. His friends who had been captured and were about to be marched off to prison, came in to bid him good-by; but he declared he would not be left behind, that he could and would go with them. Both his comrades and the Federal surgeons and nurses, who were kind and attentive, protested that this was absolutely out of the question—that he would die on the road.

"Very good," said McDaniel, "I'll die then. I am certainly going, and if you don't bring a litter and put me on it and carry me, then I will simply get up and walk till I drop."

Finally the surgeons yielded, saying that, in his condition, it would be as fatal to confine him forcibly in bed as to lift him out and attempt to transport him; that either course was certain death. So the litter was brought, he was placed upon it, his friends sadly took hold of the bearing poles and started, feeling that the marching column of prisoners was really McDaniel's funeral procession.

The journey would have been trying enough, even for a sound, strong man, but for one in McDaniel's condition it was simply fearful. Why he did not die they could not see, yet he did seem to grow weaker and weaker, until at last, as the column halted in a little Pennsylvania town and his bearers put the litter gently down in the shade, his eyes were closed, his face deadly pale, and the majority of those about him thought he was gone. The whole population was in the streets to see the Rebel prisoners go by, and some stared, with gaping curiosity, at the dead man on the stretcher.

His most intimate friend, Colonel Nesbit, stood nearest, keeping a sort of guard over him, and just as he made up his mind to examine and see if it was indeed all over, McDaniel opened his eyes, and then beckoned feebly for Nesbit to come close to him. As he reached his side and bent over him, McDaniel took hold upon the lapel of Nesbit's coat and drew him yet closer down, until their faces well nigh touched, and then, with a great effort and in a voice scarcely audible, McDaniel whispered his name—"Nesbit!"

Nesbit says he confidently expected some last message for his family, or some tender farewell to his friends, when, with extreme difficulty, his supposed-to-be-dying friend, pointing with trembling finger, uttered just these words:

"Nesbit, old fellow! Did you ever see such an ungodly pair of ankles as that Dutch woman standing over there on that porch has got?"

Of course such a man could not be killed and would not die; and it was not a matter of surprise to me when, a few years later, he was elected Governor of Georgia by a hundred thousand majority.

CHAPTER XVII

BETWEEN GETTYSBURG AND THE WILDERNESS

Lee Orders His Generals of Division to Report the Condition of Their Troops—McLaws Makes the Rounds of His Division—Back in the Old Dominion—Tuck and Marse Robert, Dragon and Logan—Meade an Able and Wary Opponent—The Homes of the People Within the Lines of the Army—A Preacher-Captain Metes Out Stern and Speedy Justice—Lee Smarting Under the *Tete-de-pont* Disaster— Pegram Meets Two of His Old Troopers—Mine Run—Mickey Free and the Persimmons—Horses Under Artillery Fire—Two Important Movements of the Federal Forces.

I confess I have not read current war literature very closely, but certainly I have never seen, in any publication, any allusion to what is related below; indeed I cannot recall any mention of it even in conversation with comrades—and yet my recollection of what transpired is clear and vivid.

Much has been said, and justly, of the unshaken condition of the Army of Northern Virginia when it retired from the Federal front at Gettysburg; and yet it is equally true that army had been through a most trying experience, and as it was still in hostile territory and a swollen and at the time impassable river flowed between it and the friendly soil of Old Virginia, Lee had great cause for anxiety, and it behooved him to be thoroughly informed and certified as to the real condition and spirit of his troops. With this view he directed his generals, particularly his generals of division, to make prompt and thorough investigation in this regard, and to report results to him. McLaws, our division general, made a special tour around the camp fires of his men one evening, while we were in line of battle at Hagerstown, Md., waiting for Meade to attack, or for the Potomac to fall, so that we might in safety cross it, and I was at special pains to follow, and to see and hear what I could.

McLaws was rather a peculiar personality. He certainly could not be called an intellectual man, nor was he a brilliant and aggressive soldier; but he was regarded as one of the most dogged defensive fighters in the army. His entire make-up, physical, mental and moral, was solid, even stolid. In figure he was short, stout, square-shouldered, deep-chested, strong-limbed; in complexion, dark and swarthy, with coal-black eyes and black, thick, close-curling hair and beard. Of his type, he was a handsome man, but the type was that of the Roman centurion; say that centurion who stood at his post in Herculaneum until the lava ran over him. It should be mentioned in his honor that when General Lee, with scant 14,000 muskets, held the front of Hooker's 92,000 at Chancellorsville, McLaws commanded one of the two divisions he had with him.

He was a Georgian, and his division, consisting of two Georgia brigades, one from South Carolina and one from Mississippi, was as stalwart and reliable as any in the service. Nothing of course could repress our Mississippians, but the general effect and influence of the man upon his command was clearly manifest in the general tenor of the responses he elicited. His men were respectful, but not enthusiastic on this occasion. For the most part they kept right on with what they happened to be doing when the General arrived—cooking, cleaning their arms and accoutrements, or whatever else it might be. He was on horseback, riding, as I remember, a small, white pony-built horse, and as he rode up into the circle of flickering light of camp fire after camp fire to talk with the men, he made quite a marked and notable figure. The conversation ran somewhat in this line:

"Well, boys, how are you?"

"We are all right, General!"

"They say there are lots of those fellows over the way there."

"Well, they can stay there; we ain't offerin' to disturb 'em. We've had all the fighting we want just now; but if they ain't satisfied and want any more, all they've got to do is to come over and get their bellies full."

"Suppose they do come, sure enough, boys. What are you going to do with them?"

"Why, just make the ground blue with 'em, that's all; just manure this here man's land with 'em. We ain't asking anything of them, but if they want anything of us, why, just let 'em come after it, and they can get all they want; but they'll wish they hadn't come."

"Well, now, I can rely upon that, can I?"

"You just bet your life you can, General. If we're asleep when they come, you just have us waked up, and we'll receive 'em in good style."

"Well, good-night, boys. I'm satisfied."

McLaws' "boys" had no occasion upon that field to vindicate their own account of themselves. The enemy did not attack, the river did fall, and we returned to our own side of the Potomac, but not until the 13th of July. The day we got there, or perhaps the day following, "Tuck," the redoubtable wagon driver of the old battery, had a memorable experience which he never tired of telling.

Tuck was a unique character. Up to the date of his enlistment his horizon had been perhaps more contracted and his opportunities fewer and lower than those of any other man among us. Naturally he gravitated to the wagon; but the man made the position. He was so quiet and steady and perfect in the discharge of its humble duties, that I question whether there was another private soldier in the battery as useful, or one more universally liked and respected, and he was as loyal and devoted to the company and his comrades as they were to him. He had a fine pair of mules, and his affection for them amounted almost to a passion. Indeed, his entire outfit—mules, harness and wagon—was always in better condition than any other I ever saw in the army, and if there was forage or food, for man or beast, to be had anywhere, Tuck was sure to get at least our share for us.

As above said, it was the very day we reached the soil of old Virginia, or the day after, that Tuck, or Tucker,—I believe the latter was really his name,—was dragging along with his wagon, through the mud and mist, considerably in rear of the battery, grieving that his two faithful mules had gone supperless to bed the last night and taken breakfastless to the road that morning, when, glancing to the left, his eye lit upon a luxuriant field of grass he was just passing, and there, right abreast of his wagon, was an enticing set of draw-bars.

On the instant he turned out to the side of the road, unhitched his mules, and taking them by their long, strong halter reins—the best I ever saw upon the harness of an army team—let down the bars and led them into the field, and was enjoying their breakfast as much perhaps as the mules were, when a fine-looking officer, with a rubber cape over his shoulders, rode up to the fence and said in a kindly, pleasant voice:

"My man, I like that. I am glad to see you taking such good care of your mules, and they like it, too. What a fine breakfast they are making! They are fine mules, too!"

"What, my mules? You bet they are fine! Marse Robert ain't got no better mules in his army than these two."

"What are their names?"

"This here gray one, he's named Dragon, and that 'ere black one, his name's Logan. Dragon, he's a leetle the best of the two, but either one of 'em's good enough."

"Yes indeed, I can well believe that, and I am glad to see you taking such good care of this man's property, too; keeping your mules in hand with the lines. I wish all the drivers in the army were as careful of their teams and of other people's property as you are. Now this is all right, but I wouldn't stay here too long. There are some gentlemen in blue, back here on the road a little way; and—"

"What's that! the damn Yankees coming? Come, Dragon, come, Logan, we must git out o' this!"

"O, I wouldn't be in quite such a hurry. There is no danger yet awhile. Let them finish their breakfast. I only meant—"

"No, sir; I ain't taking no chances. The infernal Yankees sha'n't never git my mules! Come on here, Dragon and

Logan,"—leading them toward the bars,—"we must git out o' this, and mighty quick, too!"

As he got his pets out in the road and was hitching them up again, Colonel Taylor and Colonel Marshall and the rest of General Lee's staff rode up and reported to Tuck's friend and took orders from him, and Tuck waked up to the fact that he had been talking with Marse Robert himself for the last five minutes.

"Great Scott!" said he, in relating his adventure, "I felt that I had been more impudent than the devil himself, and I wanted to get out o' sight as fast as ever I could; but I didn't feel like letting no common man speak to me for two or three days after that."

There is a delicious sequel to this story, which seems too good to be true, and yet I have every reason to believe it is as true as it is good.

When the final collapse came, Tuck, Dragon and Logan were down in North Carolina, where they had been many a time before, foraging for themselves and the rest of us— horses and men. The returning train of heavily-loaded wagons, inadequately protected, was attacked by Federal raiders. The shooting, plundering, and burning was going on front and rear and rapidly approaching from both directions. So Tuck halted his wagon, got out all the provisions he could carry for himself and them, unhitched Dragon and Logan, and took to the woods, and he kept going until he got so far away that the braying of his companions could not be heard from the road. Then he made himself comfortable by the side of a little stream and awaited developments.

The next day it rained and he kept close, but the day following was bright and clear, and he took an early morning scout to "the big road." There was the blackened débris of burnt wagons, but there had not been a track upon the road since the rain, and Tuck concluded that the coast was clear. So he went back to his bivouac, mounted Dragon and, leading Logan, returned to the road and took the direction of Richmond.

At last he emerged from the dank, sombre pine forest into a clearing, where was a comfortable farm house, and not far from the woods he ran upon an old fellow seated on the top rail of an old Virginia snake fence, with his spinal column comfortably supported by one of the cross stakes, a short-stemmed, blackened corncob pipe in his mouth, his neglected, stubby beard bristling all over his face, and his entire figure and bearing expressive of ill-temper and despair.

"Good morning," said Tuck.

"Mornin'," responded the old chap.

"Seen anything of the Yankees?"

"Yes, the infernal thieves cleaned me out day before yestiddy."

"What's that plow doin' standing in that 'ere furrow?"

"Why, the damn Yankees stole the mules right out of it. Didn't leave me a hide or hoof on the place."

"I've got a good pair of mules here," said Tuck.

"Well, go there to the gate, come right in and hitch up, and we'll go snacks on the crap."

The bargain was closed as promptly as proposed. Tuck plowed until the dinner horn blew. Then he and Dragon and Logan went to the sound of it, as if they had been "bred and born" on the place. Tuck watered and fed his mules at the stable and himself at the house, touching his hat to the old man's pretty daughter as he entered.

In due course of time he married her, and he owns that farm to-day.

Thus the house of Tucker rode into home and fortune upon "my mules," which its illustrious founder swore "the infernal Yankees sha'n't never git!"

Some little time since, in a conversation with Mr. George Cary Eggleston, he remarked that, years ago, perhaps during the war, I mentioned to him an estimate of General Meade which I had heard General Lee express, about the time of Meade's appointment to succeed Hooker in command of the Army of the Potomac. I do not now quite see how I could have overheard the remark precisely at the time indicated, but I have no doubt the story, as far as Lee's estimate of Meade is concerned, is essentially true. As the story goes, someone was congratulating Lee upon having "a mediocre man like Meade" as his opponent, suggesting that he would have an easy time with him. But Lee interrupted the speaker, saying with emphasis that General Meade was the most dangerous man who had as yet been opposed to him; that he was not only a soldier of intelligence and ability, but that he was also a conscientious, careful, thorough and painstaking man; that he would make no such mistake in his (Lee's) front as some of his predecessors had made, and that if he made any mistake in Meade's front he would be certain to take advantage of it.

It is noteworthy how exactly this estimate was fulfilled and confirmed, not only at Gettysburg, but in the campaign of the succeeding autumn upon Virginia soil, in which Meade showed himself to be able and cautious, wary and lithe; incomparably superior to Pope or Burnside, or even Hooker. In October, at Bristoe Station, when we were attempting to outflank him, as we had done Pope, he not only escaped by giving such attention to his "lines of retreat" as the latter had boasted he would not give, but he actually inflicted upon us a decided defeat, accentuated by the almost unparalleled capture of five pieces of artillery; and that, when his force engaged was inferior to ours. In November, at the *tête-de-pont* at Rappahannock Bridge, he wrote for us what Colonel Taylor calls "the saddest chapter in the history of this army," by snapping up two brigades, of twelve or fifteen hundred men, and four pieces of artillery, which had been exposed, by an arrangement of his lines more nearly questionable perhaps than any other General Lee was ever known to make. In December, at Mine Run, while he failed in his main design of turning our flank and forcing us to abandon our fortified line on the Rapidan, and so pushing us back on Hanover Junction, and while he got decidedly the worst of the fighting, yet he succeeded in getting away without the overwhelming defeat we hoped to have inflicted upon him; and, upon the whole, no preceding Federal commander of the Army of the Potomac had made anything like as good a showing in an equal number of moves against their great Confederate opponent.

Apropos of the time and the region in which the operations just commented upon occurred,—being the great battlefield of central Virginia, threshed over for three years by the iron flail of war,—Billy sends me what he very justly terms "the most pathetic and harrowing incident of my service in the Army of Northern Virginia." I give it substantially in his own words:

"One day while we were encamped in the Poison Fields of Spottsylvania County, Tom Armistead and I were summoned to Captain McCarthy's quarters. We found him talking to a woman very poorly but cleanly dressed, who seemed in bitter distress. The captain ordered us to go with the woman and bury her child. We went with her to her home, a small house with but two rooms. There we found her mother, an aged woman, and the child, a boy of ten, who had just died of a most virulent case of diphtheria. The father, a soldier in some Virginia regiment, was of course absent, and of neighbors there were none in that war-stricken country.

"Armistead and I bathed and dressed the little body and then had to rip planks off part of the shed room of the house to make something to bury it in, tearing off the palings of the garden to get nails, having no saw and being compelled to cut and break the planks with an axe. Before we had finished the box the battery bugle sounded 'Harness and hitch up.' We stayed long enough to finish the box and place the body in it, but could not stay to dig the grave. We had to leave these two poor women alone with the unburied child.

"There was not a farm animal, not even a fowl, on the place. How these women and many others in the track of both those great armies lived was then, and always has been, a mystery to me. War truly is *hell;* how utterly devilish are those who, by cruelty and license, add to its horrors."

Another incident of this same period and locality occurs to me.

One of the Georgia batteries of our battalion—"Frazier's," as it was called—was composed largely of Irishmen from Savannah—gallant fellows, but wild and reckless. The captaincy becoming vacant, a Georgia Methodist preacher, Morgan Calloway, was sent to command them. He proved to be, all in all, such a man as one seldom sees—a combination of Praise God Barebone and Sir Philip Sidney, with a dash of Hedley Vicars about him. He had all the stern grit of the Puritan, with much of the chivalry of the Cavalier and the zeal of the Apostle.

No man ever gave himself such a "send-off" as Calloway did with his battery. He gripped their very souls at the first pass.

Not long after he took command the battalion spent a few days in these Poison Fields of Spottsylvania. The very evening we arrived, before we had gotten fixed for the night, a woman of the type of the one above described by Billy came to battalion headquarters and complained that one of the men in "that company over yonder"—pointing to where Calloway's guns were parked—had gone right into her pig pen, before her very eyes, and killed and carried off her pig.

The colonel directed me to look after the matter, and the woman and I walked over to the battery and laid the complaint before Calloway, who asked her whether she thought she could point out the man. She said she could, and he ordered his bugler to blow "an assembly."

When the line was formed he gave the command, "To the rear, open order, march!" the rear rank stepping back two paces further to the rear, and he and I and the woman started to walk down the front rank; he, as was his wont when on duty, having his coat buttoned to the chin and his sabre belted about his waist.

When we had gotten a little more than half way down the line some lewd fellow of the baser sort, *sotto voce,* made some improper remark about the woman, and his comrades began to titter. With a single sweep of his right arm, Calloway drew his sabre and delivered his blow. The weapon flashed past my face and laid open the scalp of the chief offender, who dropped in his tracks, bleeding like a stricken bullock. There was a shuffle of feet moving to his aid.

"Stand fast in ranks! Eyes front!" cried Calloway, the sabre dripping with blood still in his sword hand. Needless to say they did stand, as if carved out of stone, while in absolute silence Calloway, the woman, and I, completed our inspection of the front, and when about midway of the rear rank she, without hesitation, confidently identified the thief. His manner and bearing under the charge convicted him, and Calloway had him bucked and gagged and sequestered his pay to reimburse the woman. He then gave the order, "break ranks!" and sent the surgeon to attend the wounded man.

I never saw a company of men more impressed. Indeed, I was myself as much impressed as any of them, and was at considerable pains to catch the feelings and comments of the men.

"Whew!" said a big fellow, who had been a leader in all the lawlessness of the battery, "what sort of a preacher do you call this? Be-dad! and if he hits the Yankees half as hard as he hit Dan, it'll be all right. We'll have to watch him about that, boys. We'll get his gait before long."

As several times remarked, I have not been able to determine exactly when and where I rejoined the old battalion as its adjutant; but since writing the preceding chapter I am satisfied it must have been shortly after the battle of Gettysburg, and either at or before we reached Hagerstown; as otherwise I should not have witnessed McLaws' evening visitation to the camp fires of his division.

It may be well here to say that our battalion was ordered to Hanover Junction in the autumn of 1863, about two months after our return from Gettysburg, with the view of going with Longstreet's corps to the West; but, either from lack of transportation or from some other cause, we did not go, but passed some weeks on or near the Central Railroad, gradually working our way up toward the main body of the army again, and were sent, after Mine Run, to guard the middle fords of the Rapidan.

I have quoted Colonel Taylor as saying that the disaster at Rappahannock Bridge was the saddest chapter in the history of the Army of Northern Virginia, and I am confident General Lee felt it very keenly. Some weeks after we had begun our winter's watch on the Rapidan, General Ewell, who was in command of the forces picketing the stream from Clark's Mountain down, received a message from General Lee that he would come down next day, bringing two or three general officers with him, and wished General Ewell, with two or three of his artillery officers, to ride with them along the lines. General Ewell notified Colonel Cabell and myself to be at his headquarters next morning, where we met General Lee, General Early, and Gen. John Pegram, and rode with them along the hills skirting the stream, discussing chiefly positions for artillery, until we came to a hill, over against Raccoon or Somerville Ford, where we had an exceptionally fine view of the Federal camps across the river.

The party halted on the summit and General Lee was more stirred than I had ever before seen him. He either referred expressly to Rappahannock Bridge and the affair of the *tête-de-pont,* or the implied reference to it was perfectly clear. Sweeping the stretch of the enemy's camps with his gauntleted right hand he said:

"What is there to prevent our cutting off and destroying the people in these nearer camps on this side of that hill, before those back yonder on the other side could get to them to help them?"

Early at once answered, as if the question had been propounded to him alone:

"This infernal river: how are you going to cross that without giving warning?"

"Ford it, sir; ford it!"

"What are you going to do with your pneumonia patients?" whined Old Jube with a leer.

Thereupon Ewell and Pegram sided strongly with Early in deprecating such an undertaking that winter season, though the weather at the time was open and fine. General Lee said no more, and I have never thought he seriously entertained such a purpose; but he was evidently smarting under the slap in the face he had received, and he panted for some opportunity to return the blow.

While we continued to look at the Federal camps two horsemen rode down to the other bank to water their horses. Pegram seemed much interested and said he believed he would gallop down and interview "those fellows." As he started, General Lee said, in a deep voice, "You'd better be careful, sir!" Pegram was a superb horseman and splendidly mounted, and I never saw a finer equestrian figure than he presented as he dashed off down the hill, never making an uneven movement in the saddle. When he reached the flat, through which the river ran, the Federal horses raised their heads, and their riders shaded their eyes with their hands, gazing intently at the rapidly-approaching horseman and striving to make him out. As he dashed into the stream amid a cloud of spray, they advanced rapidly to meet him, and we felt a shade of uneasiness; but the next moment we saw that the meeting was not only friendly but enthusiastic, and after the first fervors of the greeting had subsided the three sat upon their horses in the middle of the stream and had a conference so long that we actually tired waiting. When Pegram returned he told us, with a glowing countenance, that the troopers had belonged to his company in the old army and that their hearts were in the same place toward him. He was a noble gentleman, and no one suggested such a thing as military information acquired or divulged under such circumstances.

I recall a trivial incident of Mine Run which may serve as an introduction to what may prove of interest. I had been sent with a message to Gen. William N. Pendleton, chief of artillery of the army, and told only that he was on the lines. So I had to ride from one end to the other while the artillery fire was heavy, and did not find the general after all. But just as I go to the end of the lines I did find, a little back of them, a fine tree full of ripe persimmons, the first I had seen that autumn, in perfect condition for eating. I dismounted, threw my bridle rein over the pommel of the saddle, climbed the tree and gave it a good shake. Meanwhile several shells whistled not far above my head and I distinctly recall laughing to myself at the difference two and a half years had wrought. Just after I was mustered

into service I should have considered that I had made a narrow escape from shells passing as near as these, and that it
was little less than profane to have so much as thought of
persimmons "under such solemn circumstances."

But my horse, "Mickey Free," and I had come to a more
practical state of mind. We were badly in need of lunch—
the persimmons would furnish a very acceptable one, and it
never occurred to either of us that the shells constituted any
serious obstacle to our gathering and eating luncheon. I recall vividly how he raised his head and pricked up his ears,
watching where the persimmons fell thickest and going there
and gobbling them up with the greatest gusto. After I
had shaken off all that were ready to drop, I proceeded to
gather my portion, which I thought, under the circumstances, should be the lion's share; but Mickey evidently
thought differently. I can see the dear old fellow now trotting ahead of me to the spots where the fruit lay thickest,
and as I tried to dart in and pick up my share, backing his
ears, wheeling his rear upon me and executing a sort of continuous kick with one hind leg, just to bully me a little and
without any intention of really doing me harm. Many
horses and most dogs are very fond of persimmons, and
Mickey and I had the fullest and finest feed of them that
morning at Mine Run that we ever enjoyed during our army
comradeship.

I have always been fond of what we are pleased to term
"the lower animals," particularly of horses and dogs, and
have already devoted several pages to the biographies of the
only two dogs I was intimately acquainted with during the
war. I ask permission now to say a few words about the
horses, whose starvation and sufferings and wounds and
death I really believe used to affect me even more than the
like experience of my human fellow-beings; and this because, as Grover said, at Ball's Bluff, the men " 'listed ter git
killed," and the horses didn't.

Some of these sensitive creatures were mortally afraid of
artillery fire. I have seen the poor brutes, when the shells
were flying low and close above their backs, squat until their
bellies almost touched the ground. They would be per-

fectly satisfied during battle, or at least entirely quiet, if their drivers remained with them, especially on their backs; and when the men were compelled to absent themselves for a time and returned again to their teams, I have heard the horses welcome them with whinnies of satisfaction and content, and have seen them, under fire, rub their heads against their drivers with confiding and appealing affection.

And the poor animals loved not only their drivers but each other. I have heard and seen a horse, whose mate was killed at his side, utter an agonized and terrified neigh, meanwhile shuddering violently, and have known a horse so bereaved persistently refuse to eat, and pine away and die.

A few horses, the grand progeny of Job's horse, may "mock at fear * * * and say among the trumpets, ha! ha!" But it should be remembered that Job's horse probably did not have artillery fire to face. However, I have known horses which seemed to be thrilled rather than terrified even by the thunder of the guns. Mickey was a horse of this class, and I used to say of him that, however he might be dragged out with fatigue, under fire he moved like a steam engine on steel springs, and that any coward could be a hero on his back. Even wounds had no power to daunt him. He was struck repeatedly and very dangerously, but it never dampened his martial ardor at all. He was withal a horse of great intelligence and sensibility, as stories I have yet to tell of him will show.

There were only two important movements of the Federal forces in Virginia which intervened between Mine Run and the opening of the great campaign of 1864, and neither of them requires extended comment from me. The first was the pushing of a corps across the Rapidan, at Morton's Ford, immediately in front of the Howitzers. I cannot recall the exact date—though I think it was early in February—or what corps it was; nor was the object or purpose of the movement at all clear. It may have been with the view of ascertaining whether General Lee had recently detached and sent off to other fields any considerable bodies of troops; or it may have been thought that the main body of his infantry was encamped so far back of the lines that the artillery on the river and its small infantry support could be snapped up before adequate reinforcement could reach them. But if such an opportunity ever existed, the invaders did not act with vigor in availing themselves of it. The Howitzers maintained a determined front, the infantry arrived and poured into the works, and the Federals, after suffering some little loss, withdrew, leaving the object of the movement shrouded in mystery, and returned across the river.

I may be pardoned for relating in this connection an amusing flurry of my good friend, General Ewell, which forced me for a few moments into rather an awkward position. The General was somewhat excited over the length of time the troops took to enter the works after getting upon the ground, and particularly over the performance of a stiff old Georgia colonel, whose regiment was facing the works and who was actually side-stepping it to the right, to clear the right flank of another regiment that had just entered the works, and this while the enemy was advancing up the slope in our front, and there was not a man in the lines to our right.

The General was storming at the colonel, and I, sitting on my horse near-by, could not repress a titter. Suddenly "Old Dick" turned to me and exclaimed:

"Mr. Stiles, for the Lord's sake, take that regiment and put it into the works!"

Somewhat startled, I asked, "Do you really mean that, General?"

"Of course I do!"

Putting spurs to my horse, I trotted down the line of the regiment, calling out as I reached its right flank, "Right face, forward, run—march!" In a moment or so I had the men in the works, and returning, reached the General just as the old colonel got there and tendered his sword. General Ewell declined to receive the sword, ordered him back to his command, and turning to me said:—

"Do you still insist, sir, that you don't know tactics enough to justify your being promoted?"

The other movement was what is generally known as "the Dahlgren raid," which started in three co-operating cavalry columns, under Kilpatrick, Dahlgren and Custer, about the last of February, 1864, having Richmond for its objective, with the intention to sack and burn the city and kill the prominent Confederate officials. The history of the expedition is familiar. I did not come into personal contact with it in any way, and it cannot therefore be said to fall within the domain of reminiscence. If, however, the generally-accepted version of the famous "Dahlgren orders" be correct,—which would seem to be beyond question,—then it would be mild characterization to term them "infamous!"

It is a pleasure in this connection to note that General Lee's adjutant general has put on record the statement that "The disclaimer of General Meade was most candid and emphatic."

CHAPTER XVIII

CAMPAIGN OF '64—THE WILDERNESS

Grant—His Rough Chivalry—His Imperturbable Grit—His Theory of
Attrition—Its Effect Upon the Spirit of Lee's Army—An Artillery-
man of That Army in Campaign Trim—Sundown Prayer-meetings—
The Wilderness an Infantry Fight—A Cup of Coffee with Gen.
Ewell in the Forest—Ewell and Jackson—Longstreet Struck Down.

Without recanting the statement that Chancellorsville is
the most brilliant of Lee's single battles, I do not hesitate to
say that in my opinion—that is, if and so far as I am entitled to an opinion on the subject—the campaign of 1864,
from the Wilderness to Cold Harbor, inclusive, is the greatest of all Lee's campaigns—incomparably the greatest exhibition of generalship and soldiership ever given by the great
leader and his devoted followers.

Manifestly, one of the indispensable elements in any estimate of this campaign is the man now, for the first time, opposed to us. I do not propose to enter upon any extended
discussion or analysis of General Grant's powers. In common with the majority of the more intelligent soldiers of
the Army of Northern Virginia, I thought and think well
of him as a soldier, both as to character and capacity. We
all felt that he behaved handsomely, both to General Lee
and to his men, at Appomattox, and that, later, in standing
between Lee and his leading officers and the threatened
prosecutions for treason, he exhibited strong manhood and
sense of right. Many of us, too, have heard of other instances in his career of a rough chivalry always attractive
to men.

Just before the surrender, on my way to Petersburg as a
prisoner of war, I was standing on the roadside near General
Custis Lee when he was shocked by a report of the death of

his mother. I reminded him that, at such times, the wildest rumors were apt to be in circulation, and suggested his applying, by field telegraph, to Grant for leave to go to Richmond to ascertain the truth. He did so, and at once received leave, with transportation to Richmond. Upon finding there was nothing in the rumor, he reported promptly at the office of the provost marshal, but was there told that orders had been sent by General Grant that General Custis Lee should not be received as a prisoner of war, and he never succeeded in getting back into prison or any sort of captivity, though he made earnest efforts to do so.

As to Grant's grit and determination, all his predecessors together did not possess as much of these manly qualities, and we used to hear fine tales, too, of his imperturbability; for instance, that soon after he crossed the Rapidan in '64, when someone dashed up to his headquarters and announced with great excitement the capture of his pontoons, everyone else seemed to be shattered; but Grant deliberately removed his cigar from his mouth, blew a very fine smoke wreath or ring, and said quietly, "If I beat General Lee I sha'n't want any pontoons; and if General Lee beats me I can take all the men I intend to take back across the river on a log."

As to his capacity and our estimate of it, we did not think much of him as a strategist, but we did credit him with the vigor and trenchancy of mind that cut right through to the only plan upon which, as I believe, we ever could have been overcome—and the nerve to adhere to that plan relentlessly, remorsely to the very end, in spite of all the suffering and shrinking and weeping of the people. That plan was the simple but terrible one of *attrition*. As Colonel Taylor says:

If one hundred and forty thousand men are made to grapple in a death struggle with sixty thousand men; of the former, twenty thousand should survive the total annihilation of the latter, even though the price exacted for such destruction be in the ratio of two to one. Behold the theory of the Federal commander and an epitome of his construction of strategy, as exemplified on the sanguinary field extending from the Wilderness to James River.

But there were two other subordinate or rather preparatory points that were indispensable to the efficient working
of this scheme, and these also were settled by Grant, as we
understood at the time, before he would consent to take
charge of the main Federal army, the Army of the Potomac.
These points were, *first,* that he should have all the men he
wanted to fight the Army of Northern Virginia, and to that
end should control all the armies and levies of the Union, as
well as have access to all the recruiting grounds of the
world; and *second,* that the Confederate armies should not
be recruited from the only ground from which they could
possibly draw reinforcements—the military prisons of the
North—and to this end there should be no exchange of prisoners; that he did not wish to be reinforced from a source
that must give Lee man for man with him; that it would
be cheaper and more merciful in the end that Northern
soldiers should starve and rot in Southern prisons, the Confederate authorities, as he well knew, not having the resources to prevent this result.   And so he held right on to—
Appomattox.

If anyone deems this a shallow or weak or self-evident
scheme, then I for one do not agree with him.   It is not
the scheme or plan of a great military genius, and it is one
as to the moral justification of which I feel serious question;
but upon this basis, such as it is, we all felt Grant's power,
and I for one am willing to admit his greatness.

So much for the new theory of the struggle and the iron-
nerved and iron-souled man who had now taken charge of its
enforcement, and at the same time of our old antagonist, the
Army of the Potomac.

What effect, if any, did the new scheme, so far as it was
divulged or foreshadowed, have upon the spirits of our soldiery before the first shot was fired?   I find my comrades
differ radically as to this—I mean the more intelligent, observant and thoughtful of them, those whose views upon
such a subject should be worth most.   Willy Dame, one of
the best men of the old battery,—No. 4 at the fourth gun,
now the Rev. William M. Dame, D. D., of Baltimore, Md.,—
who has written a charming reminiscence or personal narra-

tive of this campaign, which ought to be in print, is emphatic in stating that the same old familiar spirit of light-hearted jollity and fun characterized the men of the battery, and of the commands they encountered and passed on the 4th and 5th of May, as we all poured from our winter quarters down into the Wilderness fight.

Billy, on the contrary,—my Billy, who has already appeared frequently in these reminiscences,—is of very different mind and memory touching this point. His recollection is that he was deeply impressed with the change, and as he had just made his way back from furlough through the army, and passed the night with an infantry regiment from his own county that contained many of his former schoolmates and friends and neighbors, he had enjoyed rather unusual opportunities for testing the matter. He did not detect any depression, or apprehension of disaster, or weakness of pluck or purpose; but he says he did miss the bounding, buoyant spirit, the effervescent outbursts, the quips, the jests, the jokes, the jollities, such as had usually characterized the first spring rousings of the army and the first meetings and minglings of the different commands as they shouted their tumultuous way to battle. He says that there seems to have sifted through the ranks the conviction that the struggle ahead of us was of a different character from any we had experienced in the past—a sort of premonition of the definite mathematical calculation, in whose hard, unyielding grip it was intended our future should be held and crushed.

Billy mentions as a fact, which tends to demonstrate that his analysis of the views and feelings of the men is correct, that every man in our battery who was absent on furlough the 1st of May, '64, returned instantly, some of them having just reached home. I cannot forbear mentioning that Billy was one of these latter, and my youngest brother, who had joined us from Georgia some months before, another. Some of these men arrived before we left camp at Morton's Ford; and others walked many hours, following the solemn sound of the firing, and found us in the midst of the sombre Wilderness, and two at bloody Spottsylvania. One of these two, a Petersburg boy, was delayed because of having fought at home one day under Beauregard against Butler. To this I may add the fact that another man of the battery, wounded during the campaign, apologized humbly to the captain for the imprudence which led to his wound, because, as he said, he well understood what the loss of one man meant to us now.

Upon the whole, while not formally deciding, as the Supreme Court of Texas recently did in a telegraph case,—as to the inherent difference between "Willy and Billy,"—yet I am inclined to think in this particular that Billy is right— that in the spring of 1864 there was very generally diffused throughout the army a more or less definite realization or consciousness that a new stage in the contest had been reached and a new theory broached; the mathematical theory that if one army outnumbers another more than two to one, and the larger can be indefinitely reinforced and the smaller not at all, then if the stronger side will but make up its mind to stand all the killing the weaker can do, and will keep it so made up, there can be but one result. Billy says the realization of this new order of things did not affect the resolution of the men, but that it did affect their spirits. I can only say I believe he is exactly correct.

Willy Dame, in his reminiscences above mentioned, gives a graphic account of the break up on the 4th of May of the winter camp of the Howitzers at Morton's Ford, in the course of which he presents this excellent picture of the full dress of a Confederate artilleryman in campaign fighting trim:

"In less than two hours after the order was given, the wagon was gone and the men left in 'campaign trim.' This meant that each man had one blanket, one small haversack, one change of underclothes, a canteen, cup and plate of tin, a knife and fork, and the clothes in which he stood. When ready to march, the blanket, rolled lengthwise, the ends brought together and strapped, hung from left shoulder across under right arm; the haversack—furnished with towel, soap, comb, knife and fork in various pockets, a change of underclothes in the main division, and whatever rations we happened to have in the other—hung on the left hip; the canteen, cup and plate, tied together, hung on the right; toothbrush, at will, stuck in two button holes of jacket or in haversack; tobacco bag hung to a breast button, pipe in pocket. In this rig, into which a fellow could get in just two minutes from a state of rest, the Confederate soldier considered himself all right and all ready for anything; in this he marched and in this he fought. Like the terrapin, 'all he had he carried on his back,' and this 'all' weighed about seven or eight pounds."

It will be noted that I have prefaced this catalogue by the expression "full dress." If I may be allowed, I would criticise the list as a little too full. I cannot recall ever having eaten out of a plate, or with a knife and fork, or having owned any or either of these articles while a private soldier, certainly not after the first few months of the war. And even after I became an officer, as adjutant of the battalion, I never carried plate, knife, or fork with me on my horse after the campaign opened. Colonel Cabell and I often ate out of the same tin cup or frying pan. Indeed, I carried nothing on my horse save a pair of very contracted saddle pockets and the cape of my overcoat, and Colonel Cabell carried his pockets, his overcoat, and an oil cloth. We slept together, lying on his oil cloth, he wearing his overcoat when cold, and both of us covered with my cape.

Another feature of Willy Dame's account of the Howitzer good-by to winter quarters, at the opening of the campaign of '64, is well worthy of record. He says that the very last public and general act of the men was, of their own account, to gather for a farewell religious service,—Bible reading, singing of a hymn, prayer, words of exhortation and cheer, —and that this meeting closed with a solemn resolution to hold such a service daily during the campaign when practicable, and as near as might be to the sunset hour, and then he adds:

"But however circumstanced, in battle, on the battle-line, in intervals of quiet, or otherwise, we held that prayer hour nearly every day, at sunset, during the entire campaign. And some of us thought and think, that the strange exemption our battery experienced, our little loss in the midst of unnumbered perils and incessant service during that awful campaign, was that in answer to our prayers the God of Battles 'covered our heads in the day of battle,' and was merciful to us, because we 'called upon Him.' If any think this is a 'fond fancy,' *we don't."*

Lee's ready acceptance of the gage of battle flung down by Grant, his daring and unexpected attack upon him in the thickets of the Wilderness, while it appeared to be the height of reckless audacity, was really the dictate of the wisest and most balanced prudence. In such a country the advantage of Grant's overwhelming preponderance of numbers was reduced to a *minimum*, and his great parks of artillery were absolutely useless. Besides, to retire and fall back upon an inner line was just what Grant desired and expected Lee to do, and would have been in exact furtherance of Grant's plans. In this instance, as usual, Lee's audacity meant the exercise of his unerring military instinct and judgment.

As just intimated, the Wilderness was essentially, yes, almost exclusively, an infantry fight, and we of the artillery saw, in fact, next to nothing of it, but hovered around its edge, thrilled and solemnized by the awful roar and swell and reverberation of the musketry and by the procession of wounded men and prisoners that streamed past.

The first incident of the march or the battle-field that impressed itself upon my memory is that early on the morning of the 5th of May, while riding ahead of the battalion, I came upon my old friend, General Ewell, crouching over a low fire at a "cross roads" in the forest, no one at the time being nigh except the two horses, and a courier who had charge of them and the two crutches. The old hero, who had lost a leg in battle, could not mount his horse alone and never rode without at least one attendant, who always followed close after him, carrying his "quadruped pegs," or rather his tripod pegs. The General was usually very thin and pale,— unusually so that morning,—but bright-eyed and alert. He was accustomed to ride a flea-bitten gray named Rifle, who was singularly like him—so far as a horse could be like a man. I knew Rifle well and noted that both he and his master looked a little as if they had been up all night and had not had breakfast.

I have before mentioned the General's great kindness to me. When we were alone he often called me "My child," and he embarrassed me by repeated recommendations for promotion. We were captured very late in the war, in the same battle and about the same time, and he not only honored and touched me greatly by expressing on the field and in the presence of several general officers, also prisoners, his high estimate of and strong affection for me, but he wrote me in prison one or two kind letters giving me earnest advice as to my immediate future.

On this morning he asked me to dismount and take a cup of coffee with him. He was a great cook. I remember on one occasion, later in the war, I met him in the outer defenses of Richmond, and he told me someone had sent him a turkey leg which he was going to "devil;" that he was strong on that particular dish; that his staff would be away, and I must come around that evening and share it with him. I willingly accepted on both occasions, and on both greatly enjoyed a chat with the General and the unaccustomed treat. On this Wilderness morning, while we were drinking our coffee, I asked him if he had any objection to telling me his orders, and he answered briskly, "No, sir; none at all—just the orders I like—to go right down the plank road and strike the enemy wherever I find him."

It is glory enough for any man to have been Stonewall Jackson's trusted lieutenant. Ewell simply worshiped his great commander; indeed, it was this worship that led him to the highest. He worshiped Jackson, and yet they were not exactly kindred spirits. The following little story, which I quote from Dr. McGuire, but which I heard many times before reading it in print, well illustrates one of the points of difference between them.

At the battle of Port Republic an officer commanding a regiment of Federal soldiers and riding a snow-white horse was very conspicuous for his gallantry. He frequently exposed himself to the fire of our men in the most reckless way. So splendid was this man's courage that General Ewell, one of the most chivalrous gentlemen I ever knew, at some risk to his own life, rode down the line and called to his men not to shoot the man on the white horse. After a while, however, the officer and the white horse went down. A day or two after, when General Jackson learned of the incident, he sent for General Ewell and told him not to do such a thing again; that this was no ordinary war, and the brave and gallant Federal officers were the very kind that must be killed. "Shoot the brave officers and the cowards will run away and take the men with them?"

I do not say Jackson was not right, but I do say that in this double picture dear Old Dick's is the most lovable.

It is a little singular that though nominally attached to his command longer than any other, yet I probably had less acquaintance and association with General Longstreet than with any other of the more prominent generals of the Confederate army in Virginia. Indeed I do not recall ever having spoken to him or having heard him utter so much as one word. True, he was several times sent off on detached service, upon which we did not accompany him, and while nominally of his corps we had just been for some five months under Ewell's command; yet, after making allowance for all this, I could not but feel that there must be something in the nature of the man himself to account for the fact that I knew so little of him. Colonel Freemantle, of the Cold Stream Guards, who wrote a very charming diary entitled, I think, "Two Months in the Confederate Lines," says, however, if I rightly remember, that the relations between Longstreet and his staff were exceptionally pleasant, and reminded him more of those which obtained in the British service than any others he observed in America. In this Wilderness fight I was suddenly brought in contact with a scene which greatly affected my conception of the man under the regalia of the general.

It may not have been generally observed that Jackson and Longstreet were both struck down in the Wilderness, just one year apart, each at the crisis of the most brilliant and, up to the moment of his fall, the most successful movement of his career as a soldier, and each by the fire of his own men. I had been sent forward, perhaps to look for some place where we might get into the fight, when I observed an excited gathering some distance back of the lines, and pressing toward it I heard that General Longstreet had just been shot down and was being put into an ambulance. I could not learn anything definite as to the character of his wound, but only that it was serious—some said he was dead. When the ambulance moved off, I followed it a little way, being anxious for trustworthy news of the General. The members of his staff surrounded the vehicle, some riding in front, some on one side and some on the other, and some behind. One, I remember, stood upon the rear step of the ambulance, seeming to desire to be as near him as possible. I never on any occasion during the four years of the war saw a group of officers and gentlemen more deeply distressed. They were literally bowed down with grief. All of them were in tears. One, by whose side I rode for some distance, was himself severely hurt, but he made no allusion to his wound, and I do not believe he felt it. It was not alone the general they admired who had been shot down—it was, rather, the man they loved.

I rode up to the ambulance and looked in. They had taken off Longstreet's hat and coat and boots. The blood had paled out of his face and its somewhat gross aspect was gone. I noticed how white and dome-like his great forehead looked and, with scarcely less reverent admiration, how spotless white his socks and his fine gauze undervest, save where the black red gore from his breast and shoulder had stained it. While I gazed at his massive frame, lying so still, except when it rocked inertly with the lurch of the vehicle, his eyelids frayed apart till I could see a delicate line of blue between them, and then he very quietly moved his unwounded arm and, with his thumb and two fingers, carefully lifted the saturated undershirt from his chest, holding it up a moment, and heaved a deep sigh. He is not dead, I said to myself, and he is calm and entirely master of the situation—he is both greater and more attractive than I have heretofore thought him.

Some years after the war I read in a newspaper a short paragraph which brought this scene vividly to my mind. Longstreet, at the Wilderness, was wounded in the shoulder, fighting Hancock's corps; Hancock had previously been wounded in the thigh, fighting Longstreet's. One evening while Hancock was in command in New Orleans, he and Longstreet entered Hancock's theatre box together. The entire audience rose and burst into enthusiastic cheers, and refused to be seated or to be quiet until the two generals advanced together to the front of the box, when Hancock said: "Ladies and Gentlemen—I have the pleasure of presenting to you my friend, General Longstreet, a gentleman to whom I am indebted for an ungraceful limp, and whom I had the misfortune to wing in the same contest."

Both sides suffered severely in the Wilderness, but except perhaps upon the basis of Grant's mathematical theory of attrition, the Confederates got decidedly the best of the fighting. Next came the race for Spottsylvania Court House, and the checkmate of Warren's corps by Stuart's dismounted cavalry. Such were the prominent features of the entire campaign. It was a succession of death grapples and recoils and races for new position, and several times during the campaign the race was so close and tense and clearly defined that we could determine the exact location of the Federal column by the cloud of dust that overhung and crept along the horizon parallel to our own advance.

CHAPTER XIX

SPOTTSYLVANIA

Death of a Gallant Boy—Mickey Free Hard to Kill—The 10th and 12th of May—Handsome Conduct of the "Napoleon Section" of the Howitzers—Frying Pan as Sword and Banner—Prayer with a Dying Federal Soldier—"Trot Out Your Deaf Man and Your Old Doctor"—The Base of the Bloody Angle—The Musketry Fire—Majestic Equipoise of Marse Robert.

At Spottsylvania Court House, when the artillery and infantry arrived and took the place of the gallant cavalrymen, who had saved the day and the place for us, the guns of our battalion, as I remember, were the first to reach the field. As adjutant, I had ridden with the old battery to its selected position, and, these guns in place, had returned to the column and was aiding in locating another of the batteries, when the fire upon the Howitzer position became so heavy that I galloped back to see how they were faring and if they needed anything. As I rode rapidly in rear of the first gun of the battery, at which my youngest brother, Eugene, had been made a driver, I noted that the fire had slackened considerably, but that one of his horses had been killed; that he had very practically pulled the dead horse around into proper position, and he and the driver of the other team were fast constructing quite a passable earthwork over and about him. Just as I observed this, "Genie" caught sight of me, and springing up, shouted after me, in fine voice and good old Georgia nursery phrase:

"Bubba, Bubba, I wasn't scared a bit—not a bit!"

A line of stalwart veteran infantry was lying down behind the guns, and as the plucky, but uninitiated, boy shouted this reassuring greeting, several of these seasoned old fellows raised up partly and looked around, and one of them called out, "Where's that fellow that wasn't scared a bit? He must be some greenhorn or fool!" And then there was a burst of laughter at the lad's expense. But I shouted back to him that he musn't mind them; that they were just guying him, and were glad enough to be behind his gun and his dead horse, too.

At one of the positions the Howitzers took on these lines I witnessed a striking scene, or rather the climax of it—the rest was told me shortly after I reached the guns.

There was a tall, black-haired, pale-faced boy in the company, named Cary Eggleston, a cousin, I think, of George Cary Eggleston, whom he strongly resembled. He was No. 1 at the third gun; said to be the best No. 1 in the battery, and even before his heroic end, known to be a fellow of most gallant spirit. He was one of that small class of men who really love a fight for its own sake. He was not yet fully developed, and ordinarily appeared rather gangling and loose-jointed, but it required only the thrill of action to inspire him and to make his movements as graceful as they were powerful and effective. His "manual of the piece" was really superb when his gun was hotly engaged.

At the very height of a fierce flurry his left arm was nearly severed from his body by a fragment of shell. At that moment a comrade, who had returned while on furlough and had walked in all nearly forty miles to reach us, came running up to his gun. The disabled No. 1 handed him the rammer, saying:

"Here, Johnny, take it! You haven't had any fun yet." When he had thus surrendered his scepter and appointed his own successor, he had a crude tourniquet applied to his arm; but insisted upon walking to the field hospital, refusing a litter or even a man to accompany him.

I had been with another of the batteries of the battalion, but hearing the rapid firing about the Howitzer position, was galloping down there, when I saw Eggleston walking out. He had his unwounded side toward me, and I called to him to know where and why he was going. He answered by turning his other side and holding up the stump, from which his shattered arm hung by ragged shirt sleeve and torn tendon, and then he shook the clenched fist of his sound arm toward the Federal lines, shouting to me that he would soon be back to fight them with that. The unconquerable boy died the following evening.

I have spoken several times of the "Howitzer position" in the Spottsylvania lines. Up to the 12th of May I think only two of their guns were on the main or front line, and even on the 12th the four were not together. Prior to the 12th two rifles of this battery and two of the Troupe Artillery were some distance back upon a hill, having been so placed with a view of engaging certain of the enemy's batteries to the relief of our front line, and of having a wider range and sweep of the attacking lines and columns.

One evening, about the 9th of May, I was riding into the position of some of our guns on the front line and passing through a little copse of woods, there being at the time quite a sharp musketry fire on the lines, and bullets clinking against the resinous boles of the pine trees about me, when suddenly my horse, Mickey Free, was shot, the ball making a loud slap when it struck. He sprang aside, but settled right down again to his course, and it was some little time before I could find any trace of the shot. I soon discovered, however, that the ball had cut into one of my saddle pockets, but not through it, and there it was, inside. A moment later he was struck again, and this time reared and plunged violently. Glancing around I saw that the ball had entered back of my legs about the mid line of his body one side and had come out about opposite on the other, and, as he persisted in lying down and rolling, I concluded that the poor fellow was mortally hurt, and sprang off, endeavoring to remove saddle and bridle, which I finally accomplished, with some difficulty and at some peril of being kicked or rolled upon. I looked at him a few moments in great distress, but the fire becoming really heavy, I threw saddle and bridle across my shoulder and toddled into the works on foot.

My recollection is that when the attack had been repulsed I went back to see if Mickey was dead, or if I could do anything for him, but that he had disappeared; that I could not track him far and soon gave it up, concluding I would never see him again. I certainly laid down that night one of *"Lee's Miserables,"* as we used to term ourselves, after reading Victor Hugo's great novel—a soldier edition of his works in Confederate "sheep's wool paper" having been distributed largely throughout the army the preceding winter. Judge of my surprise and delight at learning, early in the morning, that Mickey had in some mysterious way found our headquarter wagon and was being cared for there, and that he did not seem to be contemplating immediate death, but on the contrary had drunk copiously and eaten sparingly, as was a Confederate artillery horse's duty to do. As soon as I could get off I went back to see the dear old fellow, and there he was, as good as ever, except that a rope appeared to have been drawn around the lower part of his body, just under the skin, and a little back of the proper line of the saddle girth. The Minie bullet had of course been deflected, and had passed beneath the skin, half around his body, without penetrating the cavity.

My dear friend, Willy Dame, in his reminiscences already quoted, says some very pleasant and complimentary things of "our old adjutant." These things I do not pretend to gainsay or deny. It would be easy to deny and not hard, perhaps, to disprove them; but motive is lacking. Why should I? The fact is, I shouldn't and I won't. But there are other things, or at least there is one other thing he says, and says elaborately, with date and circumstance,—the date is the 10th of May—calculated to bring my gray hair into ridicule and contempt, which, of course, I deny, even if I cannot disprove. The difficulty of proving a negative is well understood. I certainly go as far as this—I have no recollection whatever of such occurrence or utterance as he mentions, barring the nasty performances of those twenty-pounder Parrott shells. I recollect a good many of these quite similar to what Willy describes. But here is what he says:

Robert Stiles, the adjutant of the battalion, who had been until lately a member of our battery and was very devoted to it and his comrades in it, had come to the line to see how we were getting on, and gave us news of other parts of the line. He, Beau Barnes, and others of us, were standing by our guns talking, when a twenty-pounder Parrott shell came grazing just over our guns, passed on, and about forty yards behind us struck a pine tree about two and a half to three feet in diameter. The shell had turned. It struck that big tree sideways and cut it entirely off, and threw it from the stump. It fell in an upright position, struck the ground, stood for an instant and then came crashing down. It was a very creepy suggestion of what that shell might have done to one of us. A few moments after, another struck the ground right by us and ricochetted. After it passed us, as was frequently the case, we caught sight of it and followed its upward flight until it seemed to be going straight to the sky.

Stiles said, "There it goes, as though flung by the hand of a giant." Beau Barnes, who was not poetical, exclaimed, "Giant be darned; there ain't any giant can fling 'em like that!" He was right!

If the foregoing was not written with malicious intent to expose me to the scorn of all sensible and practical people, then my belief is that Willy Dame dreamed the absurd story; but if Barnes and I did speak under the circumstances mentioned, and both are correctly quoted, then I admit the redoubtable "Beau" had decidedly the best of it, and I apologize humbly.

The 10th of May, '64, was preeminently a day of battle with the Army of Northern Virginia. I know, of course, that the 12th is commonly regarded as the pivotal day, the great day, and the Bloody Angle as the pivotal place, the great place, of the Spottsylvania fights, and that for an hour or so, along the sides and base of that angle, the musketry fire is said to have been heavier than it ever was at any other place in all the world, or for any other hour in all the tide of time. But for frequency and pertinacity of attack, and repetition and constancy of repulse, I question if the left of General Lee's line on the 10th of May, 1864, has ever been surpassed. I cannot pretend to identify the separate attacks or to distinguish between them, but should think there must have been at least a dozen of them. One marked feature was that, while fresh troops poured to almost every charge, the same muskets in the hands of the same men met the first attack in the morning and the last at night; and so it was that the men who in the early morning were so full of fight and fun that they leaped upon the breastworks and shouted to the retiring Federals to come a little closer the next time, as they did not care to go so far after the clothes and shoes and muskets—were so weary and worn and heavy at night that they could scarcely be roused to meet the charging enemy.

The troops supporting the two Napoleon guns of the Howitzers were, as I remember, the Seventh (or Eighth) Georgia and the First Texas. Toward the close of the day everything seemed to have quieted down, in a sort of implied truce. There was absolutely no fire, either of musketry or cannon. Our weary, hungry infantry stacked arms and were cooking their mean and meagre little rations. Someone rose up, and looking over the works—it was shading down a little toward the dark—cried out: "Hello! What's this? Why, here come our men on a run, from—no, by Heavens! it's the Yankees!" and before anyone could realize the situation, or even start toward the stacked muskets, the Federal column broke over the little work, between our troops and their arms, bayonetted or shot two or three who were asleep before they could even awake, and dashed upon the men crouched over their low fires—with cooking utensils instead of weapons in their hands. Of course they ran. What else could they do?

The Howitzers—only the left, or Napoleon section, was there—sprang to their guns, swinging them around to bear inside our lines, double-shotted them with canister and fairly spouted it into the Federals, whose formation had been broken in the rush and the plunge over the works, and who seemed to be somewhat massed and huddled and hesitating, but only a few rods away. Quicker almost than I can tell it, our infantry supports, than whom there were not two better regiments in the army, had rallied and gotten to their arms, and then they opened out into a V-shape, and fairly tore the head of the Federal column to pieces. In an incredibly short time those who were able to do so turned to fly and our infantry were following them over the intrenchments; but it is doubtful whether this would have been the result had it not been for the prompt and gallant action of the artillery.

There was an old Captain Hunter,—it seems difficult to determine whether of the Texas or the Georgia regiment,— who had the handle of his frying pan in his hand, holding the pan over the hot coals, with his little slice of meat sizzling in it, when the enemy broke over. He had his back to them, and the first thing he knew his men were scampering past him like frightened sheep. He had not been accustomed to that style of movement among them, and he sprang up and tore after them, showering them with hot grease and hotter profanity, but never letting go his frying pan. On the contrary, he slapped right and left with the sooty, burning bottom, distributing his favors impartially on Federal and Confederate alike—several of his own men bearing the black and ugly brand on their cheeks for a long time after and occasionally having to bear also the captain's curses for having made him lose his meat that evening. He actually led the counter-charge, leaping upon the works, wielding and waving his frying pan, at once as sword and banner.

When it became evident that the attack had failed, I suggested to the chaplain—who happened to be with the Howitzer guns, perhaps for that sundown prayer meeting which Willy Dame mentioned—that there might be some demand for his ministrations where the enemy had broken over; so we walked up there and found their dead and dying piled higher than the works themselves. It was almost dark, but as we drew near we saw a wounded Federal soldier clutch the pantaloons of Captain Hunter, who at that moment was passing by, frying pan in hand, and heard him ask, with intense eagerness: "Can you pray, sir? Can you pray?" The old captain looked down at him with a peculiar expression, and pulled away, saying, "No, my friend, I don't wish you any harm now, but praying's not exactly my trade."

I said to the chaplain, "Let's go to that man." As we came up he caught my pants in the same way and uttered the same words: "Can you pray, sir? Can you pray?" I bent over the poor fellow, turned back his blouse, and saw that a large canister shot had passed through his chest at such a point that the wound must necessarily prove mortal, and that soon. We both knelt down by him, and I took his hand in mine and said: "My friend, you haven't much time left for prayer, but if you will say after me just these simple words, with heart as well as lips, all will be well with you: 'God have mercy on me, a sinner, for Jesus Christ's sake.'"

I never saw such intensity in human gaze, nor ever heard such intensity in human voice, as in the gaze and voice of that dying man as he held my hand and looked into my face, repeating the simple, awful, yet reassuring words I had dictated. He uttered them again and again, with the death rattle in his throat and the death tremor in his frame, until someone shouted, "They are coming again!" and we broke away and ran down to the guns. It proved to be a false alarm, and we returned immediately—but he was dead, yes, dead and half-stripped; but I managed to get my hand upon his blouse a moment and looked at the buttons. He was from the far-off State of Maine.

It was long before I slept that night. It had been an unparalleled day. The last hour, especially, had brought together elements so diverse and so tremendous, that heart and brain were overstrained in attempting to harmonize and assimilate them. This was the first time in all my career as a soldier that I had heard from a dying man on the battle-field any expression that indicated even so much as a belief in the existence of any other world than this.

What did it all mean? When that Federal soldier and I had our brief conference and prayer on the dividing line between the two worlds, neither of us felt the slightest tremor of uncertainty about it. To both of us the other world was as certainly existing as this, and infinitely greater. Would I ever see him again? If so, would both of us realize that our few moments of communion and of prayer had meant more perhaps than all the struggles, that day, of the great embattled armies? I went to sleep at last that night, as I shall go this night, feeling that it all was and is too much for me, and committing myself and all my perplexities to the One Being who is "sufficient for these things," and able to lead us safely through such a world and such experiences.

It is an interesting coincidence that on this very day, the 10th of May, '64, at the point christened two days later as "The Bloody Angle," the Second Howitzers rendered a service even more important and distinguished perhaps than the gallant conduct of the First Company just recorded; a service which, in the opinion of prominent officers thoroughly acquainted with the facts and every way competent and qualified to judge, was deemed to have saved General Lee's army from being cut in twain.

There is one other feature or incident of the closing fight of the 10th of May which may be worthy of record, not alone because of its essentially amusing nature, but also because of a very pleasant after-clap or remainder of it later on. There were two men in the First Howitzers, older than most of us, of exceptionally high character and courage, who, because of the deafness of the one and the lack of a certain physical flexibility and adaptation in the other, were not well fitted for regular places in the detachment or service about the gun. For a time one or both of them took the position of driver, but this scarcely seemed fitting, and finally they were both classed as "supernumeraries," but with special duties as our company ambulance corps, having charge, under the surgeon of the battalion, of our company litters and our other simple medical and surgical outfit. For this and other reasons, the elder of these two good and gritty soldiers was always called "Doctor."

When the break occurred these two men, always on the extremest forward verge of our battle line, were overwhelmed with amazement, not so much at the irruption of the enemy, as at what seemed to be the demoralized rout of the Georgians and Texans. They ran in among them asking explanation of their conduct, then appealing to them and exhorting them—the Doctor in most courteous and lofty phrase: "Gentlemen, what does this mean? You certainly are not flying before the enemy! Turn, for God's sake; turn, and drive them out!" Then, with indignant outburst: "Halt! you infernal cowards!" and suiting the action to the word, these choleric cannoneers tore the carrying poles out of their litters, and sprang among and in front of the fugitives, belaboring them right and left, till they turned, and then turned with them, following up the retreating enemy with their wooden spears.

Some weeks later, after we had reached Petersburg, in the nick of time to keep Burnside out of the town, and had taken up what promised to be a permanent position and were just dozing off into our first nap in forty-eight hours, an infantry command passing by, in the darkness, stumbled over the trail handspikes of our guns and broke out in the usual style:

"O, of course! Here's that infernal artillery again; always in the way, blocking the roads by day and tripping us up at night. What battery is this, any way?"

Some fellow, not yet clean gone in slumber, grunted out: "First Company, Richmond Howitzers."

What a change! Instantly there was a perfect chorus of greetings from the warm-hearted Texans.

"Boys, here are the Howitzers! Where's your old deaf man? Trot out your old Doctor. They're the jockeys for us. We are going to stay right here. We won't get a chance to run if these plucky Howitzer boys are with us."

Billy tells me that he remembers, word for word, the last crisp sentence Col. Stephen D. Lee uttered the morning he complimented the old battery on the field of Frazier's Farm; that he said, "Men, hereafter when I want a battery, I'll know where to get one!" Two years later, at the base of the Bloody Angle, General Ewell seems to have been of the same opinion. He held our centre, which had just been pierced and smashed and his artillery captured. He wanted guns to stay the rout and steady his men, and he sent to the extreme left for Cabell's Battalion. I do not mean that the old battalion, or either of its batteries, was counted among the most brilliant artillery commands of the army, but I do claim that the command did have and did deserve the reputation of "staying where it was put," and of doing its work reliably and well.

The 11th had been a sort of off-day with us, very little business doing; but the 12th made up for it. As I remember, it was yet early on the morning of the 12th that we were sent for. We went at once, and did not stand upon the order of our going, though I think two guns of the Howitzers led the column, followed by two guns of Carlton's battery, the Troupe Artillery. If I remember correctly, our other guns occupied positions on the line from which they could not be withdrawn. As Colonel Cabell and I rode ahead, as before mentioned in another connection, to learn precisely where the guns were to be placed, we passed General Lee on horseback, or he passed us. He had only one or two attendants with him. His face was more serious than I had ever seen it, but showed no trace of excitement or alarm. Numbers of demoralized men were streaming past him and his voice was deep as the growl of a tempest as he said: "Shame on you, men; shame on you! Go back to your regiments; go back to your regiments!"

I remember thinking at the moment that it was the only time I ever knew his faintest wish not to be instantly responded to by his troops; but something I have since read induces me to question whether he did not refer to some special rendezvous, somewhere in the rear, appointed for the remnants of the shattered commands to rally to. Be this as it may, every soldier of experience knows that when a man has reached a certain point of demoralization and until he has settled down again past that point, it is absolutely useless to attempt to rouse him to a sense of duty or of honor. I have seen many a man substantially in the condition of the fellow who, as he executed a flying leap over the musket of the guard threatening to shoot and crying "Halt!"—called back, "Give any man fifty dollars to halt me, but can't halt myself!"

When we came back to our four guns and were leading them to the lines and the positions selected for them, just as we were turning down a little declivity, we passed again within a few feet of General Lee, seated upon his horse on the crest of the hill, this time entirely alone, not even a courier with him. I was much impressed with the calmness and perfect poise of his bearing, though his centre had just been pierced by forty thousand men and the fate of his army trembled in the balance. He was completely exposed to the

Federal fire, which was very heavy. A half dozen of our men were wounded in making this short descent. In this connection I have recently heard from a courier—who, with others, had ridden with the General to the point where we saw him—that, observing and remarking upon the peril to which they were subjected, he ordered all his couriers to protect themselves behind an old brick kiln, some one hundred and fifty yards to the left, until their services were required, but refused to go there himself. This habit of exposing himself to fire, as they sometimes thought, unnecessarily, was the only point in which his soldiers felt that Lee ever did wrong. The superb stories of the several occasions during this campaign when his men refused to advance until he retired, and, with tears streaming down their faces, led his horse to the rear, are too familiar to justify repetition, especially as I did not happen to be an eye-witness of either of these impressive scenes.

Our guns were put in at the left base of the Salient, and there, in full sight and but a short distance up the side of the angle, stood two or three of the guns from which our men had been driven, or at which they had been captured. The Howitzers had two clumsy iron three-inch rifles, and Captain McCarthy and I offered, with volunteers from that company, to draw these captured guns back into our lines, provided we were allowed to exchange our two iron guns for two of these, which were brass Napoleons. This would have given the battery a uniform armament and prevented the frequent separation of the sections. There was not at the time a Federal soldier in sight, and some of us walked out to or near these guns without being fired upon. It might have been a perilous undertaking, yet I think General Ewell would have given his consent; but the officer to whose command the guns belonged protested, saying he would himself have them drawn off later in the day. If it ever could have been done, the opportunity was brief; later it became impracticable, and the guns were permanently lost.

Barrett, Colonel Cabell's plucky little courier, rode almost into the works with us, and we had left our horses with him, close up, but in a position which we thought afforded some protection. In a few moments someone shouted to me that Barrett was calling lustily for me. I ran back where I had left him and was distressed to see my good horse, Mickey, stretched on the ground. Barrett said he had just been killed by a piece of shell which struck him in the head. The poor fellow's limbs were still quivering. I could see no wound of any consequence about the head or anywhere else; while I was examining him he shuddered violently, sprang up, snorted a little blood and was again "as good as new." As soon as practicable, however, we sent Barrett and the three horses behind that brick kiln back on the hill, or to some place near by of comparative safety. I was afraid that Mickey, who seemed to have "gotten his hand in," might keep up this trick of getting "killed," as Barrett said, once too often. I may as well say. right here that the noble horse got safely through the war, but was captured with his master at Sailor's Creek.

When our guns first entered the works, or rather were stationed on the line just back of the little trench, there seemed to be comparatively few infantrymen about. One thing that pleased us greatly was, that our old Mississippi brigade, Barksdale's, or Humphreys', was supporting us; but it must have been just the end of their brigade line, and a very thin line it was. We saw nothing of the major-general of our division. General Rodes, of Ewell's corps, was the only major-general we saw. He was a man of very striking appearance, of erect, fine figure and martial bearing. He constantly passed and repassed in rear of our guns, riding a black horse that champed his bit and tossed his head proudly, until his neck and shoulders were flecked with white froth, seeming to be conscious that he carried Cæsar. Rodes' eyes were everywhere, and every now and then he would stop to attend to some detail of the arrangement of his line or his troops, and then ride on again, humming to himself and catching the ends of his long, tawny moustache between his lips.

It had rained hard all night and was drizzling all day, and everything was wet, soggy, muddy, and comfortless. General Ewell made his headquarters not far off, and seemed busy and apprehensive, and we gathered from everything we saw and heard, especially from General Lee's taking his position so near, that he and his generals anticipated a renewal of the attack at or about this point. From the time of our first approach, stragglers from various commands had been streaming past. I noticed that most of them had their arms and did not seem to be very badly shattered, and I tried hard to induce some of them to turn in and reinforce our thin infantry line. But they would not hearken to the voice of the charmer, charming never so wisely, and finally I appealed to General Rodes and asked him for a detail of men to throw off a short line at right angles to the works so as to catch and turn in these stragglers. He readily assented, and we soon had a strong, full line, though at first neither Rodes' own men nor our Mississippians seemed to appreciate this style of reinforcement.

One point more, with regard to our experience at the left base of the Salient, and we have done with the "Bloody Angle." Every soldier who was there, if he opens his mouth to speak or takes up his pen to write, seems to feel it solemnly incumbent upon him to expatiate upon the fearful fire of musketry. What I have to say about the matter will doubtless prove surprising and disappointing to many; but first let me quote Colonel Taylor's account of it, from pages 130 and 131 of his invaluable work, so frequently referred to:

* * * The army was thus cut in twain, and the situation was well calculated to test the skill of its commander and the nerve and courage of the men. Dispositions were immediately made to repair the breach, and troops were moved up to the right and left to dispute the further progress of the assaulting column. Then occurred the most remarkable musketry fire of the war—from the sides of the Salient, in the possession of the Federals, and the new line forming the base of the triangle, occupied by the Confederates, poured forth from continuous lines of hissing fire an incessant, terrific hail of deadly missiles. No living man nor thing could· stand in the doomed space embraced within those angry lines; even large trees were felled, their trunks cut in twain by the bullets of small arms.

Every intelligent soldier, on either side, is aware of Colonel Taylor's deserved reputation for careful and unprejudiced observation and investigation, and for correct and accurate statement, and General Fitz Lee, in his "Life of General Robert E. Lee," at p. 335, fully agrees with him, saying: "The musketry fire, with its terrific leaden hail, was beyond comparison the heaviest of the four years of war. In the bitter struggle, trees, large and small, fell, cut down by bullets."

Still, I am bound to say I saw nothing that approached a justification of these vivid and powerful descriptions. Of course the fire was at times heavy, but at no time, *in front of our position,* did it approximate, for example, the intensity of the fire during the great attack at Cold Harbor, a few weeks later. One singular feature of the matter is that we appear to have been at the very place and the very time where this fire is said to have occurred; for we were sent for by General Ewell, as I recollect, early on the morning of the 12th, and we remained at the left base of the Salient and within sight of some of the captured guns all that day and until the line was moved back out of the bottom, to the crest of the little ridge above mentioned. The only explanation I can suggest is that the fighting must have been much hotter *further to the right.*

It may be well just here to explain, while we cannot excuse, the existence not alone of the great Salient of Spottsylvania, with its soldier nickname of "Bloody Angle," and its fearful lesson of calamity, but also of other like faulty formations in our Confederate battle lines.

It was noticeable toward the close of the war what skilful, practical engineers the rank and file of the Army of Northern Virginia had become; how quickly and unerringly they detected and how unsparingly they condemned an untenable line—that is, where they were unprejudiced critics, as for instance, where fresh troops were brought in to reinforce or relieve a command already in position. I seem to hear, even now, their slashing, impudent, outspoken comment:

"Boys, what infernal fool do you reckon laid out this line? Why, anyone can see we can't hold it. We are certain to be enfiladed on this flank, and the Yankees can even take us in reverse over yonder. Let's fall back to that ridge we just passed!"

But where troops had themselves originally taken position, it was a very different matter. This was one point where Johnny was disposed to be unreasonable and insubordinate—not to consider consequences or to obey orders. He did not like to fall back from any position he had himself established by hard fighting, especially if it was in advance of the general line. So well recognized was his attitude in this regard that it had well nigh passed into a proverb:

"No, sir! *We fought for this dirt, and we're going to hold it.* The men on our right and left ought to be here alongside of us, and would be if they had fought as hard as we did!"

Of course, Johnny would not violate or forget the fundamental maxim of geometry and war, that *a line must be continuous;* that his right must be somebody's left and his left somebody's right; but the furthest he would go in recognition of the maxim was the compromise of bending back his flanks, so as to connect with the troops on his right and left who had failed to keep up. So, this was done, he did not seem to care how irregular the general line of battle was. One cannot look at a map of any of our great battles without being impressed with the tortuous character of our lines.

I have myself heard a major-general send a message back to Army Headquarters, by a staff officer of General Lee, that he didn't see why his division should be expected to abandon the position they had fought for just to accommodate General ———, whose troops had fallen back where his had driven the enemy. On that very occasion, if my memory serves me, this selfish, stupid obstinacy cost us the lives of hundreds of men.

One word more in connection with the straightening of our lines. Of course we moved after dark, and, as I remember, but a short distance. After we got to our new position I discovered that I had lost my pocket-knife, or some such trivial article of personal outfit, but difficult to replace; so, contrary to Colonel Cabell's advice—he didn't forbid my going—I went back on foot and in the dark to look, or feel, for it. I had no difficulty in finding the spot where we had been lying, and began to grope and feel about for the knife, having at the time an unpleasant consciousness that I was running a very foolish and unjustifiable risk, for the minies were hissing and singing and spatting all about me. There was a man near me, also on his hands and knees, looking or feeling for something. While glancing at the shape, dimly outlined, I heard the unmistakable thud of a bullet striking flesh. There was a muffled outcry, and the crouching or kneeling figure lay stretched upon the ground. I went to it and felt it. The man was dead. In a very brief time I was back in our new position and not thinking of pocket-knives.

CHAPTER XX

Another Slide to the East, and Another, and Another—The Armies Straining Like Two Coursers, Side by Side, for the Next Goal— Grant Waiting for Reinforcements—Lee Seriously Indisposed—One of His Three Corps Commanders Disabled by Wounds, Another by Sickness—Mickey and the Children—"It Beats a Furlough Hollow" —A Baby in Battle—Death of Lawrence M. Keitt and Demoralization of His Command—Splendid Services of Lieut. Robt. Falligant, of Georgia, with a Single Gun—Hot Fighting the Evening of June 1st—Building Roads and Bridges and Getting Ready June 2d— Removal of Falligant's Lone Gun at Night.

After feeling our lines, feinting several times, and making, on the 18th, what might perhaps be termed a genuine attack, Grant, on the evening of the 20th, slid off toward Bowling Green; but although he got a little the start of Lee, yet, when he reached his immediate objective, Lee was in line of battle at Hanover Junction, directly across the line of further progress. It is the belief of many intelligent Confederate officers that if Lee had not been attacked by disabling disease, the movements of the two armies about the North Anna would have had a very different termination. Grant ran great risk in taking his army to the southern bank of the river with Lee on the stream between his two wings; it is fair to add that he seems to have realized his peril and to have withdrawn in good time.

General Lee's indisposition, about this time, was really serious. Some of us will never forget how shocked and alarmed we were at seeing him in an ambulance. General Early, in his address before mentioned, says of this matter:

One of his three corps commanders had been disabled by wounds at the Wilderness, and another was too sick to command his corps, while he himself was suffering from a most annoying and weakening disease. In fact nothing but his own determined will enabled him to keep the field at all; and it was there rendered more manifest than ever that he was the head and front, the very life and soul of his army.

It was about this date that General Lee, as I remember a second time, broached the idea that he might be compelled to retire—an idea which no one else could contemplate with any sort of composure; happily, as soon as the disease was checked his superb physical powers came to his aid, and he soon rallied and regained his customary vigor and spirits.

Perhaps no other position of equal labor and responsibility can be mentioned, nor one which makes such drafts upon human strength and endurance, as the command of a great army in a time of active service. I recall during the Gettysburg campaign being equally impressed with the force of this general proposition, and with the almost incredible physical powers of General Lee. On two occasions, just before and just after we recrossed the Potomac, I was sent upon an errand which required my visiting army, corps, and division headquarters, and, so far as practicable, seeing the respective commanding officers in person. On the first round I did not find General Lee at his quarters, and was told that he had ridden down the road to the lines. When I reached the lines I heard he had passed out in front. Following him up, I found him in the rain with a single piece of horse artillery, feeling the enemy. My second ride was made largely at night, and, as I remember, every officer I desired to see was asleep, except at Army Headquarters, where I found Colonel Taylor in his tent on his knees, with his prayer-book open before him, and General Lee in his tent, wide-awake, poring over a map stretched upon a temporary table of rough plank, with a tallow candle stuck in a bottle for a light. I remember saying to myself, as I delivered my message and withdrew, "Does he never, never sleep?"

Again General Grant slid to the east, and we moved off upon a parallel line. I think it was during this detour—or it may have been an earlier or a later one—that I was sent ahead, upon a road which led through a tract of country which had not been desolated by the encampments or the battles of armies, to select a night's resting place for the battalion. Forests were standing untouched, farm lands were protected by fences, crops were green and untrampled, birds were singing, flowers blooming--Eden everywhere. Even my horse seemed to feel the change from the crowded roads, the deadly lines, the dust, the dirt, the mud, the blood, the horror. We were passing through a quiet wood at a brisk walk, when suddenly he roused himself and quickened his gait, breaking of his own accord into a long trot, his beautiful, sensitive ears playing back and forth in the unmistakable way which, in a fine horse, indicates that he catches sounds interesting and agreeable to him. It was, perhaps, several hundred yards before we swung around out of the forest into the open land where stood a comfortable farm house, and there in a sweet and sunny corner were several chubby little children chatting and singing at their play. Mickey, dear old Mickey, trotted right up to the little people, with low whinnies of recognition and delight, and rubbed his head against them. They did not seem at all afraid, but pulled nice tufts of grass for him, which he ate with evident relish and gratitude.

If I remember correctly, it was the evening of the same day, after Mickey and I had kissed and left the children, and I had found a beautiful camping ground for the battalion— a succession of little swells of land crowned with pine copses and covered with broom-sedge, with a clear, cool stream flowing between the hills; and after the batteries were all up and located in this soldier paradise—guns parked, horses watered and fed and all work done—I say, I think it was after all this, that the bugles of each of the batteries blew such sweet and happy notes as I never heard from any one of them before, and then, while I was lying on the broom-sedge, bathing my soul in this peace, and Mickey was browsing near-by, over across the stream, the Howitzer Glee Club launched out into a song, the first they had sung since we broke camp at Morton's Ford, three weeks before.

As the song ceased and the day was fading into the twilight, I caught, up the road, the low murmur of conversation and the rattle of canteens, and following the sound with my eye, saw two infantrymen, from a command that had followed us and camped further back from the stream, wending their way to water. Just as they came fully within sight and hearing, two of the Howitzer Club struck up "What are the Wild Waves Saying?"—one of them, in a fine falsetto, taking the sister's part. As the clear, sweet female voice floated out on the still evening air my two infantrymen stood transfixed, one putting his hand upon the other's arm and saying with suppressed excitement, "Stop, man; there's a woman!" They were absolutely silent during the singing of the sister's part, but when the brother took up the song they openly wondered whether she would sing again. "Yes, there she is; listen, listen!"

And so, until the song was done, and they had waited, and it had become evident she would sing no more—and then a deep sigh from both the spell-bound auditors, and one of them, making use of the strongest figure he could command, exclaimed, from the bottom of a full heart, "Well, it beats a furlough hollow!"

We almost began to hope that Grant had gotten enough. Even his apparent, yes, real, success at the Salient did not embolden him to attack again at Spottsylvania. He had retired without any serious fighting at Hanover Junction or North Anna, and after feeling our position about Atlee's, he had once more slipped away from our front. Where was he going? What did he intend to do? Anyone of his predecessors would have retired and given it up long ago. Was he about to do so?

The fact is, Grant was waiting for reinforcements. He had been heavily reinforced at Spottsylvania after the 12th of May, but not up to the measure of his desires, or of his needs, either; for he really needed more men—and more, and more. He needed them, he asked for them, and he got them. He had a right to all he wanted. His original contract so provided; it covered all necessary drafts. He wanted especially Baldy Smith and his men from the transports, and they were coming. They were stretching out hands to each other. When they clasped hands, then Grant would attack once more; would make his great final effort. When and where would it be?

When Grant slid away from Lee at Atlee's, we felt satisfied that he was, as usual, making for the south and east, so Hoke was ordered toward Cold Harbor, and Kershaw (now our division general, McLaws never having returned from the West) toward Beulah Church. Colonel Cabell received orders on the evening of the 31st of May, or early on the morning of the 1st of June, to make for the latter point; but he was not upon the same road as Kershaw's division, and our orders said nothing about joining it. They seemed to contemplate our going by the most direct route, and we went —that is, as far as we could. No infantry apparently had received any orders to go with us, certainly none went, and we soon passed beyond the apparent end of our infantry line, at least on the road we were traveling. Very soon we reached a stout infantry picket, which I interviewed, and they said there were no Confederate troops down that road, unless perhaps a few cavalry videttes.

I was on very intimate terms with my colonel, and I went to him and suggested whether there was not danger in our proceeding as we were, a battalion of artillery unaccompanied by infantry, out and beyond the last picket post. The colonel was a strict constructionist, and he shut me up at once by saying: "Stiles, that is the responsibility of the general officer who sent me my orders. I am ordered to Beulah Church and to Beulah Church I am going. This is the nearest road." I looked up at him in some little surprise, but said no more; having fired, I now fell back on my reserves, in pretty fair order, but slightly demoralized.

My reserves were the officers and men of the battalion, all of whom I think were fond of me. If I mistake not, Frazier's battery led the column. I am certain it did a little later. Calloway, its commanding officer, to whom we have already been introduced, was one of the very best of soldiers, as the reader will soon be prepared to admit. He was the first man I fell in with as I fell back, Colonel Cabell and little Barrett, his courier, being ahead of the column. Calloway asked me if I didn't think we were running some risk, entirely unsupported as we seemed to be, and outside our lines. I told him what had occurred, and he smiled grimly.

Then I fell back further to the old battery. The column was pretty well closed up that morning; everybody seemed to feel it well to be so. I was strongly attached to the old company and particularly to the captain, who was a magnificent fellow. It was early on a beautiful spring morning, and we were again passing through a tract of undesolated, undesecrated country—greenness, quiet, the song of birds, the scent of flowers, all about us. Captain McCarthy was on foot, walking among his men, his great arms frequently around the necks of two of them at once—a position which displayed his martial, manly figure to great advantage. I dismounted, one of the fellows mounting my horse, and walked and talked and chatted with the men, and particularly with the captain.

He was altogether an uncommon person, marked by great simplicity, sincerity, kindliness, courage, good sense, personal force, and a genius for commanding men. He had been rather a reckless, pugnacious boy, difficult to manage, impatient of control. The war had proved a real blessing to him. It let off the surplus fire and fight. Its deep and powerful undertone was just what was needed to harmonize his nature. His spirit had really been balanced and gentled and sweetened by it. He was not essentially an intellectual man, nor yet a man of broad education, and he had under him some of the most intellectual and cultivated young men I ever met, yet he was easily their leader and commander; in the matter of control and for the business in hand, "from his shoulders and upward, taller than any of the people." And these intellectual and cultivated men freely recognized his supremacy and admired and loved him. He seemed to be somewhat subdued and quiet that morning; even more than ordinarily affectionate and demonstrative, but not cheerful or chatty. Several of us noticed his unusual bearing and speculated as to the cause.

As the morning wore on and we were leaving our infantry further and further behind, my uneasiness returned; and besides, I had been away long enough from the colonel, so I remounted and rode forward to the head of the column. He had been very emphatic in repelling my suggestions, but l thought it my duty to renew them, and I did. He was even more emphatic than before, saying he had been ordered to take that battalion to Beulah Church, and he proposed to do it, and he even added that when he wanted any advice from me he would ask it. I felt a nearer approach to heat than ever before or after, in all my intercourse with my friend and commander, and I assured him I would not obtrude my advice again.

I reined in my horse, waiting for Calloway, and rode with him at the head of his battery. I had scarcely joined him, when Colonels Fairfax and Latrobe, of Longstreet's staff, and Captain Simonton, of Pickett's, dashed by, splendidly mounted, and disappeared in a body of woods but a few hundred yards ahead. Hardly had they done so, when pop! pop! pop! went a half dozen carbines and revolvers; and a moment later the three officers galloped back out of the forest, driving before them two or three Federal cavalrymen on foot—Simonton leaning over his horse's head and striking at them with his riding whip. On the instant I took my revenge, riding up to Colonel Cabell, taking off my hat with a profound bow, and asking whether it was still his intention to push right on to Beulah Church? Meanwhile, minie balls began to drop in on us, evidently fired by sharpshooters from a house a short distance to our left and front. The Colonel turned toward me with a smile, and said, in a tone that took all the sting out of his former words, if any was ever intended to be in them: "Yes, you impudent fellow, it is my intention, but let's see how quickly you can drive those sharpshooters out of that house!"

Scarce sooner said than done. I sprang from my horse. Calloway's guns were in battery on the instant, I, by his permission, taking charge of his first piece as gunner. Making a quick estimate of the distance, I shouted back to No. 6 at how many seconds to cut the fuse, and the shell reached the gun almost as soon as I did. A moment—and the gun was loaded, aimed and fired; a moment more and the house burst into flame. The shell from the other three guns were exploded among the retiring skirmishers, who ran back toward the woods; while from the side of the house nearest to us

two women came out, one very stout and walking with
difficulty, the other bearing a baby in her arms and two
little children following her. Calling to the gunner to
take charge of his piece, I broke for these women, three or
four of the men running with me. There was a fence between us and them that could not have been less than four
and a half feet high, which I cleared, "hair and hough,"
while the rest stopped to climb it. I took the baby and
dragged the youngest child along with me, telling the other
to come on, and sent the younger woman back to help the
elder. When the reinforcements arrived we re-arranged our
convoys, I still keeping the baby. By the time we reached the
battery more of the guns were in action, shelling the woods,
and I became interested in the firing. The number fives as
they ran by me with the ammunition would stop a moment
to pat the baby, who was quite satisfied, and seemed to enjoy
the racket, cooing and trying to pull my short hair and
beard. This thing had been going on for several minutes,
and I had not been conscious of any appeal to me, until one
of the men ran up, and, pulling me sharply around, pointed
to the two women, who were standing back down the hill,
and as far as possible out of the line of the bullets, which
were still annoying us. There was a rousing laugh and
cheer as I started back to deliver the little infant artilleryman to his mother. It turned out that the elder of the two
women was the mother of the other, and had been bedridden
for several years. We were exceedingly sorry to have burned their little house, but some of the boys suggested that if
the cure of the mother proved permanent, the balance, after
all, might be considered rather in our favor.

I do not recall the events of the next few hours with any
distinctness, or in any orderly sequence, nor how we got
into connection with our division, Kershaw's; but we did so
without serious mishap; so, perhaps, Colonel Cabell may
have been more nearly right than I after all. The first definite recollection I have, after what I have just related, is of
the breaking of Col. Lawrence M. Keitt's big South Carolina regiment, which had just come to the army and been entered in Kershaw's old brigade, and probably outnumbered

all the balance of that command. General Kershaw had put this and another of his brigades into action not far from where we had burned the house to dislodge the skirmishers. Keitt's men gave ground, and in attempting to rally them their colonel fell mortally wounded. Thereupon the regiment went to pieces in abject rout and threatened to overwhelm the rest of the brigade. I have never seen any body of troops in such a condition of utter demoralization; they actually groveled upon the ground and attempted to burrow under each other in holes and depressions. Major Goggin, the stalwart adjutant-general of the division, was attempting to rally them, and I did what I could to help him. It was of no avail. We actually spurred our horses upon them, and seemed to hear their very bones crack, but it did no good; if compelled to wriggle out of one hole they wriggled into another.

So far as I recollect, however, this affair was of no real significance. Our other troops stood firm, and we lost no ground. I think none of the guns of the battery were engaged. Meanwhile the three divisions of our corps—the First, since Longstreet's wounding, under command of Major-General R. H. Anderson—had settled into alignment in the following order, beginning from the left: Field, Pickett, Kershaw. On the right of Kershaw's was Hoke's division, which had been under Beauregard and had joined the Army of Northern Virginia only the night before. The ground upon which our troops had thus felt and fought their way into line was the historic field of Cold Harbor, and the day was the first of June, 1864.

In the afternoon a furious attack was made on the left of Hoke and right of Kershaw; and Clingman's, the left brigade of Hoke and Wofford's, the right brigade of Kershaw gave way, and the Federal troops poured into the gap over a marshy piece of ground which had not been properly covered by either of these two brigades. Both Field and Pickett sent aid to Kershaw, and several of the guns of our battalion—I am not sure of which batteries, though I think two belonged to the Howitzers, came into battery on the edge of a peach orchard which sloped down to the break, and poured in a hot enfilade fire on the victorious Federals, who, after a manly struggle, were driven back, though we did not quite regain all we had lost, and our lines were left in very bad shape.

While Wofford was bending back the right of his line to connect with Hoke, who, even with the aid sent him, had not quite succeeded in regaining his original position, Kershaw's old brigade, which had more perfectly recovered from its little contretemps, was pressing and driving the enemy, both advancing and extending its line upon higher and better ground, a feat it would never have been able to accomplish but for the aid of one of Calloway's guns, which, under command of Lieutenant Robert Falligant, of Savannah, Ga., held and carried the right flank of the brigade, coming into battery and fighting fiercely whenever the enemy seemed to be holding the brigade in check, and limbering up and moving forward with it, while it was advancing; and this alternate advancing and firing was kept up until a fresh Federal force came in and opened fire on the right flank, and all of Falligant's horses fell at the first volley. The enemy made a gallant rush for the piece, but they did not get it. It was in battery in a moment and belching fire like a volcano, and very hot shot, too. The brigade, whose flank it had held, now sprang to its defense, and after a furious little fight the gun was for the present safe, and everyone began to dig and to pile up dirt.

The brigade did not, however, advance one foot after Falligant's horses were shot; but it was already considerably in advance of Wofford's left, with which it was not connected at all, until the entire line was rectified on the night of the 2d—nor was there at any time a Confederate infantry soldier to the right of this piece, nor a spadeful of earth, except the little traverse we threw up to protect the right of the gun. It may just as well be added now that this lone gun held the right of Kershaw's brigade line that evening and night—it was getting dark when the extreme advanced position was reached—and all the next day, and was moved back by hand the night of the 2d of June. I have no hesitation in saying that in all my experience as a soldier I never witnessed more gallant action than this of Lieutenant Falligant and his dauntless cannoneers, nor do I believe that any officer of his rank made a more important contribution than he to the success of the Confederate arms in the great historic battle.

Both sides anticipated battle on the 3d, as it really occurred. General Grant in his memoirs says in express terms, "The 2d of June was spent in getting troops into position for attack on the 3d;" and the "Official Journal" of our corps says, under date of June 3d, "The expected battle begins early." This journal also notes the weakness of "Kershaw's Salient," and that the enemy was aware of it, and was "massing heavily" in front of it. Three brigades were sent to support Kershaw—Anderson's, Gregg's, and Law's. We also set to work to rectify the lines about this point. Gen. E. M. Law, of Alabama, is probably entitled to the credit of this suggestion, which had so important a bearing upon our success. He laid off the new line with his own hand and superintended the construction of it during the night of the 2d. The record of the 3d might have been a very different one if this change had not been made. Under Colonel Cabell's instructions and with the aid of the division pioneer corps, I opened roads through the woods for the more rapid and convenient transmission of artillery ammunition, and put up two or three little bridges across ravines with the same view.

While I was superintending this work, the fire at the time being lively, I heard someone calling in a most lugubrious voice, "Mister, Mister, won't you please come here!" I glanced in the direction of the cry and saw a man standing behind a large tree in a very peculiar attitude, having the muzzle of his musket under his left shoulder and leaning heavily upon it. Supposing he was wounded, I went to him and asked what he wanted. He pointed to the butt of his gun, under which a large, vigorous, venomous copperhead snake was writhing; and the wretched skulker actually had the face to whine to me, "Won't you please, sir, kill that snake?" I knew not what to say to the creature, and fear what I did say was neither a very Christian nor a very soldierly response; but no one who has not seen a thoroughly demoralized man can form the slightest conception of how repulsive a thing such a wretch is.

The headquarters of General Kershaw at Cold Harbor was close up to the lines and just back of the position of some of our guns. It was but a short distance, too, from where the caissons bringing in ammunition turned to the right, on a road I had cut, running along the slope of a declivity at the crest of which our guns were stationed, some of them before and all of them after the lines were rectified. He might have found a safer place, but none nearer the point of peril and the working point of everything. The position, however, was so exposed that he found himself compelled to protect it, which he did by putting up a heavy wall of logs, back of which the earth was cut away and pitched over against the face, which was toward the lines. His quarters were thus cut deep into the hillside, and had besides, above the surface and toward the enemy, this wall of logs faced with earth. Thus he had a place where he and his officers could safely confer and at a very short distance from their commands; but it was after all a ghastly place, and very difficult and dangerous of approach. All the roads or paths leading to it were not only swept by an almost continuous and heavy fire of musketry, but I had to keep a force of axe-men almost constantly at work cutting away trees felled across the ammunition roads by the artillery fire of the enemy. Col. Charles S. Venable, reputed to be one of the roughest and most daring riders on General Lee's staff,— later, professor of mathematics at the University of Virginia, and chairman of the faculty,—told me he believed this headquarter position of Kershaw's at Cold Harbor was the worst place he was ever sent to. Colonel Cabell was necessarily a great part of the time at these headquarters, and I also, when not engaged at some special work, or with some of the guns, or on the way from one to another. At Cold Harbor these journeys had to be made on foot, and necessarily consumed a good deal of time, an artillery battalion frequently covering, say, half a mile of the line.

Up to the night of the 2d of June, when it was moved back, every time Falligant's gun fired while I was at headquarters, General Kershaw would repeat his admiration of his courage, and ask me to explain to him again and again the isolated and exposed position of the piece, and then he would express his determination that Falligant's gallantry and services should receive their merited reward. Once, when I happened to be there, a soldier from a South Carolina regiment in Kershaw's old brigade, one of those supporting Falligant's gun, came in, reporting that his part of the line was almost out of ammunition, and asking that some be sent in at once. He may have had a written order, but at all events he represented that the case was urgent; that they could not trust to getting it into the line at some safe point and having it passed along by hand, because it would take too long, and besides all the troops were scantily supplied and it would never get to his regiment; and lastly, because the officer who sent him had ordered him to bring it himself. The man was intelligent, self-possessed, and determined. I well remember, too, how pale and worn and powder-begrimed he looked. He confirmed all I had said as to the position and services of Falligant's gun, and was enthusiastic about him and his detachment.

I told him I was going down there and would help him. Boxes of ammunition were piled up in a corner of the cellar, as it might be called, in which we were sitting, and we knocked the top from one, and putting two good, strong oilcloths together, poured into them as many cartridges as either of us could conveniently carry at a pretty good rate of speed. We then tied up the cloths, making a bag of double thickness and having two ends to hold by. Together we could run quite rapidly with it, and in case either of us should be killed or wounded, the other could get along fairly well. We then took the course I had already several times taken in reaching the gun—that is, we went down behind Wofford's left flank, and from that point ran across a field covered with scattering sassafras bushes, to a point on Kershaw's line, a little to the left of our gun. This route afforded the best protection, but after we left Wofford's position the "protection" amounted to nothing. The sharpshooters had two-thirds of a circle of fire around the piece, and they popped merrily at us as we stepped across the field, but they never touched either of us; we got in safe and each of us "counted a *coup*," as the French Canadian trappers used to say.

After shaking hands with the infantry, hearing my plucky comrade complimented on his quick and successful trip, and seeing the men draw their rations of powder and ball, I made my way to the gun, told Bob and his gallant detachment what the General had said about them, looked to their fortification and ammunition, and was just about to take the perilous trip back again when the enemy began to press us in a very determined way. There was heavy timber immediately in front, and their mode of attack was to thicken a skirmish line into a line of battle behind the trees, and then try to rush us at very short range. The infantry ammunition had been replenished just in time, but it must be remembered there was not an infantry soldier to our right. If the woods had been as close upon us in that direction they would undoubtedly have captured the piece, but they did not relish coming out into the open.

I was struck with the splendid fighting spirit of Campbell, the tall, lean, keen-eyed, black-haired gunner of the piece; but he was entirely too reckless, standing erect except when bending over the handspike in sighting the piece, and not much "sighting" is done at such short range. Every time the gun belched its deadly contents into the woods Campbell would throw his glengary or fez cap around his head and yell savagely. I cautioned him again and again, reminding him that the other men of the detachment were fighting, and fighting effectively, on their hands and knees. When his commanding officer or I ordered him to "get down" he would do so for a moment, but spring up again when the gun fired. Suddenly I heard the thud of a minie striking a man, and Campbell's arms flew up as he fell backward, ejaculating, "Oh, God! I'm done forever!" We lifted the poor fellow around, across the face of the little work, under the mouth of the piece, and Falligant kneeled by him and pressed his finger where the blood was spouting, while I took the gunner's place at the trail. Every time the gun was discharged I noticed how Campbell's face—which was almost directly under the bellowing muzzle—was contorted, but he urged me to keep up the fire, until finally, observing a sort of lull in the fight, I proposed to cease firing and note the effect, and the poor fellow said brokenly, "Well, if you think it's safe, Adjutant!" Then he added, "Tell my mother I died like a soldier"—and he was gone.

During this flurry one of the enemy bounded over the work and landed right in among us; but he ran on toward the rear and brought up in a sitting posture on a pile of earth one of the infantry had thrown out of a hole he had dug to cook in—a sort of safety-kitchen. The man's back was turned toward us, his elbows were on his knees, and his head sunk in his hands. After Campbell's death, as he was still sitting there, thinking he must be wounded, I proposed to one of the men to run out and bring him back into the work. We tried it, but he cast off our hands and we had to leave him to his fate. In a few moments he was shot in the head and tumbled in upon the cook in the kitchen—dead.

The 2d of June, 1864, was the heaviest, the hardest-worked and the most straining day of my life. Not only did I have my ordinary duties of a day of battle to perform, but I had, in addition, to open and to keep open roads for getting in ammunition, to bridge two or three ravines, to visit Falligant's gun several times and to keep it supplied with ammunition, which had to be passed along the infantry line by hand for quite a long distance. When night came I believe I was more nearly wornout than on any other occasion during the entire war. Colonel Cabell insisted I should go back to our headquarters camp, which was about midway between the lines and the drivers' camp, and sleep; and, in view of what impended on the morrow, I consented to do so. But first, and just before dark, I took Calloway over all the confusing and obscure part of the road to Falligant's gun and the road by which he was to bring it out later. I omitted to say that General Kershaw highly approved our determination to save that piece, if at all possible. I greatly disliked not going with the party to fetch the gun out, but Calloway and everyone concerned insisted that I must not think of attempting it, fearing that I would utterly give way if I did so. So I yielded, and after showing and explaining everything to Calloway, I went back to camp and laid down.

I had scarcely gotten to sleep when I had to get up to pilot an officer who had important orders for General Kershaw, and had been unable to find his headquarters. Once more I stretched out and dozed off. How long I dozed or slept I cannot say, but I was awakened by Calloway bending over me and saying, "Adjutant, I never was so sorry about anything, but in those woods it is now as dark as Erebus! Nobody but yourself can find and keep the road you showed me, and I don't believe even you can do it."

The noble fellow was evidently much mortified and troubled at being compelled to rouse me, but he well knew I had much rather this should be done than that the chance of saving the gun should be abandoned. So I got up and mounted Mickey, and off we started.

It was very dark. Just before reaching the point where the road turned to the right along the slope of the hill we found the gun horses and drivers, Calloway and I passing and directing them to follow us, and to keep absolutely quiet. I experienced little difficulty in finding the road, having superintended the cutting of it and being very familiar with it, and we passed on over the little bridge, and were just passing out from behind Wofford's left flank and heading for Kershaw's line, when someone seized my bridle rein and abruptly stopped my horse; at the same time asking who I was and what I intended to do, and what I meant by bringing artillery horses through his lines without his permission.

The manner and tone of this address was irritating, but suspecting who my interlocutor was and knowing something of his temperament, I answered quietly that I was adjutant of Cabell's Battalion of Artillery, and that the commanding officer of one of our batteries was with me; that the gun out there, which had protected this part of the line all day, belonged to his battery; that we proposed to save it, and that we had brought the horses for the purpose of hauling it off. I could see nothing, but by this time my suspicion had become conviction and I felt sure I was talking with General

Wofford. He positively forbade the attempt, and did not seem disposed to yield until my cousin, Col. Edward Stiles, of the Sixteenth Georgia, of his brigade, who knew the General well, joined us and suggested as a compromise that we should make the attempt without taking the horses any further; to which I agreed, upon condition that he would furnish me with, say twenty men, to get the gun off by hand, and that in the event of their failing I should then make the effort with the horses, as we had General Kershaw's positive orders to save the gun if possible.

We got the men and started up the hill, leaving drivers and horses to await our return. It was now absolutely dark. I remember putting my hand before my face and being unable to see it. Calloway and I rode side by side, inclining to the left, so as to guard against running out into the enemy through the gap in the lines. There was absolute silence, save the soft tread of our horses' feet in the sandy soil. In a few moments their heads rustled against dry leaves—the leafy screen which the troops had put up to protect themselves from the baking sun. We knew we were at the infantry line and turned to the right and toward the gun. There was a good deal of smoke in the air from the woods afire out in front, and we soon became conscious of an insufferable odor of burning flesh. My horse being a rapid walker, I kept a little ahead of Calloway, and very soon was stopped again, by someone who spoke almost in a stage whisper. It turned out to be the commanding officer of Kershaw's old brigade, and he, too, forbade our attempt and ordered us back; but the direct authority of his major-general satisfied him, and he begged only that we should wait until his men could be thoroughly roused and ready to resist any attack that might be made; adding that the poor fellows were utterly exhausted by the unrelieved strain of the past thirty-six hours. All true; yet it was fearful to contemplate the risk they ran in sleeping. The colonel told us, too, what we already suspected, that the odor which so offended our nostrils was that of human bodies roasting in the forest fires in front. We plainly heard the officers passing along the lines and rousing the men, and we feared the enemy heard it, too; but preferred this risk to that of a sudden rush upon a slumbering brigade just as we were drawing the gun off.

Soon after we started again, my horse snorted and sprang aside. I knew this meant we had reached the dead horses, and told Calloway we were almost upon the gun. He dismounted, handing his bridle rein to me, and I heard him enter the little trench and feel and fumble his way along it for a few steps, and then heard him call, in a low tone, "Falligant, Falligant!" Then I heard the sort of groan or grumble a tired man gives out when he is half roused from a sound sleep, and after that a low hum of conversation. Then Calloway came up out of the trench, and, groping his way to me, said: "Adjutant, do you know every man in that detachment was fast asleep and the enemy is lying down in line of battle between here and that low fire out there!" I said he must be mistaken, that I could toss a cracker into that fire. He insisted he was right and urged me to dismount and go into the trench and stoop till I could see under the smoke. I did so, and there, sure enough, was a continuous line of blue which the flickering of the flames beyond enabled me to see. My heart stopped beating at the sight, but this was no time for indulgence of over-sensibility, physical or emotional.

As quietly and rapidly as possible we got everything ready for fight or retreat. Our twenty men had brought their muskets and Kershaw's brigade was up in the trench and on their knees. The gun was backed out of the little work, limbered up, and the ammunition chest replaced; some of the men took hold of the wheels and some of the tongue, and the piece was soon moving after us almost noiselessly, along the sassafras field toward Wofford's line. In a few moments we reached the goal, returning our thanks to the General, and to my cousin and the sturdy, gallant men they lent us; the horses were hitched up and we were rolling over the little bridges and up to the new line and the position selected for this now distinguished piece.

I trust I am not small enough to indulge in any vulgar pride in my part of the trying experiences of this day; yet I scarce recall another day for which I so thank God, or which has had a greater influence on my life. Often, when depressed and disposed to question whether there is, or ever was, in me the salt of a real manhood, I have looked back to the first three days of June, 1864, and felt the revival of a saving self-respect and the determination not to do or suffer anything unworthy of this heroic past of which I was a part.

CHAPTER XXI

COLD HARBOR OF '64.

The Great Fight of June 3d—Unparalleled in Brevity, in Slaughter, and in Disproportion of Loss—Grant Assaults in Column, or in Mass—His Troops Refuse to Renew the Attack—Effect at the North—Confederate "Works" in the Campaign of '64—The Lines—Sharpshooting—The Covered Way—The Spring—Death of Captain McCarthy, of the Howitzers—How It Occurred on the Lines—How It Was Received in the City—My Brother Loses an Eye—"Alone in the World"—A Last Look at the Enemy—Buildings Felled and Scattered by Artillery—Gun Wheels Cut Down by Musketry—Bronze Guns Splotched and Pitted Like Smallpox—Epitome of the Campaign of '64—Maneuvering of No Avail Against Lee's Army—Did That Army Make Lee, or Lee That Army?

There were two battles at Cold Harbor, one in '62 and one in '64. In '62 the Confederates attacked and drove the Federals from their position; in '64 the Federals attacked, but were repulsed with frightful slaughter. It is undisputed that both McClellan's army and Grant's outnumbered Lee's,—Grant's overwhelmingly,—and it is asserted that the position occupied by the Federals in '62 and the Confederates in '64 was substantially the same.

We were in line of battle at Cold Harbor of '64 from the 1st to the 12th of June—say twelve days; the battle proper did not last perhaps that many minutes. In some respects, at least, it was one of the notable battles of history—certainly in its brevity measured in time, and its length measured in slaughter—as also in the disproportion of the losses. A fair epitome of it in these respects would be that in a few moments more than thirteen thousand men were killed and wounded on the Federal side and less than thirteen hundred on the Confederate. As to the time consumed in the conflict, the longest duration assigned is sixty minutes and the shortest less than eight. For my own part, I could scarcely say whether it lasted eight or sixty minutes, or eight or sixty hours—to such a degree were all my powers concentrated upon the one point of keeping the guns fully supplied with ammunition.

The effect of the fighting was not at all appreciated on the Confederate side at the time. Why we did not at least suspect it, when the truce was asked and granted to allow the removal of the Federal dead and wounded, I cannot say, although I went myself with the officers on our side, detailed to accompany them, on account of my familiarity with the lines. I presume the ignorance, and even incredulity, of our side as to the overwhelming magnitude of the Federal losses resulted from two causes mainly—our own loss was so trivial, so utterly out of proportion, and the one characteristic feature of the fight on the Federal side was not then generally known or appreciated by us, namely, that Grant had attacked in column, in phalanx, or in mass. The record of the Official Diary of our corps (Southern Historical Society Papers, Vol. VII., p. 503), under date of June 3, 1864, is very peculiar and is in part in these words: "Meantime the enemy is heavily massed in front of Kershaw's salient. Anderson's, Law's, and Gregg's brigades are there to support Kershaw. Assault after assault is made, and each time repulsed with severe loss to the enemy. At eight o'clock A. M., fourteen had been made and repulsed (this means, I suppose, fourteen lines advanced)."

This is obviously a hurried field note by one officer, corrected later by another, in accordance with the facts known to the writer, that is, to the officer who made the later note, but not generally known at the time to the public. We suppose, however, it will to-day be admitted by all that there was *but one attack* upon Kershaw up to eight A. M., and that at that hour the order was issued to the Federal troops to renew the attack, but they failed to advance; that this order was repeated in the afternoon, when the troops again refused to obey, and that at least some of Grant's corps generals approved of this refusal of their men to repeat the useless sacrifice.

Here, then, is the secret of the otherwise inexplicable and incredible butchery. A little after daylight on June 3, 1864, along the lines of Kershaw's salient, his infantry discharged their bullets and his artillery fired case-shot and double-shotted canister, at very short range, into a mass of men twenty-eight (28) deep, who could neither advance nor retreat, and the most of whom could not even discharge their muskets at us. We do not suppose that the general outline of these facts will be denied to-day, but it may be as well to confirm the essential statement by a brief extract from Swinton's "Army of the Potomac," p. 487:

The order was issued through these officers to their subordinate commanders, and from them descended through the wonted channels, but no man stirred and the immobile lines pronounced a verdict, silent, yet emphatic, against further slaughter. The loss on the Union side in this sanguinary action was over thirteen thousand, while on the part of the Confederates it is doubtful whether it reached that many hundreds.

To like effect, as to the amount and the disproportion of the carnage, is the statement of Colonel Taylor, on page 135 of his book, that:

I well recall having received a report after the assault from General Hoke—whose division reached the army just previous to this battle—to the effect that the ground in his entire front over which the enemy had charged was literally covered with their dead and wounded; and that up to that time he had not had a single man killed.

So much for the amount, the disproportion, and the cause of the slaughter. A word now as to the effect of it upon others than the immediate contestants. Is it too much to say that even Grant's iron nerve was for the time shattered? Not that he would not have fought again if his men would, but they would not. Is it not true that he so informed President Lincoln; that he asked for another army; that, not getting it, or not getting it at once, he changed his plan of campaign from a fighting to a digging one? Is it reasonable to suppose that when he attacked at the Bloody Angle or at Cold Harbor, he really contemplated the siege of Petersburg and regarded those operations as merely preparatory? Is it not true that, years later, Grant said—looking back over his long career of bloody fights—that Cold Harbor was the only battle he ever fought that he would not fight over again under the same circumstances? Is it not true that when first urged, as President, to remove a certain Democratic office-holder in California, and later, when urged to give a reason for his refusal, he replied that the man had been a standard-bearer in the Army of the Potomac, and that he would—allow something very unpleasant to happen to him—before he would remove the only man in his army who even attempted to obey his order to attack a second time at Cold Harbor? Is it not true that General Meade said the Confederacy came nearer to winning recognition at Cold Harbor than at any other period during the war? Is it not true that, after Grant's telegram, the Federal Cabinet resolved at least upon an armistice, and that Mr. Seward was selected to draft the necessary papers, and Mr. Swinton to prepare the public mind for the change? And finally, even if none of these things be true, exactly as propounded—yet is it not true, that Cold Harbor shocked and depressed the Federal Government and the Northern public more than any other single battle of the war?

A few words as to some of the prominent features, physical and otherwise, of fighting in "the lines," as we began regularly to do in this campaign of '64, particularly at Cold Harbor. Something of this is necessary to a proper understanding and appreciation of some of the incidents that occurred there. And first, as to "the works" of which I have so often spoken. What were they? I cannot answer in any other way one-half so well as by the following vivid quotation from my friend Willy Dame's "Reminiscences," already mentioned and quoted. Says Mr. Dame:

Just here I take occasion to correct a very wrong impression about the field works the Army of Northern Virginia fought behind in this campaign. All the Federal writers who have written about these battles speak about our works as "formidable earthworks," "powerful fortifications," "impregnable lines;" such works as no troops could be expected to take and *any troops* should be expected to hold.

Now about the parts of the line distant from us, I couldn't speak so certainly—though I am sure they were all very much the same—but about the works all along our part of the line I can speak with exactness and certainty. I saw them, I helped with my own hands to make them, I fought behind them, I was often on top of them and both sides of them. I know all about them. I got a good deal of the mud off them on me (not for purposes of personal fortification, however). Our works were a single line of earth about four feet high and three to five feet thick. It had no ditch or obstruction in front. It was nothing more than a little heavier line of "rifle pits." There was no physical difficulty in men walking right over that bank. I did it often myself, saw many others do it, and twice saw a line of Federal troops walk over it, and then saw them walk *back* over it with the greatest ease, at the rate of forty miles an hour; i. e. except those whom we had persuaded to stay with us, and those the angels were carrying to Abraham's bosom at a still swifter rate. Works they could go over like that couldn't have been much obstacle! They couldn't have made better time on a dead level.

Such were our works actually, and still they seemed to "loom large" to the people in front. I wonder what could have given them such an exaggerated idea of the strength of those modest little works! I wonder if it could have been the *men* behind them! There wasn't a great many of these men! It was a very thin gray line along them, back of a thin red line of clay. But these lines stuck together, very hard, and were very hard indeed to separate. The red clay was "sticky" and the men were just as "sticky," and as the two lines "stuck" together so closely, it made the whole very strong indeed. Certainly it seems they gave to those who tried to force them apart an impression of great strength.

Yes, it must have been the *men!* A story in point comes to my aid here. A handsome, well dressed lady sweeps with a great air past two street boys. They are much struck. "My eye, Jim, but ain't that a stunning dress?" says Jim with a superior air. "O get out, Bill, the dress ain't no great shakes; it's the woman in it that makes it so killing!" That was the way with the Spottsylvania earthworks. The "works wa'n't no great shakes." It was the men in 'em that made them so "killing."

The men behind those works, such as they were, had perfect confidence in their own ability to hold them. And this happy combination of "faith" and "works" proved as strong against the world and the flesh as it does against the devil. It was perfectly effectual, it withstood all assaults.

The original intent of such "works" is to afford protection against regular attack by the full line of battle of the opposite side, advancing out of their works to attack yours. This, of course, everyone understands. But this is only an occasional and comparatively rare thing. The constant and wearing feature of "the lines" is the sharpshooting, which never ceases as long as there is light enough to see how to shoot; unless the skirmishers or sharpshooters of the two sides proclaim, or in some way begin, a temporary truce, as I have known them to do. I have also known them to give explicit warning of the expiration of such a truce.

Sharpshooting, at best, however, is a fearful thing. The regular sharpshooter often seemed to me little better than a human tiger lying in wait for blood. His rifle is frequently trained and made fast bearing upon a particular spot,— for example, where the head of a gunner must of necessity appear when sighting his piece,—and the instant that object appears and, as it were, "darkens the hole," crash goes a bullet through his brain.

The consequence of the sharpshooting is the "covered-way," which, when applied to these rough and ready temporary lines, means any sort of protection—trenches, ditches, traverses, piles of earth, here and there, at what have proved to be the danger points, designed and placed so as to protect as far as possible against the sharpshooters. Only in regular and elaborate lines of "siege," such as we had later about Petersburg, is seen the more perfect protection of regularly covered galleries and ways for passing from one part of the line to another inside; just as, outside and on the face toward the enemy, such elaborate and permanent lines of works are protected by ditches, abattis or felled trees, friezes or sharpened stakes, to make the "works" more difficult of approach, of access, and of capture.

One can readily understand, now, the supreme discomfort and even suffering of "the lines." Thousands of men cramped up in a narrow trench, unable to go out, or to get up, or to stretch or to stand without danger to life and limb; unable to lie down, or to sleep, for lack of room and pressure of peril; night alarms, day attacks, hunger, thirst, supreme weariness, squalor, vermin, filth, disgusting odors everywhere; the weary night succeeded by the yet more weary day; the first glance over the way, at day dawn, bringing the sharpshooter's bullet singing past your ear or smashing through your skull, a man's life often exacted as the price of a cup of water from the spring. But I will not specify or elaborate further; only, upon the canvas thus stretched, let me paint for you two or three life and death pictures of Cold Harbor of '64.

The reader may recall our "Old Doctor," the chief of our ambulance corps, who helped to rally the Texans and Georgians on the 10th of May at Spottsylvania, first exhorting them as "gentlemen," then berating and belaboring them as "cowards." No man who was ever in the Howitzers but will appreciate the grim absurdity of this man's feeling a lack of confidence in his own nerve and courage; but he did feel it. When the war broke out he was in Europe enjoying himself, but returned to his native State, serving first in some, as he considered it, "non-combatant" position, until that became unendurable to him, and then he joined the Howitzers as a private soldier; and that final flurry of the 10th of May was the first real fight he ever got into. Hearing someone say just as it was over that it had been "pretty hot work," he asked with the greatest earnestness whether the speaker really meant what he said, and when assured that he did, he asked two or three others of his comrades, whom he regarded as experienced soldiers, whether they concurred in this view of the matter, and on their expressing emphatic concurrence, he expressed intense satisfaction at having at last a standard in his mind, and a relieving standard at that; saying that he had feared he would disgrace his family by exhibiting a lack of courage; but if this was really "hot work," he felt that he would be able to maintain himself and do his duty. The story is almost too much for belief, but it is the sober truth and vouched for by gentlemen of the highest character.

I think it was the evening after the big fight at Cold Harbor that I was sitting in the works, with one of the Howitzer detachments, when the Doctor announced his intention of going to the spring for water. I reminded him that it was not quite dark and the sharpshooters would be apt to pay their respects to him; but he said he must have some water, and offered to take down and fill as many canteens as he could carry. His captain was present and I said no more. He was soon loaded up and started off, stepping right up out of the trench on the level ground. I could not help urging him to take the "covered way," but he replied, "I can't do it, Adjutant. It is dirty; a gentleman can't walk in it, sir."

Away he went, walking bolt upright and with entire non-chalance, down the hill; to my great relief reaching the spring in safety, where he was pretty well protected. In due time he started back, loaded with the full canteens and having a tin cup full of water in his right hand. I heard the sharp report of a rifle and saw the Doctor start forward or stumble, and sprang up to go to his relief, but he steadied himself and came right on up the hill without further attention from the sharpshooters, and stepped down into the work. As he did so he handed the captain the cup of water, in the quietest manner apologizing for having spilled part of it, adding that he had met with a trivial accident. The upper joint of his thumb had been shot away, yet he had not dropped the cup. Then he turned to me and asked my pardon for his disregard of my warning and his imprudence in getting shot, protesting still, however, that it was very hard indeed for a gentleman to walk in those filthy, abominable covered ways.

The spring was perhaps the point of greatest power and pathos in all the weird drama of "The Lines." About this date, or very soon after, a few of us were sitting in the part of the trenches occupied by the Twenty-first Mississippi, of our old brigade,—Barksdale's, now Humphreys',—which was supporting our guns. There had been a number of Yale men in the Twenty-first—the Sims, Smiths, Brandon, Scott, and perhaps others. A good many were "gone," and those of us who were left were talking of them and of good times at Old Yale, when someone said, "Scott, isn't it your turn to go to the spring?" "Yes," said Scott, submissively, "I believe it is. Pass up your canteens," and he loaded up and started out. There was a particularly exposed spot on the way to water, which we had tried in vain to protect more perfectly, and we heard, as usual, two or three rifle shots as Scott passed that point. In due time we heard them again as he returned, and one of the fellows said, "Ha! they are waking up old Scott, again, on the home stretch."

The smile had not died upon our faces when a head appeared above the traverse and a business-like voice called:

"Hello, Company I; man of yours dead out here!" We ran around the angle of the work, and there lay poor Scott, prone in the ditch and almost covered with canteens. We picked him up and bore him tenderly into the trench, and, as we laid him down and composed his limbs, manly tears dropped upon his still face. Each man disengaged and took his own canteen from the slumbering water-carrier. We did not "pour the water out to the Lord," as David did when the "three mightiest brake through the host of the Philistines and drew water out of the well of Bethlehem that was by the gate"—albeit, in a truer sense than David spoke, this water was the very "blood of this man."

It was about six o'clock in the evening of one of the days that followed close upon the great fight that there befell the company the very saddest loss it had yet experienced. An order had come to Captain McCarthy, from General Alexander, commanding the artillery corps, directing that the effect of the fire of several Howitzers, which were operating as mortars, from a position immediately back of the Howitzer guns, should be carefully observed and reported to him. The captain, appreciating at once the responsibility and the peril of the work, with characteristic chivalry, determined to divide it between himself and one of the most competent and careful men in the company. He was not the man to shrink, or slur over, or postpone his own part in any duty, and immediately stationed himself where he could thoroughly discharge it. He had taken his stand but a few moments when he fell back among his men, his brain pierced by a sharpshooter's bullet. The detachment sprang to his aid, but too late even to prevent his fall. His broad breast heaved once or twice as they knelt about him, and it was all over. The men broke down utterly and sobbed like children.

We never found his hat. While his boys were still gazing at him through their tears a Mississippi soldier came working his way along the lines, from a point some one hundred feet or more to the right, holding in his hand a little piece of brass, and as he approached the group said: "This here thing has just fell at my feet. I reckon it belongs to some of you artillery fellows;" and then, looking at the noble figure stretched upon the ground, he asked in the dry, matter-of-fact soldier style, "Who's that's dead?" When we told him Captain McCarthy, of the Howitzers, he said musingly: "McCarthy, McCarthy; why, that's the name of the folks that took care o' me, when I was wounded so bad last year. Well, here's the cannons from his hat." And so it was; his hat, as we suppose, had gone over the works, and his badge of cross cannon, dislodged from it by the shock, had fallen at the feet of a man who had been nursed back to life by his mother and sisters in his boyhood's home.

In a few moments his men bore him to where he could be placed in an ambulance, and then all, save his cousin, Dan, afterwards Lieutenant McCarthy, who went into Richmond with his body, turned back to the lines with such choking of grief and heaviness of heart as they had never before felt.

It is seldom a man is so beloved or so deserves to be. I can truly say I never heard him utter an evil word concerning anyone, and never heard from anyone either adverse criticism or complaint of him. A day or two before, on that very spot, he had shown what a true hero he was. Just after the great repulse, and while a fearful fire was pouring upon us from the Federal batteries and such of their assaulting infantry as had succeeded in reaching their own works, a poor wretch, who had fallen just outside our works, was shrieking for help. The captain, deeply stirred, cried: "Boys, I can't stand this. I don't order any of you to accompany me; but, as I can't well manage him alone, I call for one volunteer to go with me and bring in that poor fellow." Several volunteered, but Sergeant, afterwards Lieutenant, Moncure said, "You can't go, boys; I am chief of this piece," and he and the captain went right over the works, and, picking up the man, brought him back inside, but he was dead before they laid him down. He had been killed by the fire of his own friends.

Such was death upon the lines; but let me show what all this meant to the people at home. General Kershaw very willingly furnished Dan an ambulance and a man from his old brigade to drive it, and the two started on their melancholy journey. Counting the necessary turn-outs in the road, which was badly cut up by army wagons, they had some twelve or thirteen miles to travel, and it must have been after seven o'clock before they started. Meanwhile, at the captain's father's home, in the northern part of the city, were his mother and sisters, his father, an aged man, suffering from a disease which had robbed him of the power of speech and forced him to breathe through a tube, and a younger brother, under military age, who was his father's constant attendant and nurse; and who slept with him at night. This brother was roused that night from his first nap by loud shouts on the street and a rough, startling, disagreeable noise made, as he thought, by running a stout stick backwards and forwards across the wooden palings of the front fence. Going to the window the lad hesitated for a moment to throw up the sash, the streets of a beleaguered city at night being, of course, not entirely free from prowlers and disorder. What he saw was a man holding a horse, from which he had evidently just dismounted, and who had been making these noises for the purpose of rousing the people in the house. As the sash went up the man said: "Captain McCarthy was killed on the lines awhile ago. If you want his body you had better send for it to-night, or it may be buried on the field." As he said this he remounted and was gone.

The house was instantly in a turmoil, but the inmates soon recovered reasonable balance, and in a short time the lad was off after a horse and wagon for the sad errand. At first he could not think where he might get one, but it soon occurred to him that he had seen upon the streets within a few days a new wagon of "John and George Gibson, Builders," and he went to Mr. George Gibson's house and waked him. Upon hearing the sad news, Mr. Gibson kindly consented not only to let him have the wagon, but to go with him to the lines. He added, however, that the horse and vehicle were kept at a considerable distance from his house and that, as the night threatened to be stormy, young McCarthy had better go home and get some proper wraps and protections and meet him at an appointed place and time. As the boy reached home, or soon after, an ambulance drove up to the door and his Cousin Dan and the South Carolina soldier bore the captain's body into the house. As soon as they had deposited it and helped the family to arrange it as they desired, Dan kissed his uncle, aunt, and cousins, and was bidding them good-by, when the old gentleman made signs for him to remain a moment and asked for pencil and paper. When these were given him he wrote just these words and handed them to Dan—"Since it was God's will to take him, I am glad he died at his post."

Dan was back at his post by daylight, and sent word to the captain's two brothers, who were in another corps, when he would be buried. These young men walked into town, attended the funeral, and walked out again to their posts the same night, and in a very short time the lad who had been his father's nurse was regularly mustered into the company to which his elder brothers belonged. Such was death, and also life, in the devoted city back of the lines.

My younger brother was a great favorite in the company. As before stated, he had been a sailor, and as we had come from New England to Virginia, he was nicknamed "Skipper." He had a beautiful tenor voice and a unique repertoire of songs from almost every clime and country. Whenever "Skipper" deigned to sing, "the Professor," the trainer of the Glee Club, would enforce absolute silence throughout the camp, under penalty of a heavy battery of maledictions.

The day after Captain McCarthy's death, my brother, being in almost the exact position the captain occupied when killed, was shot in the left temple, and fell just where the captain had fallen. I was not present at the moment, but the boys reported that as they bent over him, thinking him dead, he raised his head and said, "If you fellows will stand back and give me some air, I'll get up!"—which he not only did, but walked out to the hospital camp, refusing a litter. He also refused to take chloroform, and directed the surgeons in exploring the track of the ball, which had crushed up his temple and the under half of the socket of his eye, and lodged somewhere in behind his nose. After they had extracted the ball and a great deal of crushed bone, he declared there was something else in his head which must come out. The surgeons told him it was more crushed bone which would come away of itself after awhile; but he insisted it was something that did not belong there, and that they must take it away immediately. They remonstrated, but he would not be satisfied, and finally they probed further and drew out a piece of his hat brim, cut just the width of the ball and jammed like a wad into his head; after that he was much easier. I omitted to say we never found his hat, either.

He was blind in the left eye from the moment the ball struck him, and became for a time blind in the other eye also. While in utter darkness he sang most of the time, and I remember our dear mother was troubled by a fancy that, like a mocking bird she once had that went blind in a railroad train, he might sing himself to death. But he recovered the sight of his right eye after a time, and the marvel is that the left eye did not shrink away and was not even discolored. The bony formation of the under-socket of the eye grew up and rectified itself almost entirely, and a lock of his curly hair covered the desperate-looking wound in the temple. It was a wonderful recovery.

There was a gunner in Calloway's battery named Allen Moore, a backwoods Georgian and a simple-hearted fellow, but a noble, enthusiastic man and soldier. The only other living member of Moore's family was with him, a lad of not more than twelve or thirteen years; and the devotion of the elder brother to the younger was tender as a mother's. The little fellow was a strange, sad, prematurely old child, who seldom talked and never smiled. He used to wear a red zouave fez that ill-befitted the peculiar, sallow, pallid complexion of the piney-woods Georgian; but he was a perfect hero in a fight. After the great repulse it looked for a time as if Grant had some idea of digging up to or mining our position. We had all day been shelling a suspicious-looking working party of the enemy, and about sunset I was visiting the batteries to see that the guns were properly arranged for night firing. As I approached Calloway's position the sharpshooting had almost ceased, and down the line I could see the figures of the cannoneers standing out boldly against the sky. Moore was at the trail adjusting his piece for the night's work. His gunnery had been superb during the evening and his blood was up.

I descended into a little valley and lost sight of the group, but heard Calloway's stern voice: "Sit down, Moore! Your gun is well enough; the sharpshooting is not over yet. Get down!" I rose the hill. "One moment, Captain! My trail's a hair's breadth too much to the right," and the gunner bent eagerly over the hand-spike. A sharp report and that unmistakable crash of a bullet against a man's head. It was the last rifle shot on the lines that night.

The rushing together of the detachment obstructed my view; but as I came up the sergeant stepped aside and said, "See there, Adjutant!" Moore had fallen on the trail, the blood flowing from his wound all over his face. His little brother was at his side instantly. No wildness, no tumult of grief. He knelt on the earth, and, lifting Allen's head on his knees, wiped the blood from his forehead with the cuff of his own tattered shirt-sleeve and kissed the pale face again and again, but very quietly. Moore was evidently dead, and none of us cared to disturb the child.

Presently he rose,—quiet still, tearless still,—gazed down at his dead brother, then around at us, and breathing the saddest sigh I ever heard, said: "Well, I am alone in the world!"

The preacher-captain sprang to his side, and placing his hand on the poor lad's shoulder, said confidently: "No, my child; you are not alone, for the Bible says: 'When my father and my mother forsake me, then the Lord will take me up;' and Allen was both father and mother to you; besides, I am going to take you up, too; you shall sleep under my blanket to-night."

There was not a dry eye in the group; and when, months afterwards, the whole battalion gathered on a quiet sabbath evening, on the banks of Swift Creek, to witness a baptism, and Calloway, at the water's edge, tenderly handed this child to the officiating minister, and receiving him again when the ceremony was over, threw a blanket about the little shivering form, carried him into a thicket, changed his clothing, and then reappeared, carrying the bundle of wet clothes, and he and the child walked away, hand in hand, to camp—then there were more tears, manly, ennobling tears, and the sergeant laid his hand on my shoulder and said, "Faith, Adjutant, the Captain has fulfilled his pledge to that boy!"

In one of the regiments of Kershaw's old brigade, which was supporting our guns at Cold Harbor, were three young men, brothers, whose cool daring in battle attracted our special admiration. We did not know the names of these gallant fellows, but had christened them "Tom, Dick, and Harry." A day or two after the great fight a fourth and youngest, a mere lad, who had been wounded at the Wilderness, came on his crutches to visit his brothers, and they had a hard time getting him safely into the trench. We noticed they called him "Fred." He was going home on what the soldiers called "a wounded furlough;" that is, a furlough granted because of a wound, to last until the man should be fit for service again; and as the lines were quiet in the sultry noon, except, of course, the spiteful sputter of the sharp-shooters, all the men from his neighborhood were soon busy painfully scribbling on scraps of paper and in the cramped trenches, letters for Fred to carry home.

Meanwhile, "Tom, Dick and Harry" surrounded their pet, as he evidently was; and indeed he was a lovely thing. We had not specially noted that the other young men were gentlemen. In fact, that did not so specially appear through the dirt and rags. We had readily seen they were "men," and that was what counted in those days.

But Fred—all the dirt was off of him, and the rags, too, and the sunburn, and the squalor—they were all gone. The Richmond ladies who had attended to his wounds in the hospital had seen to his toilet as well, which was simple and strictly military, but of the best material and fitted perfectly his perfect figure. His thin skin, his blue veins, his small, finely-formed hands and feet, his beautiful manners—everything, in fact—indicated that he was the scion of a noble house, the flower of South Carolina chivalry. In short, he was the most thoroughbred and aristocratic-looking thing any of us had seen for many a day. Compared with the rest

of us and in the midst of our surroundings, he glowed like
a fair seraph.

After a while he warned the writers that the mail was
about to close and they must bring in their letters; that his
"old leg" was hurting him and he must be off. The men
gathered around. His haversack was filled with the priceless
letters, head and heart crowded to confusion with trite messages, inestimably precious to those at home. He rose with
a smile of weariness and pain, yet bright anticipation, and
as he did so said, "Well, let me take a good look at those
rascals over the way; for it will be a long time before I get
another chance."

"Look out, Fred!" Too late! The sharp shock of the
bullet against the skull—he sprang up wildly, his cap flew
off and his brothers caught him in their arms and laid him
gently down. The home letters tumbled out of the full
haversack and were dabbled with the blood of the postman;
his brothers knelt about him, in a silent grief awful to look
upon, and heavy-hearted comrades gathered up each his
blood-stained package and gazed vacantly at it.

During the great gathering of Confederate soldiers at the
dedication of the Lee Monument, in Richmond, I told this
story of his Cold Harbor lines and his old brigade to General Kershaw, when Gen. Joseph E. Johnston happened to
be sitting near. It was too much for General Johnston.
Tears started to his eyes and he reproved me sharply for telling a story that had in it only dead, unrelieved pain. He
added that he must "take the taste of that thing out of our
mouths as quickly as possible;" and, as sharpshooting seemed to be the theme, he would repeat to us a practical lecture
on that subject which he once heard delivered by an expert
to a novice.

He said it was during the Atlanta campaign that he was
sitting in a clump of laurel on the north face of a mountain,
out beyond the bounds of his own lines, sweeping with a
glass the lines and camps of Sherman's army, which were
spread out before him upon the plain below. He had been
deeply absorbed and was suddenly startled by hearing conversation in a low tone comparatively near him. He sat

absolutely still and peered about, until, to his great relief, he saw two gray-brown figures stretched out side by side on the leaves but a little distance in front of him. One was a grizzled, fire-seamed veteran, and the other a beardless youth, and the elder addressed the younger, in substance, as follows:

"Now, Charley, when you ain't in a fight, but just shootin' so; of course you ought to get a fellow off by himself, before you let fly. Then the next thing is to see what you need most of anything. If it's clothes, why, of course, you choose a fellow of your own size; but if it's shoes you want, you just pick out the very littlest weevil-eaten chap you can find. Your feet would slide 'round in the shoes of a Yankee as big as you are like they was in flat-boats. Why, no longer ago than last evening I had drawed a bead on a fine, great big buck of a fellow, but just as I was about to drop him I looked around and found I didn't have no shoes. So I let him pass, and pretty soon here come along a little cuss of an officer, and"—raising his right foot, as the old general did his, by way of vivid recital and illustration— *"there's the boots."*

A word or two as to the volume, intensity, and effect of the fire at Cold Harbor. So far as the Confederate fire is concerned, nothing can be needed to supplement the fearful record of the slaughter upon the Federal side. But now as to the Federal fire, and first, of artillery. I think the barn just back of the positions of Manly's guns and two of the Howitzers' was Ellyson's. It was cut down, cut up and scattered, and the very ground so torn and ploughed by artillery fire that it was really difficult, after the battle was over, to say just where the barn had stood. Just back of this barn trees were so constantly felled across the road opened for the purpose of bringing in ammunition that it was necessary to have axe-men constantly at hand, and they were chopping almost continuously. Once or twice the falling trees and limbs actually drove the division pioneer corps from the work, and I was forced to get a detail from the Howitzers to do the necessary chopping.

As to musketry fire, I remember counting ninety odd bullet holes through a "dog tent," which was stretched immediately back of Calloway's guns, and he walked backward and forward between this tent and his pieces during the great attack. Though he did not leave the field, he was wounded in several places, and his clothes looked as if he had been drawn through a briar patch. His field glasses were smashed by a bullet and the guard of his revolver shot away. It is fair to say the same ball may have made two holes through Calloway's little tent; but on the other hand, many balls may have passed through the same hole.

When we left Cold Harbor all our bronze guns looked as if they had had smallpox, from the striking and splaying of leaden balls against them. Even the narrow lips of the pieces, about their muzzles, were indented in this way. One of the guns, I think of Manly's battery, was actually cut down by musketry fire, every spoke of both wheels being cut. Indeed, I had an extra wheel brought and substituted for that which first became useless, and this also shared the same fate. It is my desire and purpose to speak accurately, and therefore I take occasion to say that I do not intend to imply that all the spokes were completely severed and cut in two separate parts. Some of them were and others were not, but these latter were so frayed and splintered that the wheel would not stand straight and could no longer be used as a wheel. Much of the other wood work of this and other guns was badly split and splintered by musket balls, and some of the lighter iron parts and attachments were shot away.

The particular gun referred to was finally rendered absolutely useless for the rest of the fight. The men had worked it, for the most part, upon their hands and knees. How many of them were killed and wounded I do not recall; but one lieutenant was killed and one wounded, while directing, if I remember rightly, the fire of this gun and the one next to it.

After the fight it was necessary for some purpose to tip this gun, when a quantity of lead, exactly how much I would not like to say, but I should think more than a handful,

poured out of the muzzle upon the ground.   The gun carriage, with two of its wheels, was carried into Richmond
and hung up in the arsenal as an evidence of what musketry
fire might be and do.   Dr. Gaines, of Gaines' Mill, whom I
knew very well, had the other wheel carried to his house.   I
saw it there a few years later.   The hub and tire had actually
fallen apart.

A brief epitome of some of the salient features and results of the campaign of 1864, from the Wilderness to Cold
Harbor, inclusive, may not be devoid of interest.

The campaign covered, say sixty miles of space and thirty
days of time.   General Lee had a little under 64,000 men of
all arms present for duty at the outset, and he put *hors de
combat* of Grant's army an equal number man for man.   Mr.
Swinton, p. 482 of his "Army of the Potomac," puts Grant's
loss at "above sixty thousand men;" so that Grant lost in
killed and wounded and prisoners more than a thousand men
per mile and more than two thousand men per day during the
campaign.

Again, Lee had, as stated, at the start, present for duty,
less than 64,000 men, and the reinforcements he received
numbered 14,400 men; so that, from first to last, he had
under his command in this campaign, say 78,400 men; while
Grant had at the start, present for duty, 141,160 men, and
the reinforcements he received numbered 51,000 men; so
that from first to last he had under his command in this
campaign, say 192,160 men.

Now, Grant's one desire and effort was to turn Lee's
either flank, preferably his right flank, and thus get between
him and Richmond.   To accomplish this purpose, with his
preponderance of numbers, he might have left man for man
in Lee's front, and at the same time thrown an army of
77,000 to 114,000 on his flank, and yet he utterly failed to
get around or to crush that inevitable, indomitable flank.

From what I have read and heard of Grant, and the opinion I have formed of him, it is my belief that if this proposition had been put to him he would have admitted candidly
that he would not have dared to leave man for man in Lee's
front; that it would have been utterly unsafe for him to do

so—a statement I am certainly not prepared to dispute. Well, then; he might have left two for one in front of Lee, and yet have free from 13,000 to 36,000 men with which to turn his flank—and yet he failed utterly to turn it.

The figures here used are those of Col. Walter Taylor, and are less favorable to Lee than those of most of the Confederate authorities upon the war. General Early, for example, says that Lee, at the outset, had less than 50,000 effectives of all arms under his command.

It is not my purpose to accentuate this contrast in any unfair or unpleasant way, and yet an intelligent soldier of the Army of Northern Virginia, who fought at Chancellorsville in 1863, and again from the Rapidan to Cold Harbor in 1864, cannot but set opposite to the picture just sketched that of Lee holding the front of Hooker's 92,000 with "scant 14,000 muskets," while with about one-third (1-3) his numbers he utterly crushed in the right flank and rear of Hooker's great host. It should not be forgotten in this connection, and in endeavoring to form a just estimate of Lee's operations throughout this campaign of '64, that in the death of Jackson, Lee had lost his great offensive right arm, to which, at Chancellorsville and theretofore, he had looked to carry into execution his confounding strategies and his overpowering, resistless attacks.

This last suggestion was made as bearing upon a just and balanced view of the campaign in general, as well as an estimate of the ability displayed by Lee in the conduct of it. I ask leave to submit one other reflection of like general bearing, as well as tending to explain and relieve what may be regarded as adverse criticism of Grant. I said the soldiers of the Army of Northern Virginia did not generally consider Grant as a great strategist or maneuverer. His friends have entered for him a plea by way of confession and avoidance of this negative indictment—a good, sound plea. We cannot demur to it, and the Court of Impartial History will never strike it out as immaterial or improper, nor record a verdict that it is false.

I have not before me just now General Badeau's life of his chief, but in it he, in effect, says that Grant did not maneuver against the Army of Northern Virginia, because he found maneuvering of no avail against that army. Other Federal generals have made in substance the same remark. Maneuvering differs from fighting as a force in war, in this, that fighting is purely physical, while maneuvering gets in its work largely upon the moral plane. Its most deadly and disastrous effect is wrought by the destruction of confidence; confidence of the out-maneuvered general in himself and in his army, of the out-maneuvered army in itself and in its general.

In the case of Lee's army none of these consequences followed, when, for example, its huge adversary overlapped it upon one flank or upon both; or even turned its flank and took it in reverse—a thing which actually happened at least once in this campaign, when Hancock, on the 10th of May, at Spottsylvania, marched clean and clear around our left flank, and even, for a time, drove us in the fighting there. The men in our line fully appreciated what was happening, and yet there was not the slightest trepidation. Billy chanced to be standing near two intelligent infantry soldiers who were listening to and looking at the steady progression of the fire and the smoke of the fight, further and further in our rear, and quietly discussing the situation. At a sudden swell of musketry one of them, removing his pipe from his mouth and spitting upon the ground, said, "Look here, Tom, if those fellows should get much further around there we would be in a bad fix here; we'd have to get out of this."

"Law, John!" said his friend, "Marse Robert'll take care of those fellows. He knows just what to do."

So we all felt, and if he had deemed it best and so ordered, we would have fought just as steadily in two lines, back to back and facing both ways.

Two days later the gallant Hancock made further and, if possible, higher proof of the soundness of Grant's plea, and of the steadfast, indomitable courage of the Army of Northern Virginia,* when after bursting through its center with 40,000 men, and taking and holding the "Bloody Angle," embracing, perhaps, counting both sides, approximately two miles of its line, and capturing the infantry and the artillery that defended it, he yet found himself unable to advance one foot beyond the point where the first impulse had carried him, in the darkness and surprise, and he encountered, across the base of the salient and at each extremity of the captured line, troops as staunch and sturdy and unconquerable as any he had ever met in battle.

It is this quality or condition, or habit of mind and conduct, of which different Federal officers have spoken under different names, in expressing their high estimate of the Army of Northern Virginia. It is this which General Hooker terms "discipline," in his remarkable testimony before the Committee on the Conduct of the War, already quoted, in the course of which, speaking of Lee's army, he said "* * * that army has by discipline alone acquired a character for steadiness and efficiency unsurpassed, in my judgment, in ancient or modern times."

It has been said, and it may be true in a certain sense, to the honor and glory of the private soldiers of that immortal army, that the army made the general and made for him his world-wide fame; that General Lee throughout his great career wielded an unrivalled weapon, a weapon of perfect temper and of finest edge,—but it has also been said, and it is also true, perhaps in a yet higher sense, that the general made the army; that the weapon was wielded by an unrivalled swordsman, a swordsman of dauntless courage and of matchless skill.

We are free to admit that, in our view, the explanation of all this is to be found largely in the fact that the relation between our general and our army was constant and permanent, undissolved and indissoluble; that we grew to be, as it were, one body dominated by one great inspiring soul; and that we came to look with wonder, not unmixed with pity, upon the contrasted condition of the opposing Federal army, with generals jealous of and plotting against each other, and the Government forever pulling down one and putting up another. Nor are we small enough to be unappreciative of the manhood which could and did, even under such unfavorable circumstances, exhibit the loyalty and courage which the Army of the Potomac exhibited upon many a hard-fought field.

CHAPTER XXII

FROM COLD HARBOR TO EVACUATION OF RICHMOND AND PETERSBURG

Grant's Change of Base—Petersburg Proves to Be His Immediate Objective—Lee Just in Time to Prevent the Capture of the City—Our Battalion Stationed First in the Petersburg Lines, Then Between the James and the Appomattox—The Writer Commissioned Major of Artillery and Ordered to Chaffin's Bluff—The Battalion There Greatly Demoralized—Measures Adopted to Tone it Up—Rapid Downward Trend of the Confederacy—"A Kid of the Goats" Gives a Lesson in Pluck.

The repulse at Cold Harbor marked a crisis in the campaign. If Richmond was to continue to be Grant's immediate objective, there was but one thing for him to do, and that was to fight, to renew his attack upon Lee's lines. He was as close to Richmond as he could get by the old process of sliding southward and eastward. Every foot of further progress in that direction would be progress away from the goal. He must decide, then, between another effort to force his men to the imminent deadly breach and the abandonment of Richmond as his immediate objective. It took him nine days to decide, and then he folded his tents, like the Arabs, and silently stole away—at night, the night of June 12th.

He was just in time. It was not Lee's habit to give his adversary the choice of moves, especially if he took long to choose. He seldom abandoned the initiative—that is where at all practicable for him to retain it. He had only seemed to abandon it this time. It would have been, even for him, an astounding piece of audacity, with his worn and wasted little army, to march out from his intrenchments and attack Grant's overwhelming numbers, yet he had determined to do this very thing. On page 37 of his address, so often quoted, General Early says:

Notwithstanding the disparity which existed, he was anxious, as I know, to avail himself of every opportunity to strike an offensive blow; and just as Grant was preparing to move across James River, with his defeated and dispirited army, General Lee was maturing his plans for taking the offensive; and in stating his desire for me to take the initiative with the corps I then commanded, he said: "We must destroy this army of Grant's before he gets to James River. If he gets there it will become a siege, and then it will be a mere question of time.

It was the startling intelligence of Hunter's operations in the Valley which prevented the contemplated movement against Grant. It became necessary to detach, first Breckenridge, and then Early, to meet this new peril threatening Lee's communications. As Early's corps was to have led the attack, and because it was worse than hopeless to attack at all with his army thus seriously reduced, Lee was compelled to abandon his cherished plan, and Grant retired unmolested from Lee's front on the very night that Early received his orders to move at three o'clock next morning for the Valley; so close and critical was the sequence of events in these later days of the struggle.

When we waked on the morning of the 13th and found no enemy in our front we realized that a new element had entered into this move—the element of uncertainty. Thus far, during the campaign, whenever the enemy was missing, we knew where, that is, in what direction and upon what line, to look for him; he was certainly making for a point between us and Richmond. Not so now—even Marse Robert, who knew everything knowable, did not appear to know what his old enemy proposed to do or where he would be most likely to find him.

I remember I went across to the Federal works and was surprised to see what a short distance they were from ours, and how enormous and elaborate they looked in comparison. I have been all over the opposing lines at Cold Harbor since the war,—so far as they remain undisturbed,—and this latter impression has been confirmed and strengthened. At some points it really seems as if the Federal army had anticipated attack from every point, except the skies, and fortified against them all.

I have little or no recollection of our search for Grant, except that there was nothing about it calculated to make an impression—that it seemed rather a slow, stupid affair. Of course we crossed the Chickahominy, and then we worked down toward Malvern Hill. I am not even sure, however, whether we left the vicinity of Cold Harbor on the 13th or waited a day or two in that neighborhood. We did not cross the James River, I think, until the night of the 17th; but from that time everything seemed to have waked up, and though we saw no enemy, yet we knew where he was, and that Petersburg was his immediate objective and not Richmond, nor any point on James River.

We made a rapid all-night march, which was a very trying one, on account of the heat and the heavy dust which covered everything and everybody and rendered breathing all but impossible. We stopped an hour or so to rest the horses—we did not so much regard the men—and arrived in Petersburg in the early morning, our division and our battalion being among the first of Lee's troops to arrive. We were just in time to prevent Burnside from making an assault, which would probably have given him the city. General Beauregard had made admirable use of the scant force at his command and had successfully repulsed all previous attacks, but he did not have a garrison at all adequate to resist the countless thousands of Grant's main army, which had now begun to arrive, and which seems to have been deterred from the assault by the knowledge of our arrival.

The whole population of the city appeared to be in the streets and thoroughly alive to the narrow escape they had made. Though we had done nothing save to come right along, after we found out where to come, they seemed to be overflowing with gratitude to us. Ladies, old and young, met us at their front gates with hearty welcome, cool water, and delicious viands, and did not at all shrink from grasping our rough and dirty hands. There is nothing more inspiring to a soldier than to pass through the streets of a city he is helping to defend, and to be greeted as a deliverer by its women and children. He would be a spiritless wretch indeed who could not be a hero after passing through a scene like this. Grant's men did not seem to yearn for close contact with us immediately after such an experience, and they did wisely to defer that pleasure.

We were not at once placed upon the lines, and some of us witnessed scenes yet more intense when a command passed through the streets which had in it what was left of several companies originally recruited in Petersburg. Every now and then along the line of march some squalid, tattered fellow, with dust-begrimed and sweat-stained face, would dart out of the column, run up the steps to the pillared porch of a fine old mansion and fling his arms about some lovely, silver-haired matron, and fairly smother her with kisses; she fervently returning his embrace, and following him with her blessing as he hurried to catch up with the command and resume his place in the ranks.

My recollection is that we were placed in the works about noon and remained only a few hours, never firing a shot nor seeing an enemy; and then followed an experience unparalleled since we left Leesburg in the spring of '62. Our guns were withdrawn late in the night and we passed back through Petersburg, recrossed the Appomattox River, and were stationed on the lines, between that and the James, near the Dunn house, the Howitzers quartered in the house; and there the battalion remained from say the 20th of June, 1864, until the 2d of April, 1865, *without ever so much as firing a shot or being fired at by an enemy,* except that I have an indistinct recollection of our taking a rifled gun, I think of Manly's battery, a little in advance and to the left of our regular position, and taking a shot or two at the astronomer or observer in General Butler's tower. This was really a little hard on that gentleman, as I am confident he never did us any harm; but then I am equally confident we did not do him any. On the contrary, we gave him a little respite from his high and exalted position and his exhausting observations.

I said the experience was unparalleled. I refer of course to our being placed in such a safe and easy position. Both the preceding winters we had passed upon the advanced picket line of the army—while most of the artillery was quartered on the railroad in comfortable winter camps. We were not responsible for being now, as it were, "mustered out of service;" yet we could not repress a vague feeling that, somehow, we were not doing our full duty. Especially was this feeling intensified when, a few months later, Mahone's division, which had been manning a very trying part of the Petersburg lines, was brought over between the Appomattox and the James to relieve Pickett's, which was sent north of the James. We thought we had before seen men with the marks of hard service upon them; but the appearance of this division of Mahone's, and particularly of Finnegan's Florida brigade, with which we happened to be most closely associated, made us realize, for the first time, what our comrades in the hottest Petersburg lines were undergoing. We were shocked at the condition, the complexion, the expression of the men, and of the officers, too, even the field officers; indeed we could scarcely realize that the unwashed, uncombed, unfed and almost unclad creatures we saw were officers of rank and reputation in the army It was a great pleasure, too, to note these gallant fellows, looking up and coming out, under the vastly improved conditions in which they found themselves.

Sometime, I think in December, '64,—strange as it may appear, I am not certain of the date—I was promoted to be major of artillery, and ordered on duty with the battalion of heavy artillery at Chaffin's Bluff, on the north side of the James River, about ten or twelve miles below Richmond, and about a mile below Drewry's Bluff, which was on the south side. There were batteries of heavy guns on the shore at both these points, the battalions manning them being also armed with muskets, and our iron-clads were anchored in the river about and between the two land batteries. These iron-clads were manned by a body of marines and seamen under command of Admiral Tucker. At the close of the campaign proper of 1864 all the troops manning the defenses of Richmond who were not strictly of the Army of Northern Virginia were under command of Lieutenant-General Ewell, who was in charge of the Department of Richmond. The heavy artillery battalions on the river—the Chaffin's Bluff battalion among them—and the local troops manning the parts of the line adjacent thereto constituted the division of Gen. Custis Lee, eldest son of Gen. Robert E. Lee, a man of the highest character and an officer of the finest culture and a very high order of ability. He did not have a fair opportunity during the war, President Davis, of whose staff he was a member, refusing to permit him to go to the field, though he plead earnestly to do so. He was a most sensitive and modest gentleman, and would have rejoiced to command even a regiment in his father's army. After he was sent to the field, in the modified way in which he was sent near the close of the war, he more than once told me that every time he met one of his father's veteran fighting colonels he felt compromised at having the stars and wreath of a major-general on his collar.

When I first went to Chaffin's, Colonel Hardaway, of the Field Artillery of the Army of Northern Virginia, was in command, but, as I remember, he left very soon. Some time before the end, Major Gibbes, who had served with our battalion (Cabell's) during a part of the campaign of '64, was sent there, and of course ranked me; but for a considerable time I was in command of the post and of the battalion, and of course was greatly interested in becoming thoroughly acquainted with my duties and my men.

They were splendid soldiers in external appearance and bearing. I had never seen anything approximating to them in the field. Their dress-parades, inspections, reports, salutes, bearing in the presence of officers and on guard were wonderfully regular, accurate, and according to the drill and regulations. The mint, anise, and cumin were most scrupulously tithed; but the weightier matters of the soldier law— patriotism, devotion, loyalty, fidelity, courage, endurance,— how as to these? Perhaps the first day I was in command the sergeant-major and acting-adjutant brought me his report, which I looked over and found very satisfactory— until I came to the added foot-note, that a first lieutenant and several non-commissioned officers and men had "disappeared" the preceding day while on a "wood detail" down the river.

I recalled the adjutant and asked him what that entry meant. He seemed surprised and did not answer promptly. Changing the form of the question, I asked if it was possible it meant what it seemed to mean, and he replied that it did. I made him sit down and tell me all he knew of the matter, in the course of the conversation sending for his book of reports and examining them for some time back. I saw no entry quite so shocking as the report of the day, but found that entries of like character were not infrequent; that every few days these details were sent down the river to get wood and were in the habit of meeting emissaries sent by the enemy for the purpose, who offered them every inducement to desert; that these inducements were embodied also in printed circulars, one of which was shown me. I was horrified, and in the course of the next day or two made a careful investigation into the character and condition of the command, the result of which was anything but satisfactory.

I hardly knew what to do, but through the acting-adjutant, who turned out to be an excellent fellow and a trustworthy, useful, and promising officer, I was enabled to secure a conference of the best officers of the battalion, and in a long interview to secure their confidence and co-operation, and we set to work together to change the condition of things. I ingratiated myself, too, with the men by doing away with a number of petty orders and regulations which were annoying and burdensome, and instituting in their place a few which were really important. Among other things I, of course, did away with this down-the-river wood-detail.

It is not worth while to particularize further. Suffice it to say, I endeavored to impress upon the men three things: first, that I already knew a great deal about them and expected and intended to know them thoroughly; second, that I was in command of them and expected and intended to be obeyed implicitly; and third, that I was their friend and expected and intended to do the very best I could for them in every way. I will only add that I was deeply stirred, and put my whole heart and soul into the matter and into my

men, and that my efforts ultimately effected more than I had
even dared to hope; particularly in the line of securing the respect and confidence and friendly regard of the men.   The
greatest difficulty was encountered in the fact that not a few
of the officers were utterly worthless, and I determined to get
rid of these, but as to this was compelled to move slowly.

One other measure adopted certainly ought to be mentioned.   There were a good many Christian men in the command, but they seemed to have little or no social or public
religious life.   I had these assembled for special, informal conference with the commanding officer.   I talked with
them, in a general way, about the condition of the command,
and asked their interest and assistance in doing everything
possible to improve it and tone it up, and gave notice that I
would myself, whenever it was practicable, conduct a simple
religious service on Sunday evenings in our log church, to
which all were invited, but none would be compelled to attend.   I believe this little service conduced as much as any
other means or measure to such success as attended my
efforts.

I had but two difficulties with the men.   One was a simple, though aggravated, case of open disrespect to some an-
nouncement or order having to do with the new order of
things, and which was read at dress-parade.   This I punished on the spot, and severely, and we never had any repetition of it.   The other was a more complicated and trouble-
some affair.

The weather was very cold, and after I put a stop to the
wood-detail down the river, the men began cutting some of
the standing timber upon and back of the bluff; but orders
were sent me by competent authority forbidding this, and
these orders were duly read at dress-parade and also posted.
I did the best I could to provide wood, but the supply was
inadequate, and the men really suffered.   I explained how
much I   regretted the situation and added that I fared
and should fare no better than they.   I was compelled,
of course, to have fire in the adjutant's office, where writing
must be done; but I should have none in my house except
when they had it in their houses, and no more wood than

they had, and I urged the observance of the regulation against cutting wood on the bluff, to which special importance seemed to be attached by the authorities.

The men were resentful and rebellious about this regulation against felling trees. My order stopping the river wood-detail was the obvious consequence of the disgraceful action of their comrades, and that they did not seem to resent. But, one cold night, soon after my special utterance about the preservation of the timber, while lying awake in bed—very likely from cold—I heard the regular blows of two axes upon a tree. I got up, dressed, and armed myself, and made my way through the snow, guided by the sound, until I was close upon two men who were chopping at a large tree which was about toppling to its fall. I waited until it did fall and then came suddenly upon them. They started to run, but I ordered them to halt, impressing the order with my revolver, and adding that I knew them both. I reminded them that they could not possibly plead ignorance of the order and asked how they thought I ought to punish them, to which, of course, they made no response. I then expressed deep sympathy with them; adding that, though it would break up discipline to allow sympathy with suffering to excuse flagrant violation of orders, yet as it was the first offense, and they were so entirely in my power, and seemed to admit the truth and force of all I had said, I had determined to take no further notice of the matter. They thanked me profusely and were about to return to their quarters, but I ordered them to remain and cut up the tree for use; but that, of course, it should be divided among the command or distributed by the quartermaster with his other wood. I exacted from them a promise not only not to fell any more trees themselves, but to do all in their power to put a stop to tree-cutting by others. The two men told this story around the battalion, with considerable amplification and adornment. It seemed to make an unexpectedly strong and favorable impression and was one of the definite things that aided the accomplishment of my intense desire to *get hold* of my men.

Of course I greatly missed my old life, and especially its congenial and often charming companionship. This life was comparatively solitary, but it was after all a life of greater power, a life that meant more, and I was becoming deeply absorbed in it. I felt more and more what a tremendous thing it was to have almost absolute power over men and to be in a position where I could well nigh mould them to my will. Billy came over to see me after I had gotten pretty well under way in my work, and seemed thoroughly to agree with me about it; though it was shocking to him to be brought into contact with soldiers of such a stamp and standard as I have described.

Colonel Hardaway's old battalion was composed of as fine material as any in General Lee's army, and I did not wonder that he preferred to return to it. Just before or just after we abandoned our lines, General Alexander requested that both Major Gibbes and myself should be sent to him, one to serve in Hardaway's battalion and one in Haskell's. But Gen. Custis Lee, commanding our division, declined to give up both of us, and as Gibbes ranked me, he had the choice and went to Hardaway, while I remained with my Chaffin's Bluff battalion, not only in command, but the only field officer connected with it.

I recall but one incident of these lines worth relating. After the loss of Fort Harrison in September, '64, our picket line was retired and the enemy's advanced, in front of the fort; but nearer the river we still held our old line, and upon it a wooded knoll which commanded a full view of the enemy's main line, and so was very important to us and our tenure of it correspondingly annoying to them. The Federal lines at this point were manned by negro troops.

One evening, sitting on the knoll and looking toward Fort Harrison, several hundred yards distant, I observed the negro picket near the intersection of our old picket line and theirs, walking his beat upon our line, instead of theirs, and so coming directly toward me. Then he took his return beat toward the fort, but when he came again he extended his beat further in my direction, and another followed him. So the next time there were three of them upon our line, and I divined their purpose, which was by moral pressure, as it were, to crowd us back from the knoll.

I had only two men with me, but I dispatched one to General Custis Lee, with a brief note of explanation, asking that fifty men be sent me immediately. Meanwhile I mounted my remaining man on our old picket line, faced toward Fort Harrison, and ordered him to walk rapidly—I walking at his side—just inside the little curtain of earth.

When the negroes saw us coming they turned back and I could see the one nearest us was trembling as he heard our steps approaching. When we came close upon him he turned, his face actually ashy, and holding his gun in both hands horizontally, he obtruded it towards us, at the same time backing away and saying:

"'Tain't my fault. Officer ob de day tell me to come up dis way."

Noticing this revelation, but not remarking upon it, I picked up a billet of wood and laid it across the top of the little work, between my man and the negro, saying, "If that negro steps across that piece of wood, shoot him; and if he steps off the line, on either side, shoot him."

This broke up the little scheme. The negroes retired beyond the intersection of the lines and I never saw one of them pass it again.

During the seven months from September, '64, to March, '65, inclusive, no intelligent man could fail to note the trend and progress of events. The defeat of Hood, the fall of Atlanta, the unfortunate expedition into Tennessee, the march of Sherman southward through Georgia to the ocean, his march northward through the Carolinas to Goldsboro, the fall of Savannah, of Charleston, of Wilmington—all these and other defeats, losses, and calamities had left to the Confederacy little save its Capital and the narrow strips of country bordering on the three railroads that fed it. Of course I was—we all were—thoroughly aware of this, and yet, though it may be difficult now to realize it, we did not even approximate the failure of heart or of hope. One of our dreams was that Lee, having the inner line, might draw away from Grant, concentrate with Johnston, and crush Sherman, and then, turning, the two might crush Grant. Yet we relied not so much on any special plans or hopes, but rather upon the inherently imperishable cause, the inherently unconquerable man. Fresh disaster each day did not affect our confidence. We were quite ready to admit, indeed we had already contemplated and discounted anything and everything this side of the ultimate disaster; but that—*never!*

This was emphatically my position. I well remember that after the evacuation and on the retreat,—indeed but one day before Sailor's Creek,—I left the line of march for an hour to see my mother, who was refugeeing in Amelia County, at the country home of a prominent gentleman of Richmond, beyond military age, who, when he saw me, exclaimed:

"Ah, Bob, my dear boy; it is all over!"

"Over, sir?" said I, with the greatest sincerity; "over? Why, sir, it has just begun. We are now where a good many of us have for a good while longed to be: Richmond gone, nothing to take care of, foot loose and, thank God, out of those miserable lines! Now we may be able to get what we have longed for for months, a fair fight in an open field. Let them come on, if they are ready for this, and the sooner the better."

One very inclement day in the early spring of '65 I was leaving Richmond, about four or five o'clock in the evening, for the long, dreary, comfortless ride to Chaffin's Bluff. I cannot recall ever having been so greatly depressed. I passed Dr. Hoge's church and noticed the silent women in black streaming, with bowed heads, from all points, toward the sanctuary, and longed intently to enter with them; but I could not, as it would detain me too long from my post. Every face was pale and sad, but resolute and prayerful; while every window in the church—nay, every one in the doomed city—was shuddering with the deep boom of artillery.

I passed on down Main street and, where the terraced Libby Hill Park now is, then a rough, unsightly place, I observed a little kid cutting some unusual capers on the brink of a precipitous bluff. He was evidently trying to force himself to make the perilous leap to the street below, but shrank from the test. Two or three times he trotted back a little

from the brow, and ran forward, but he would swerve upon
the very brink, and then would stand, first upon his hind
legs and then his fore, and shake his pretty head, and bleat
and b-a-a. At last he went back further, and coming on
at prodigious speed, tried as before to stop himself on the
edge, but failed, and passing clear of the brow and of all
obstacles and projections, he did light, sure enough, in the
level street, and though a little shaken up, yet seemed to feel
that he had done a big thing and that all his troubles were
behind him.

The game little fellow curvetted and danced and pranced
around the very feet of my horse, seeming to strive to arrest
my attention and to say to me: "Do you not see—the jump-
ing-off place is not the end of all things? Never say die! If
you must leave your present position and jump off, do it like
a man and make the best of it. The end is not yet."

CHAPTER XXIII

THE RETREAT FROM CHAFFIN'S BLUFF TO SAILOR'S CREEK

On the Works, Sunday Evening, April 2d, '65, Listening to the Receding Fire at Petersburg—Evening Service with the Men Interrupted by the Order to Evacuate the Lines—Explosions of the Magazines. of the Land Batteries and Iron-Clads—A Soldier's Wife Sends Her Husband Word to Desert, But Recalls the Message—Marching, Halting, Marching, Day After Day, Night After Night—Lack of Food, Lack of Rest, Lack of Sleep—Many Drop by the Wayside, Others Lose Self-control and Fire into Each Other—In the Bloody Fight of the 6th at Sailor's Creek, the Battalion Redeems Itself, Goes Down with Flying Colors, and Is Complimented on the Field by General Ewell, After He and All Who Are Left of Us Are Prisoners of War.

Not many weeks later, on Sunday, the 2d of April, I stood almost all day on our works overhanging the river, listening to the fire about Petersburg, and noting its peculiar character and progression. I made up my mind what it meant, and had time and space out there alone with God and upon His day to commit myself and mine to Him, and to anticipate and prepare for the immediate future. Late in the afternoon I walked back to my quarters, and soon after, George Cary Eggleston, who was then in a command that held a part of the line near us, dropped in. He tells me now that I asked him then what effect he thought it would have upon our cause if our lines should be broken and we compelled to give up Petersburg and Richmond; and that he declined to answer the question because, as he said, the supposed facts were out of the plane of the practical, and would not and could not happen. Now, years afterwards, recalling the peculiar expression and manner with which I propounded this interrogatory, he asks whether I had then received any official information, and I answer in the negative—no, none whatever. Up to the time Eggleston left my camp for his I knew nothing beyond what my tell-tale ears and prescient soul had told me.

Indeed, we went into our meeting that night without any other information; but I had directed the acting-adjutant to remain in his office and to bring at once to me, in the church, any orders that might come to hand. Our service was one of unusual power and interest. I read with the men the "Soldier Psalm," the ninety-first, and exhorted them, in any special pressure that might come upon us in the near future—the "terror by night" or the "destruction * * * at noon-day"—to abide with entire confidence in that "Stronghold," to appropriate that "Strength."

As I uttered these words, I noticed a well-grown, fine-looking country lad named Blount, who was leaning forward, and gazing at me with eager interest, while tears of sympathy and appreciation were brimming his eyes. The door opened and the adjutant appeared. I told him to stand a moment where he was, and as quietly as possible told the men what I was satisfied was the purport of the paper he held in his hand, and why I was so satisfied. And then we prayed for the realization of what David had expressed in that Psalm—for faith, for strength, for protection. After the prayer I called for the paper and read it over, first silently and then aloud, gave brief directions to the men and dismissed them—first calling upon such officers and non-commissioned officers of the battalion as had special duties to perform in connection with the magazines, etc., to remain a few moments. The men were ordered to rendezvous at a given hour, and to fall in by companies on the parade, and the company officers were ordered to see that they brought with them only what was absolutely necessary, and a brief approximate list was given of the proper campaign outfit. But the poor fellows had been many months in garrison, and it was maddening work, within a short and fixed time, to select from their motley accumulations what was really necessary in the changed conditions ahead of us.

The orders were, in general, that the men of the fleet and of the James River defenses should leave the river about midnight of the 2d of April, exploding magazines and iron-clads, and join the Army of Northern Virginia in its retreat. Orders such as these were enough to try the mettle even of the best troops, in the highest condition, but for my poor little battalion they were overwhelming, well nigh stupefy-ing. The marvel is that they held together at all and left the Bluff, as they did, in pretty fair condition. A few months earlier I question whether they would have been equal to it.

I said they left in pretty fair condition, and so they did, except that they had more baggage piled upon their backs than any one brigade, perhaps I might say division, in Gen-eral Lee's army was bearing at the same moment. I could hardly blame them, and there was no time to correct the folly; besides, I knew it would correct and adjust itself, as it had done pretty well by morning.

The explosions began just as we got across the river. When the magazines at Chaffin's and Drury's Bluffs went off, the solid earth shuddered convulsively; but as the iron-clads—one after another—exploded, it seemed as if the very dome of heaven would be shattered down upon us. Earth and air and the black sky glared in the lurid light. Columns and towers and pinnacles of flame shot upward to an amaz-ing height, from which, on all sides, the ignited shells flew on arcs of fire and burst as if bombarding heaven. I dis-tinctly remember feeling that after this I could never more be startled—no, not by the catastrophes of the last great day.

I walked in rear of the battalion to prevent straggling, and as the successive flashes illumined the darkness the blanched faces and staring eyes turned backward upon me spoke volumes of nervous demoralization. I felt that a hare might shatter the column.

We halted at daylight at a country cross-road in Chester-field to allow other bodies of troops to pass, the bulk of my men lying down and falling asleep in a grove; but seeing others about a well in the yard of a farm house over the way, I deemed it best to go there to see that nothing was unnecessarily disturbed.

I sat in the porch, where were also sitting an old couple, evidently the joint head of the establishment, and a young woman dressed in black, apparently their daughter, and, as I soon learned, a soldier's widow. My coat was badly torn, and the young woman kindly offering to mend it, I thanked her and, taking it off, handed it to her. While we were chatting, and groups of men sitting on the steps and lying about the yard, the door of the house opened and another young woman appeared. She was almost beautiful, was plainly but neatly dressed, and had her hat on. She had evidently been weeping and her face was deadly pale. Turning to the old woman, as she came out, she said, cutting her words off short, "Mother, tell him if he passes here he is no husband of mine," and turned again to leave the porch. I rose, and placing myself directly in front of her, extended my arm to prevent her escape. She drew back with surprise and indignation. The men were alert on the instant, and battle was joined.

"What do you mean, sir?" she cried.

"I mean, madam," I replied, "that you are sending your husband word to desert, and that I cannot permit you to do this in the presence of my men."

"Indeed! and who asked your permission, sir? And pray, sir, is he your husband or mine?"

"He is your husband, madam, but these are my soldiers. They and I belong to the same army with your husband, and I cannot suffer you, or anyone, unchallenged, to send such a demoralizing message in their hearing."

"Army! do you call this mob of retreating cowards an army? Soldiers! if you are soldiers, why don't you stand and fight the savage wolves that are coming upon us defenseless women and children?"

"We don't stand and fight, madam, because we are soldiers, and have to obey orders, but if the enemy should appear on that hill this moment I think you would find that these men are soldiers, and willing to die in defense of women and children."

"Quite a fine speech, sir, but rather cheap to utter, since you very well know the Yankees are not here, and won't be, till you've had time to get your precious carcasses out of the way. Besides, sir, this thing is over, and has been for some time. The Government has now actually run off, bag and baggage,—the Lord knows where,—and there is no longer any Government or any country for my husband to owe allegiance to. He does owe allegiance to me and to his starving children, and if he doesn't observe this allegiance now, when I *need* him, he needn't attempt it hereafter when *he* wants *me*."

The woman was quick as a flash and cold as steel. She was getting the better of me. She saw it, I felt it, and, worst of all, the men saw and felt it, too, and had gathered thick and pressed up close all round the porch. There must have been a hundred or more of them, all eagerly listening, and evidently leaning strongly to the woman's side.

This would never do.

I tried every avenue of approach to that woman's heart. It was congealed by suffering, or else it was encased in adamant. She had parried every thrust, repelled every advance, and was now standing defiant, with her arms folded across her breast, rather courting further attack. I was desperate, and with the nonchalance of pure desperation—no stroke of genius—I asked the soldier-question:

"What command does your husband belong to?"

She started a little, and there was a trace of color in her face as she replied, with a slight tone of pride in her voice:

"He belongs to the Stonewall Brigade, sir."

I felt, rather than thought it—but, had I really found her heart? We would see.

"When did he join it?"

A little deeper flush, a little stronger emphasis of pride.

"He joined it in the spring of '61, sir."*

Yes, I was sure of it now. Her eyes had gazed straight into mine; her head inclined and her eyelids drooped a little now, and there was something in her face that was not pain

---

*The Stonewall Brigade was, of course, not so named until after the first battle of Manassas, and it did not exist an an organization after May, 1864; but men who had at any time belonged to one of the regiments that composed it ever after claimed membership in the brigade. Among soldiers of the Army of Northern Virginia, and yet more among their families and friends, once of "The Stonewall Brigade," always of that immortal corps.

and was not fight. So I let myself out a little, and turning to the men, said:

"Men, if her husband joined the Stonewall Brigade in '61, and has been in the army ever since, I reckon he's a good soldier."

I turned to look at her. It was all over. Her wifehood had conquered. She had not been addressed this time, yet she answered instantly, with head raised high, face flushing, eyes flashing—

"General Lee hasn't a better in his army!"

As she uttered these words she put her hand in her bosom, and drawing out a folded paper, extended it toward me, saying:

"If you doubt it, look at that."

Before her hand reached mine she drew it back, seeming to have changed her mind, but I caught her wrist, and without much resistance, possessed myself of the paper. It had been much thumbed and was much worn. It was hardly legible, but I made it out. Again I turned to the men.

"Take off your hats, boys, I want you to hear this with uncovered heads"—and then I read an endorsement on application for furlough, in which General Lee himself had signed a recommendation of this woman's husband for a furlough of special length on account of extraordinary gallantry in battle.

During the reading of this paper the woman was transfigured, glorified. No Madonna of old master was ever more sweetly radiant with all that appeals to what is best and holiest in man. Her bosom rose and fell with deep, quiet sighs; her eyes rained gentle, happy tears.

The men felt it all—*all*. They were all gazing upon her, but the dross was clean, purified out of them. There was not, upon any one of their faces an expression that would have brought a blush to the cheek of the purest womanhood on earth. I turned once more to the soldier's wife.

"This little paper is your most precious treasure, isn't it?"

"It is."

"And the love of him whose manly courage and devotion won this tribute is the best blessing God ever gave you, isn't it?"

"It is."

"And yet, for the brief ecstasy of one kiss, you would disgrace this hero-husband of yours, stain all his noble reputation, and turn this priceless paper to bitterness; for the rearguard would hunt him from his own cottage, in half an hour, a deserter and a coward."

Not a sound could be heard save her hurried breathing. The rest of us held even our breath.

Suddenly, with a gasp of recovered consciousness, she snatched the paper from my hand, put it back hurriedly in her bosom, and turning once more to her mother, said:

"Mother, tell him not to come."

I stepped aside at once. She left the porch, glided down the path to the gate, crossed the road, surmounted the fence with easy grace, climbed the hill, and as she disappeared in the weedy pathway I caught up my hat and said:

"Now, men, give her three cheers."

Such cheers! Oh, God! shall I ever again hear a cheer which bears a man's whole soul in it?

For the first time I felt reasonably sure of my battalion. It would follow me anywhere.

No Confederate soldier who was on and of that fearful retreat can fail to recall it as one of the most trying experiences of his life. Trying enough, in the mere fact that the Army of Northern Virginia was flying before its foes, but further trying, incomparably trying, in lack of food and rest and sleep, and because of the audacious pressure of the enemy's cavalry. The combined and continued strain of all this upon soft garrison troops, unenured to labor and hardship and privation and peril, can hardly be conceived and cannot be described. Its two most serious effects were *drowsiness and nervousness.* We crossed and left James River at midnight on Sunday, were captured at Sailor's Creek about sundown on the Thursday following, and I think rations were issued to us that night by our captors. I do not say there was only one, but I *recall only one issue of*

rations between those limits, and we were marching all day
and, as I remember, a large part of every night.

The somewhat disorganized condition of the troops and
the crowded condition of the roads necessitated frequent
halts, and whenever these occurred—especially after nightfall—the men would drop in the road, or on the side of it,
and sleep until they were roused, and it was manifestly impossible to rouse them all. My two horses were in almost
constant use to transport officers and men who had given
out, especially our doctor, whose horse was for some reason unavailable. Besides, I preferred to be on foot, for the
very purpose of moving around among the men and rousing
them when we resumed the march. With this view I was a
good part of the time at the rear of the battalion; but notwithstanding my efforts in this respect, individually and
through a detail of men selected and organized for the purpose of waking the sleepers, we lost, I am satisfied, every
time we resumed the march after a halt at night—men who
were not found or who could not be roused.

The nervousness resulting from this constant strain of
starvation, fatigue, and lack of sleep was a dangerous thing,
at one time producing very lamentable results, which threatened to be even more serious than they were. One evening an officer, I think of one of our supply departments,
passed and repassed us several times, riding a powerful,
black stallion, all of whose furnishings—girths, reins, etc.,
—were very heavy, indicating the unmanageable character
of the horse. When he rode ahead the last time, about
dark, it seems that he imprudently hitched his horse by tying
his very stout tie rein to a heavy fence rail which was part of
the road fence. Something frightened the animal and he
reared back, pulling the rail out of the fence and dragging
it after him full gallop down the road crowded with troops,
mowing them down like the scythe of a war chariot. Someone, thinking there was a charge of cavalry, fired his musket
and, on the instant, three or four battalions, mine among
them, began firing into each other.

I was never more alarmed. Muskets were discharged in
my very face, and I fully expected to be shot down; but

after the most trying and perilous experience, the commanding officers succeeded in getting control of their men and getting them again into formation. But while we were talking to them, suddenly the panic seized them again, and they rushed in such a wild rout against the heavy road fence that they swept it away, and many of them took to the woods, firing back as they ran. A second time the excitement was quieted and a third time it broke out. By this time, however, I had fully explained to my men that we had just put out fresh flankers on both sides of the road, that we could not have an attack of cavalry without warning from them, and that the safe and soldierly thing to do was to lie down until everything should become calm. I was much pleased that this third time my command did not fire a shot, while the battalions in our front and rear were firing heavily. A field officer and a good many other officers and men were killed and wounded in these alarms, just how·many I do not believe was ever ascertained.

When we next halted for any length of time, during daylight, I formed my men and talked to them fully and quietly about these alarms, explaining the folly of their firing, and impressing upon them simply to lie down, keep quiet, and attempt to catch and obey promptly any special orders I might give. I complimented them upon their having resisted the panicky infection the last time it broke out, and felt that, upon the whole, my men had gained rather than lost by the experience.

On Thursday afternoon we had descended into a moist, green little valley, crossed a small stream called Sailor's Creek, and, ascending a gentle, grassy slope beyond it, had halted, and the men were lying down and resting in the edge of a pine wood that crowned the elevation. A desultory fire was going on ahead and bullets began to drop in. I was walking about among the men, seeing that everything was in order and talking cheerfully with them, when I heard a ball strike something hard and saw a little commotion around the battalion colors. Going there, I found that the flag-staff had been splintered, and called out to the men that we were beginning to make a record.

Next moment I heard an outcry—"There, Brookin is killed!"—and saw one of the men writhing on the ground. I went to him. He seemed to be partially paralyzed below the waist, but said he was shot through the neck. I saw no blood anywhere. He had on his roll of blankets and, sure enough, a ball had gone through them and also through his jacket and flannel shirt; but there it was, sticking in the back of his neck, having barely broken the skin. I took it out and said: "O, you are not a dead man by a good deal. Here,"—handing the ball to him,—"take that home and give it to your sweetheart. It'll fix you all right." Brookin caught at the ball and held it tightly clasped in his hand, smiling faintly, and the men about him laughed.

Just then I heard a shell whizzing over us, coming from across the creek, and we were hurried into line facing in that direction, that is, *to the rear*. I inferred, of course, that we were surrounded, but could not tell how strong the force was upon which we were turning our backs.

I remember, in all the discomfort and wretchedness of the retreat, we had been no little amused by the Naval Battalion, under that old hero, Admiral Tucker. The soldiers called them the "Aye, Ayes," because they responded "aye, aye" to every order, sometimes repeating the order itself, and adding, "Aye, aye, it is, sir!" As this battalion, which followed immediately after ours, was getting into position, and seamen's and landsmen's jargon and movements were getting a good deal mixed in the orders and evolutions,—all being harmonized, however, and licked into shape by the "aye, aye,"—a young officer of the division staff rode up, saluted Admiral Tucker, and said: "Admiral, I may possibly be of assistance to you in getting your command into line." The Admiral replied: "Young man, I understand how to talk to my people;" and thereupon followed "a grand moral combination" of "right flank" and "left flank," "starboard" and "larboard," "aye, aye" and "aye, aye"—until the battalion gradually settled down into place.

By this time a large Federal force had deployed into line on the other slope beyond the creek, which we had left not long since; two or three lines of battle, and a heavy

park of artillery, which rapidly came into battery and opened an accurate and deadly fire, we having no guns with
which to reply and thus disturb their aim. My men were
lying down and were ordered not to expose themselves. I
was walking backward and forward just back of the line,
talking to them whenever that was practicable, and keeping
my eye upon everything, feeling that such action and exposure on my part were imperatively demanded by the history and condition of the command and my rather peculiar
relations to it. A good many had been wounded and several
killed, when a twenty-pounder Parrott shell struck immediately in my front, on the line, nearly severing a man in twain,
and hurling him bodily over my head, his arms hanging
down and his hands almost slapping me in the face as they
passed.

In that one awful moment I distinctly recognized young
Blount, who had gazed into my face so intently Sunday
night; and but for that peculiar paralysis which in battle
sometimes passes upon a man's entire being—excepting only
his fighting powers—the recognition might have been too
much for me.

In a few moments the artillery fire ceased and I had time
to glance about me and note results a little more carefully.
I had seldom seen a fire more accurate, nor one that had
been more deadly, in a single regiment, in so brief a time.
The expression of the men's faces indicated clearly enough
its effect upon them. They did not appear to be hopelessly
demoralized, but they did look blanched and haggard and
awe-struck.

The Federal infantry had crossed the creek and were now
coming up the slope in two lines of battle. I stepped in front
of my line and passed from end to end, impressing upon my
men that no one must fire his musket until I so ordered; that
when I said *"ready"* they must all rise, kneeling on the right
knee; that when I said *"aim"* they must all aim about the
knees of the advancing line; that when I said *"fire"* they
must all fire together, and that it was all-important they
should follow these directions exactly, and obey, implicitly
and instantly, any other instructions or orders I might
give.

The enemy was coming on and everything was still as the grave. My battalion was formed upon and around a swell of the hill, which threw it further to the front than any other command in the division, so that I was compelled to shape my own course, as I had received no special orders. The Federal officers, knowing, as I suppose, that we were surrounded, and appreciating the fearful havoc their artillery fire had wrought, evidently expected us to surrender and had their white handkerchiefs in their hands, waving them toward us, as if suggesting this course; and yet, so far as I remember, they did not call upon us to surrender. I do not recall any parallel to this action.

I dislike to break the flow and force of the narrative by repeated modifying references to recollection and memory; but it is not safe for a man, so many years after the event, to be positive with regard to details unless there was special reason why they should have been impressed upon him at the time. I will say, then, that my memory records no musket shot on either side up to this time, our skirmishers having retired upon the main line without firing. The enemy showed no disposition to break into the charge, but continued to advance in the same deliberate and even hesitating manner, and I allowed them to approach very close—I should be afraid to say just how close—before retiring behind my men. I had continued to walk along their front for the very purpose of preventing them from opening fire; but now I stepped through the line, and, stationing myself about the middle of it, called out my orders deliberately—the enemy, I am satisfied, hearing every word. "*Ready!*" To my great delight the men rose, all together, like a piece of mechanism, kneeling on their right knees and their faces set with an expression that meant—everything. "Aim!" The musket barrels fell to an almost perfect horizontal line leveled about the knees of the advancing front line. "Fire!"

I have never seen such an effect, physical and moral, produced by the utterance of one word. The enemy seemed to have been totally unprepared for it, and, as the sequel showed, my own men scarcely less so. The earth appeared to have swallowed up the first line of the Federal force in our

front. There was a rattling supplement to the volley and the
second line wavered and broke.

The revulsion was too sudden. On the instant every man
in my battalion sprang to his feet and, without orders, rushed, bareheaded and with unloaded muskets, down the slope
after the retreating Federals. I tried to stop them, but in
vain, although I actually got ahead of a good many of them.
They simply bore me on with the flood.

The standard-bearer was dashing by me, colors in hand,
when I managed to catch his roll of blankets and jerk him
violently back, demanding what he meant, advancing the
battalion colors without orders. As I was speaking, the
artillery opened fire again and he was hurled to the earth,
as I supposed, dead. I stooped to pick up the flag, when his
brother, a lieutenant, a fine officer and a splendid-looking fellow, stepped over the body, saying: "Those colors belong
to me, Major!" at the same time taking hold of the staff.
He was shot through the brain and fell backward. One
of the color guard sprang forward, saying: "Give them to
me, Major!" But by the time his hand reached the staff he
was down. There were at least five men dead and wounded
lying close about me, and I did not see why I should continue
to make a target of myself. I therefore jammed the color
staff down through a thick bush, which supported it in an
upright position, and turned my attention to my battalion,
which was scattered over the face of the hill firing irregularly at the Federals, who seemed to be reforming to renew
the attack. I managed to get my men into some sort of
formation and their guns loaded, and then charged the Federal line, driving it back across the creek, and forming my
command behind a little ridge, which protected it somewhat.

I ran back up the hill and had a brief conversation with
General Custis Lee,—commanding the division, our brigade
commander having been killed,—explaining to him that I
had not ordered the advance and that we would be cut off
if we remained long where we were, but that I was satisfied
I could bring the battalion back through a ravine, which
would protect them largely from the fire of the enemy's artillery, and reform them on the old line, on the right of the

naval battalion, which had remained in position. He expressed his doubts as to this, but I told him I believed my battalion would follow me anywhere, and with his permission I would try it. I ran down the hill again and explained to my men that when I got to the left of the line and shouted to them they were to get up and follow me, on a run and without special formation, through a ravine that led back to the top of the hill. Just because these simple-hearted fellows knew only enough to trust me, and because the enemy was not so far recovered as to take advantage of our exposure while executing the movement to the rear and reforming, we were back in the original lines in a few moments—that is, all who were left of us.

It was of no avail. By the time we had well settled into our old position we were attacked simultaneously, front and rear, by overwhelming numbers, and quicker than I can tell it the battle degenerated into a butchery and a confused mêlée of brutal personal conflicts. I saw numbers of men kill each other with bayonets and the butts of muskets, and even bite each others' throats and ears and noses, rolling on the ground like wild beasts. I saw one of my officers and a Federal officer fighting with swords over the battalion colors, which we had brought back with us, each having his left hand upon the staff. I could not get to them, but my man was a very athletic, powerful seaman, and soon I saw the Federal officer fall.

I had cautioned my men against wearing "Yankee overcoats," especially in battle, but had not been able to enforce the order perfectly—and almost at my side I saw a young fellow of one of my companies jam the muzzle of his musket against the back of the head of his most intimate friend, clad in a Yankee overcoat, and blow his brains out. I was wedged in between fighting men, only my right arm free. I tried to strike the musket barrel up, but alas, my sword had been broken in the clash and I could not reach it. I well remember the yell of demoniac triumph with which that simple country lad of yesterday clubbed his musket and whirled savagely upon another victim.

I don't think I ever suffered more than during the few moments after I saw that nothing could possibly affect or change the result of the battle. I could not let myself degenerate into a mere fighting brute or devil, because the lives of these poor fellows were, in some sense, in my hand, though there was nothing I could do just then to shield or save them. Suddenly, by one of those inexplicable shiftings which take place on a battle-field, the fighting around me almost entirely ceased, and whereas the moment before the whole environment seemed to be crowded with the enemy, there were now few or none of them on the spot, and as the slaughter and the firing seemed to be pretty well over, I concluded I would try to make my escape. By the way, I had always considered it likely I should be killed, but had never anticipated or contemplated capture.

I think it was at this juncture I encountered General Custis Lee, but it may have been after I was picked up. At all events, selecting the direction which seemed to be most free from Federal soldiers and to offer the best chance of escape, I started first at a walk and then broke into a run; but in a short distance ran into a fresh Federal force, and it seemed the most natural and easy thing in the world to be simply arrested and taken in. My recollection is that General Lee asked to be carried before the Federal general commanding on that part of the line, who, at his request, gave orders putting a stop to the firing, there being no organized Confederate force on the field. Thus ended my active life as a Confederate soldier, my four years' service under Marse Robert, and I was not sorry to end it thus, in red-hot battle, and to be spared the pain, I will not say humiliation, of Appomattox.

I must, however, mention an incident to which I have already briefly referred, to which it would perhaps have been more delicate not to refer at all; but the reader of this chapter can scarcely have failed to perceive that one of the most deeply stirring episodes in my soldier life was the struggle I made to lift my battalion out of the demoralization in which I found it; to make my men trust and love me, and to rouse and develop in them the true conception of soldierly duty and devotion, courage and endurance.

Looking back upon the teeming recollections of this first and last retreat and this final battle of the Army of North-

ern Virginia, amid all the overpowering sadness and depression of defeat, I already felt the sustaining consciousness of
a real and a worthy success; but it is impossible to express
how this consciousness was deepened and heightened when
General Ewell sent for me on the field, after we were all
captured, and in the presence of half a dozen generals said
that he had summoned me to say, in the hearing of these officers, that the conduct of my battalion had been reported to
him, and that he desired to congratulate me and them upon
the record they had made.

CHAPTER XXIV

FATAL MISTAKE OF THE CONFEDERATE MILITARY AUTHORITIES

The Love of Glory the Inspiration of a Soldier—Prompt Promotion the Life of an Army—How Napoleon Applied these Principles—How the Controlling Military Authorities of the Confederacy Ignored Them—The Material of the Confederate Armies Superb, Their Development as Soldiers Neglected—Decoration for Gallantry, and Promotion on the Field Unknown in the Confederate Service—Lee Himself Without Authority to Confer Such Promotion or Distinction—Contrasted Spirit and Practice of the Federal Authorities and Armies—Grotesque Absurdity of an Elective Roll of Military Honor.

If asked what I regarded as the most fatal mistake of the military authorities of the Confederacy, I should unhesitatingly answer—their utter and amazing *failure to appreciate the distinctive inspiration of the soldier, the informing spirit of an army.* That spirit, that inspiration, is best expressed in the one word "Promotion"—promotion on the spot, "on the field;" instant, responsive, rapid promotion.

I do not deny the existence of other great principles and forces, fundamental and formative, in the life of the soldier. On the contrary, I thoroughly believe in and appreciate them, and shall take pleasure in pointing them out in the last chapter of this work; but I do say that the great element of progress and development in the military life is the desire for *promotion,* or at least, for honorable *distinction* in the profession.

I do not hesitate to say the soldier cannot be highly developed without this influence. The true soldier is ever looking for opportunities to earn promotion or distinction, and the true general ever on the lookout to reward men who have well earned the one or the other. This is the way—I am willing to say, the only way—to make a soldier or an army and to develop both to the highest point of effectiveness.

Probably the greatest master of the art of war, in ancient or modern times, was the first Napoleon, and his army —if not the best that ever marched or fought—certainly reached a height of resistless power that alarmed and for a time dominated Europe.

It is well known how largely he made use of and relied upon the element we are now considering, and which we may as well characterize plainly as *the love of glory.* Countless stories are told illustrating how he stimulated this natural desire, until it became the one passionate thirst of his soldiers. They enjoyed the privilege of unrestrained access to him at all times, and he encouraged them to address him as "Sire."

In one of his greatest battles he occupied a commanding height from which, mounted on his favorite war horse and surrounded by a magnificent staff, he overlooked the drawn fight that hung in the balance on the plain below; striving, through the battle smoke, to analyze the field and to determine where to deliver his final blow. He was sitting deep in the saddle and deeply absorbed, when a young infantry soldier, from one of his favorite regiments, pressed through the gorgeous uniforms and prancing steeds of the staff until, pale, haggard, bloody, powder-begrimed, he reached the Emperor's side, and slapping his hand smartly upon his thigh, pointed eagerly to a particular part of the field and said: "Sire, send a strong column *there,* and the day is ours!"

Napoleon, startled from his reverie, turned and looked upon the hatless, breathless, but inspired boy; then breaking into a smile of appreciation and delight, and shaking his finger at him, burst out: "You little devil! Who told you my secret? Go back to your regiment, sir!"

The column was hurled upon the weak point the two Napoleons had detected; the victory was won, and the victor rode over to the spot where the fatal thrust had been made—and there, just where the head of the French column had pierced the hostile line, lay that peerless youth with a bullet through his brain, but the light of battle and of victory glorifying his countenance. The Emperor turned pale and reeled in his saddle, but quickly recovering, gazed yearningly at the dead hero, and with bitter emphasis exclaimed, "But for that accursed bullet, there lies a Marshal of France!"

Another illustration occurs to me.

On a rapid march through an unfamiliar region the head of his column halted on the bank of a river, and the Emperor, turning to the ranking engineer officer present, demanded to know its width. The colonel said he could not tell; but the Emperor instantly replied:

"But I must know."

"The instruments are in the rear, sire. I cannot tell without the instruments."

"I said nothing about instruments; I asked the width of this river, and I must be told."

"Sire, no one can tell without the instruments," said the colonel.

At this moment a young lieutenant of engineers stepped forward and saluted, saying:

"Sire, I think I can tell you near enough for all practical purposes, the width of the stream."

"Tell me then, sir!"

The lieutenant advanced to the edge of the water and faced the other shore. Drawing down the visor of his cap until it just cut the further brink, he turned his head—taking care to keep his chin at the same level—until the cap brim struck the bank they were on. Then, again addressing the Emperor, he said:

"Sire, let them measure the distance from here to yonder barn and you will have approximately the width of the river."

Recognizing the resource and quickness of the young officer, Napoleon ordered the immediate exchange of rank, making the lieutenant a colonel and the colonel a lieutenant, on the spot.

These incidents require not one word, by way either of explanation or of emphasis. It is easy to see, indeed it would seem impossible not to see, how such instant, responsive, public recognition and reward of merit and of service must inspire and develop an army.

What I mean to assert is that the Confederate military authorities—that is, the governing authorities—did absolutely nothing, in this general direction; that we did not have, as General Hooker and other Federal generals testified, material originally inferior which we toned up by admirable training and discipline; but, on the contrary, that the material of our armies, the bulk of our rank and file, was as fine as the world ever saw, as full of military capacity and aptitude and ambition, and that we steadily toned down this superb material by habitual neglect of what is most essential to the development of the soldier.

It is needless to say that the Army of Northern Virginia was under a leadership in the field as developing and uplifting as soldiers ever followed; but, with this exception, all things were against us. The controlling military authorities seem to have relied entirely upon the patriotism and character of the individual men, and did nothing to make them soldiers, or to make the aggregation of them an army. Any one of us might perform prodigies of valor, no one ever noticed it; or exhibit the most decided and even brilliant capacities for command or advancement, the advancement or command might never come.

Take the case of Lieutenant Falligant at Cold Harbor, already mentioned. Our battalion report set forth his splendid conduct in detail; General Kershaw, commanding our division, was full of enthusiastic admiration, and promised —and I have no doubt fulfilled his promise—to press Falligant's promotion; yet no notice was ever taken of the matter. If Falligant had done in Napoleon's army precisely what he did in the Army of Northern Virginia I have no doubt he would have been decorated on the field and promoted to be full colonel of artillery. He was a second lieutenant when he rendered his superb service at Cold Harbor, '64. If I mistake not, he was a second lieutenant at Appomattox.

I think it was at Suffolk that a private soldier in one of the regiments of the Confederate force investing the place proposed, and alone and single-handed, executed a brilliant and daring plan, which completely rid the investing force of the galling fire of sharpshooters concealed in tall, dry grass on the other side of a deep stream.

This gallant and ingenious fellow, when the wind was blowing from our side toward the enemy's, procured a long, thick plank, with which he entered the water, lying breast down on one end of the plank, which of course inclined the other end upward, making a sort of protection for him and especially for his head. Thus equipped, he paddled across the stream to a point projecting out toward our shore, and where the dry grass stood high above water so deep that the sharpshooters could not approach near it, and there, and as far up and down the stream as he could venture, he set fire to the grass. The flames spread rapidly, and the daring incendiary, taking advantage of the flight and confusion of the sharpshooters, swam safely back to our side of the stream.

The force was entirely relieved from the annoying and destructive fire, but their heroic deliverer was, as usual, overlooked and neglected.

I am not sure that the Federal military authorities fully recognized the principles we have been discussing, but they certainly contrasted very strongly with ours in this respect.

After the battle of Chickamauga Longstreet sent to Richmond a number of Federal flags captured by his men in the engagement, in charge of a party consisting of several private soldiers, two or three non-commissioned officers, and a lieutenant or two, who had specially distinguished themselves in the capture of the banners. They were met at the depot by a negro with a one-horse wagon, into which the captured banners were dumped, and in which they were hauled to the Capitol—and the men received transportation back to the army. Of course they were laughing-stocks to their fellows, and felt the deep sting of the lesson that gallant conduct is a matter beneath notice.

About the same time I read in the Northern papers an account of the reception accorded a similar party of Federal soldiers, sent upon a like errand, to Washington. As

I remember, they were received by the full Cabinet, assembled in the War Department.   The line officers were made majors and colonels, the non-commissioned officers received commissions, and the privates had the chevrons of sergeants and corporals sewed upon their coatsleeves.   Of course they returned to their army, themselves heroes and inspirers of heroic deeds among their comrades.

When I was captured and passed through Grant's army I felt as if I had entered a new world.   The non-commissioned officer who was first to reach me, as we were walking to find the Federal officer commanding on that part of the line, rattled off to me his military history, which was at his tongue's end.

"Major," said he, "you've helped me to my shoulder straps.   You make the fifth field officer I've been the first man to reach; twice my hand has been first on captured cannon.   You see that man yonder?   He's a private soldier still, because he hasn't the mind or education to make an officer, and he knows it and don't want a commission; but look at his medals and decorations.   There ain't a general officer in the corps but touches his hat to him."

And so it seemed to be with all the men I saw.   Each appeared fully aware of the amount of good conduct laid up to his credit, and yearning for opportunity to win further distinction.

There was nothing approximating this in our service.   I can truly say,—and thousands of my old comrades can say with me,—I never saw or heard of a medal or a ribbon being pinned on a man's jacket, or even so much as a man's name being read out publicly in orders for gallantry in battle.   With some of us, at least, it would have gone far to atone for having nothing put inside our stomachs if we had had a red ribbon or some such thing pinned outside our jackets.   Not only did I never see or hear of a promotion on the field, but I do not believe such a thing ever occurred in any army of the Confederacy, from the beginning to the end of the war.   Indeed, I am confident it never did; for, incredible as it may appear, even Lee himself did not have the power to make such a promotion.   On page 147 of his book, Colonel Taylor, the Adjutant-General of his army, says:

General Lee should have been supreme in all matters touching the movements and discipline of his Army; whereas, under the law and the regulations of the Department of War made in conformity thereto, he had not even the power to confer promotion on the field of battle.

I have myself heard other prominent Confederate leaders complain of their utter powerlessness in this regard, and it is generally understood that Jackson more than once threatened to resign if he should be further interfered with in "putting down one and setting up another" of the officers and men of his command.

In short, the error and defect upon which I am commenting was too glaring to be denied, but I have heard it apologized for upon the ground that deeds of gallantry were so common in the Confederate armies and especially in the Army of Northern Virginia, that they could not with propriety be recognized or rewarded as "distinguished." This is worse than absurd. No matter how high the average, some men and some deeds necessarily rose above it. Besides, men were sometimes promoted for gallantry in our service, and even in Lee's glorious army; but the point is, the promotion lagged and followed afar off—so far that, before the tardy recognition came, men had forgotten the heroic deeds that forced it, and the effect was almost, if not altogether, lost.

May I be pardoned for referring to my personal experience in this regard, amongst the bitterest of my life. I was recommended for promotion for conduct at "The Salient," that is, "The Bloody Angle," of Spottsylvania, of the 12th of May, '64; and the promotion came, but *more than six months later,* and then the commission gave me rank, *not from the date of the engagement,* but from the *date of its issue;* nor was there upon its face the slightest reference to or connection with the glorious 12th of May. I do not think I was ever so disappointed and indignant. I never saw the commission again; my recollection is that I tore it to tatters. I presume it is, in part at least, to the delay in issuing this commission that I am indebted for the additional wrong that my name is not mentioned in the only published list, so far as I know, of the field officers of the Confederate armies.

If anything were needed to accentuate the dismal failure of the military authorities of the Confederacy, in the general field of the inspiration and development of the soldier, it would be abundantly supplied by the remarkable record of the only attempt they ever made, so far as I am informed, in that direction. This attempt was embodied in an Act of the Congress of the Confederate States, approved October 13, 1862, and several orders of the Adjutant and Inspector-General's office: No. 93, of November 22, 1862; No. 31, of October 3, 1863, and No. 64, of August 10, 1864—all to be found in War Records, Series I., Vol. xxx., Part 2, Reports, pages 532 and 533.

The title of the Act is promising, and is as follows: "An Act to authorize the grant of medals and badges of distinction, as a reward for courage and good conduct on the field of battle;" but the outline of the scheme is grievously disappointing.

"The President," and not the general commanding in the field, was authorized to confer the medals and badges; so that, even without the distinct reference in the orders to "the regular channels," it is obvious that, in practical operation, the plan would fail utterly of that rapid, responsive recognition and reward wherein consist the life and power of decoration and promotion "on the field."

Again, the Act provided for conferring "a badge of distinction upon one private or non-commissioned officer of *each company,* after *every signal victory* it shall have assisted to achieve." Thus, by reason of the number to be decorated, the decoration would, of necessity, cease to be a distinction, and the scheme must, as it did, break down of its own weight, to say nothing of its other inherent defects.

Perhaps the most glaring of these was the mode of selecting the men who were to be recipients of the badges. It is expressly provided in the Act that: "The non-commissioned officers and privates of the company who may be present on the first dress-parade thereafter (that is, 'after every signal victory') may choose, by a majority of their votes, the soldier best entitled to receive such distinction." Could there be devised a more shocking travesty upon the essential law and character of military promotion or reward and the appropriate mode of conferring it? Such promotion or recognition means, of course, and exclusively, recognition or promotion from above; by the determination, that is, of one's superior or commanding officer. To substitute in place of this the ballot of one's fellows is a monstrous perversion—so monstrous as to be incredible but for the absolute proofs we have submitted. It was bad enough to provide for election to military office; but to elect the bravest man in the command is an incongruity still more extreme.

And yet there is one feature of this remarkable statute even more exaggerated and grotesque. The entire scheme had been delayed a year or more because of the difficulty or expense of procuring the medals and badges, and an elective "Roll of Honor" was the ingenious substituted device of someone to bridge over the difficulty. In the order of August 10, '64, it was provided that: "Should more than one soldier hereafter be selected by a company as equal in merit, the name to be entered upon the roll will be determined by lot." The imagination staggers at the task of picturing the scene where two elected heroes proceeded to draw straws to determine which of the twain should be enrolled among the immortals.

Was there ever enacted by a legislative body, or carried into effect by an executive office, a more utterly impotent scheme or as grim a farce? It seems almost beyond belief, but there it is, in black and white; and it was actually put into operation in some of our armies. It may have been to some extent operative in the Army of Northern Virginia; but I have yet to meet a soldier of that army who claimed the honor of having had his name entered upon this Elective Roll of Honor, this Roll of Elected Heroes, or who had even so much as heard of such a roll, although it was expressly ordered that the roll be read "at the head of every regiment in the service of the Confederate States."

I say again, the invention of such a scheme only accentuates the pitiful failure of the Confederate military authorities to put into operation the noble, healthful, inspiring law and practice of *genuine military recognition and promotion on the field.*   And I say further, that I believe this failure had as much to do with the failure of our cause as any other —yes, even more, than any and all other forces and influences, save and except, perhaps, the overwhelming material force arrayed against us.

CHAPTER XXV

POTPOURRI

Startling Figures as to the Numbers and Losses of the Federal Armies
During the War—Demoralizing Influence of Earth-works—Attrition and Starvation—Lack of Sleep *vs.* Lack of Food—Night Blindness in the Army of Northern Virginia—Desertions from the Confederate Armies—Prison Life—DeForest Medal—Gen. Lee's Hat.

Some years ago, during the discussion of the pension
legislation of Congress, the following statements, substantially, were published at Washington in *The National Tribune* of May 16, 1889. We do not vouch for their accuracy, but there is truth enough in the figures to make them
valuable, and power enough to startle the thoughtful reader.

The article asserts that the Federal force invading the
South from '61 to '65 was fully twice as large as was ever
put afield by any other modern nation, and that it contested
more battles, did more fighting, and lost more in killed and
wounded than all the armies of modern Europe in the last
three-quarters of a century, that is, since the close of the
Napoleonic wars in 1815.

It states that 2,320,272 men served an average of three
years during our war; that no other war of the century has
lasted so long or been filled with such continuous and sanguinary fighting; that 2,261 battles and skirmishes were
fought, many of them more destructive of human life than
any other battles in modern history; that over 400,000 men
lost their lives in the struggle—that is, double the number
of the entire army of Great Britain, 143,000 more than that
of Austro-Hungary; more than Napoleon arrayed against
the coalition of England, Russia, Prussia, Sweden and

Spain; and twice as many as he had when he began his Waterloo campaign. The article closes with these words:

"Our war lasted nearly seven times as long as the Franco-Prussian struggle, and we lost over six times as many killed on the field of battle as the Germans lost in overrunning the whole of France."

As I understand, the above figures represent the number and losses of the Federal armies alone. If so, what a story they tell of the fighting power of the little Confederacy, cut off from the world in its death grapple, opposing the great hosts of the Union with less than one-third their numbers, and meeting, among the overwhelming myriads of its foes, more imported foreigners than the entire number of the native soldiers of the South.

In my account of the campaign of '64, especially of Spottsylvania and Cold Harbor, in noting our first real experience of fighting "in the trenches" and behind the "works," I failed to mention its tendency to demoralize the men.

The protection of a little pile of earth being in front of a man and between him and his enemy, his natural tendency is to stay behind it, not only as to part, but as to the whole of his person. I have more than once seen men behind such a line fire their muskets without so much as raising their heads above the curtain of earth in front of them; fire, indeed, at such an inclination of their gun-barrels upward as to prevent the possibility of hitting an enemy unless that enemy were suspended in the sky or concealed in the tree tops.

So greatly did this desire to fight behind protection increase that I have seen men begin digging every time the column halted, until their commanding officers declared that any man caught intrenching himself without orders should be punished severely. It is fair to say that, after a while, the better men of the army, at least, learned to use without abusing the vantage ground of earth-works.

In commenting upon Grant's theory and plan of *attrition,* I should have added that one feature of it was to turn loose upon our armies and our homes the twin giant of *starvation.*

Especially was this the case after Sherman started through Georgia and our communications began to be cut by Federal raiding parties in all directions. Sometime ago, I do not remember just how long, Mr. George Cary Eggleston, in a graphic paper upon the campaign of '64, wrote in a very feeling and original way of the pains and pangs of hunger, and how deeply they depressed and deteriorated his entire being. I take no issue with him as to this statement, and yet, to me, even greater suffering and deterioration came from lack of sleep. I do not know that I have ever suffered more, physically and mentally, than from intense desire and demand of my whole being for deep, unbroken sleep, combined with inability to get more than a snatch at a time, which was almost worse than none at all. Such was frequently our experience, especially upon night marches and during long-continued battle.

I am inclined to think my unusual muscular strength saved me from that general giving way which, in the case of most men, follows quickly upon lack of sufficient food; but on the other hand, I seemed to be peculiarly susceptible to the suffering, even torture and almost madness, which accompanies or follows lack of sleep. I believe it was Napoleon who defined a soldier to be a man who could eat and sleep in one day for three. My army experience inclines me to say that a better definition could scarcely be framed, at least on the purely physical side.

Perhaps the most peculiar and striking fact or feature of the physical condition of General Lee's army during the latter half of the war was night blindness—the men affected being unable to see after sunset, or a little later.

I do not know what proportion of the men were so affected, but it is safe to say that thousands were. Many of them were as good and true men as any in the service; indeed, I have seen men led by the hand all night in order to go into battle with the command in the morning.

The doctors tell us that these symptoms were to be accounted for as among the expressions of an anæmic and scorbutic condition, which itself resulted from lack of proper and sufficient nutrition. It would be interesting to know to what extent, if at all, the Federal armies weer so affected. There may have been investigations and reports embodying this and other points of interest with regard to the matter, but, if so, I have never seen them. Indeed, my purpose is merely to record the fact, which 1 believe to be for the most part unknown even to the intelligent public of this generation.

There is one feature of our Confederate struggle, to which I have already made two or three indirect allusions, as to which there has been such a strange popular misapprehension that I feel as if there rested upon the men who thoroughly understand the situation a solemn obligation to bring out strongly and clearly the sound and true view of the matter. I refer to an impression, quite common, that *the desertions from the Confederate armies, especially in the latter part of the war, indicated a general lack of devotion to the cause* on the part of the men in the ranks.

On the contrary, it is my deliberate conviction that Southern soldiers who remained faithful under the unspeakable pressure of letters and messages revealing suffering, starvation, and despair at home, displayed more than human heroism.

The men who felt this strain most were husbands of young wives and fathers of young children, whom they had supported by their labor, manual or mental. As the lines of communication in the Confederacy were more and more broken and destroyed, and the ability, both of county and public authorities and of neighbors, to aid them became less and less—the situation of such families became more and more desperate, and their appeals more and more piteous to their only earthly helpers who were far away, filling their places in "the thin gray line." Meanwhile the enemy sent into our camps, often by our own pickets, circulars offering our men indefinite parole, with free transportation to their homes.

I am not condemning the Federal Government or military authorities for making these offers or putting out these circulars; but if there was ever such a thing as a conflict of duties, that conflict was presented to the private soldiers of the Confederate army who belonged to the class just mentioned, and who received, perhaps simultaneously, one of these home letters and one of these Federal circulars; and if ever the strain of such a conflict was great enough to unsettle a man's reason and to break a man's heart strings, these men were subjected to that strain.

Ask any Confederate officer who commanded troops during the latter part of the war and who was loved and trusted by his men. He will tell you of letters which it would have seared your very eyeballs to read, but that they could not be read without tears—letters in which a wife and mother, crazed by her starving children's cries for bread, required a husband and father to choose between his God-imposed obligations to her and to them and his allegiance to his country, his duty as a soldier; declaring that if the stronger party prove recreant to the marriage vow, the weaker will no longer be bound by it; that if he come not at once, he need never come; that she will never see him again nor recognize him as her husband or the father of her children.

In order that it may be seen that I am not drawing an imaginary or exaggerated picture, I quote from page 145 of Colonel Taylor's "Four Years with General Lee"—a passage which, by the way, I had not read until after I had penned the foregoing upon this topic. Says Colonel Taylor:

A few words in regard to this desertion. The condition of affairs throughout the South at that period was thoroughly deplorable. Hundreds of letters addressed to soldiers were intercepted and sent to the Army Headquarters, in which mothers, wives and sisters told of their inability to respond to the appeals of hungry children for bread, or to provide proper care and remedies for the sick; and in the name of all that was true, appealed to the men to come home and rescue them from the ills which they suffered and the starvation which threatened them. Surely never was devotion to one's country and to one's duty more sorely tested than was the case with the soldiers of Lee's army during the last year of the war.

Many a noble officer, reading such a letter with a poor fellow of his command at nightfall, has realized how entirely inadequate was the best sympathy, advice, and comfort he could give; and when, at next morning's roll-call that man failed to answer to his name, has felt far more of pity than of condemnation. Soldiers would not prevent the departure of a comrade who was known to have received such a letter. Officers of courts-martial, compelled by sense of duty to order the execution as a deserter of a man absent without leave under such circumstances, have confessed to me that they shuddered, as if accessories before the fact to *murder*.

Some years ago, cowering under a great rock on the edge of the Aletsch glacier, in an Alpine thunder-storm, with Prof. (Sir John) Tyndall, Lady Tyndall, and my brother-in-law, Professor Newton, of Yale University, I related a story which was told me by Dr. Hunter McGuire and other eye-witnesses, of Jackson's agonized suffering, yet refusal to interfere with a death sentence imposed by a court-martial, under circumstances such as I have described. Lady Tyndall shuddered and averted her face; but her husband, perceiving that she did so, said with emphasis:

"My dear, awful as it was, Jackson was right;" then, turning to me, he added, "Mr. Stiles, God never made a greater or a righter human soul than Stonewall Jackson. No, sir, I do not believe it within the power—even of the Lord God Almighty—to make one!"

In this general connection I cannot but refer with pride to the unshaken condition and magnificent record of my old battery, even on that fearful retreat from Richmond, and up to and at the very end. The evening before Sailor's Creek we passed them on the road near Amelia Court House, and I was delighted to find their condition about as good as I ever saw it, and their mettle quite as high. They were better supplied than we, and, for the last time, I plundered Billy's haversack for a morsel of food.

As I have always understood, and believe to be true, they went down and passed into history, with the immortal Army of Northern Virginia, with all their men, save two, present for duty, or honorably accounted for.

There are several minor and personal matters, more or less connected with my army experience, which I have been specially requested to touch upon. One of these is my prison life. It may be that I shall deem this worthy of more extended notice hereafter, so that for the present I shall confine myself to one or two points.

When it was proposed to release the field officers at Johnson's Island, in the summer of 1865, I was one of those called upon by the prison authorities to aid in the preparation of the numerous requisite "papers," and when, long after midnight, I handed in my batch, Major Lee, the courteous and kindly commandant of the post, when he had looked them over, said they were all right, except that I had been guilty of just such an omission as he would undertake to say had never before occurred, in like circumstances—that is, I had forgotten to prepare any paper for my own release.

I assured him that he was mistaken, that I certainly had not overlooked my own case, and he hastily ran through his pile of papers again.

"Yes, Major," said he, "I am right. There are no papers here for you."

"True," said I, "but you did not say there were no papers for me, but that I had forgotten to prepare any. In this you are in error. I did not forget—I never proposed to write any paper for myself—you see, I am not going to leave just yet. I have taken a great fancy to you and I propose to stay with you a while longer."

The commandant at first seemed to regard the matter as a joke; but when he found I really did not propose to submit any papers for my own release, he began to fear I had lost my mental balance, and sent me to my quarters, sending the post-surgeon after me, to see whether I was in normal condition. I assured the doctor, and he saw for himself, that I was perfectly sound in mind and body, and he so reported.

The next day, as soon as the prisoners had left, Major Lee sent for me, and I explained to him that the oath demanded of us entered into the domain of my convictions and feelings, requiring me to swear in substance that I abandoned the "heresy of secession," and regarded and woul'
continue to regard the United States with patriotic devotion. I contended that the Government had nothing to do with the exercise of my intellect or affections, and that I could not

myself voluntarily control their operations or conclusions; that I would never take an oath of the character of that demanded, and did not feel disposed to take any oath whatever under duress and imprisonment; that, in fact, I questioned whether an oath exacted under such circumstances was legally valid; but that I preferred not to subject myself to the moral strain of toning down and whittling away the obligation of any oath I might take; that, indeed, as the war was, or seemed to be, practically over, with no organized Confederate force in the field, I ought to be released upon indefinite parole not to take up arms against the United States; but that I was willing to accept a brief parole, say of thirty days, conditioned at the expiration of that time to take the simple oath of allegiance or leave the country; that as at present advised and inclined, I would join any nation, or government, or people under Heaven—even the Hottentots—to fight against the United States, if there was a fair chance of success; but if allowed to go out and mingle freely with the people of the South, and especially of Virginia, for a short time, and to see for myself that they had, as he assured me, given up all purpose and hope of independence, I might then be able to take the simple oath of allegiance intelligently and honestly, and in case I did so might well prove a better, that is, a more reliable, citizen than some who had raised no such question of conscience.

Major Lee was very kind and considerate. He attempted at first to reason me out of my position, and failing in that said he would incorporate the substance of what I had said in his report to the Government, and ask my release on parole; which he did, but the application was refused. He then suggested that perhaps I could formulate my own position more clearly and strongly than he had done, and said he would forward any paper of that character I might prepare, and he furnished me with writing materials for the purpose. Of course, with my comrades all departed, there was a great calm, a melancholy stagnation in "the prison pen," and I revelled for days, almost weeks, in applying my little knowledge of law and my large sympathy with "general principles" to the preparation of paper after paper on the laws of war, as related to my case, and bearing on my application to be released on parole. Suffice it to say these papers were all endorsed by Major Lee, "Respectfully forwarded approved"—and all backed by the Commissary-General of Prisoners, "Respectfully returned disapproved."

At last, however, Mrs. A. D. Egerton, a noble lady of Baltimore, and my sister,—having managed in some way to get hold of one of these papers, weeks after I had been removed from Johnson's Island and incarcerated in a stone casemate in Fort Lafayette, in New York Harbor,—secured an interview with the Secretary of War, and Mr. Stanton endorsed the paper with his own hand.

"Let this young officer have any parole he asks, conditioned, at its expiration, to take the oath *or go back to prison.*"

The big-brained, terrible man cut right through to my half-formed purpose of going to Maximilian—and he did not propose to leave any such loop-hole in the net in which the Government at the time held me fast. It is a pleasure to record this incident, to the honor of a man who gave few opportunities to the people of the South for kindly words or feelings.

The iron door of my cell opened to these dear ladies, armed with this "ukase of the Czar," and I walked forth a free man once more—that is, in a modified sense. This was, I think, in October, '65. At the expiration of my brief parole, being satisfied that the fond dream of Confederate independence was ended forever, I took the simple oath of allegiance to the United States, sadly turned my back upon the only great thing in my life, and dropped into the undistinguishable mass of "The People."

Another matter of a personal nature, which I mention by special request, is the post-collegiate history of the DeForest gold medal, which I had the honor to take in the class of '59, at Old Yale, and the formative influence it exercised upon my after life.

In 1859, when I took the medal, the die for it had not been cast, and the trustees or managers of the fund were advised that they were legally compellable to melt up ten gold eagles, or, at least, a hundred dollars' worth of gold, in the general form of a medal, and to have engraved upon it the legend prescribed in the legal instrument of donation. My recollection is the medal was a long time reaching me, and when it came it was in this "questionable shape." I carried the lump of gold in my pants pocket for months, and as the mighty conflict drew on and I grew more moody and unhappy, I walked much alone, and used occasionally to shy my golden disc at cats and other objects, until the inscription became battered and defaced beyond recognition.

It was probably after my return from New York in the spring of '61 that one of my uncles, a cotton manufacturer from Northern Georgia, was sitting one evening with the family in our parlor in New Haven and I was filliping the great round piece of yellow metal up to the ceiling, when he asked what it was, and I answered:

"A lump of gold."

"Nonsense, Bob," said Uncle B. "What is it, really?"

"It is really a piece of gold, Uncle. If you doubt it, examine it and see for yourself!"—tossing it to him.

"Why, I really believe it is gold. How did you come by it, boy, and what are you going to do with it?"

When I explained, my uncle said:

"Well, it is certainly good for nothing now as a medal. We don't know what is coming upon us; you'd better let me take it South and put it in cotton for you."

"All right," I replied; "only let me first have a piece clipped off to make a breast-pin for mother;" which was done next morning. The little pin was made, my mother wore it for years, my sister has it now and my little daughter is to have it. "Uncle B." took the three-quarter moon of gold with him, and I cannot recall ever thinking of it again until the fall of 1865, just after I was released from prison.

I was on the border line of Albemarle and Orange Counties, Virginia, helping my brother, Randy, to harvest a little corn crop, which he had cultivated on shares, after getting out of prison in the spring. It was toward the gloaming and I was seated on a pile of corn, which we were anxious to finish that night. A solitary horseman came riding across the open country from the direction of the railroad, evidently an ex-Confederate cavalryman, and as we all, in those days, seemed to have a sort of intuitive knowledge of each other's whereabouts, I was not surprised when he rode close to us, tossing a letter upon the corn pile as he passed, and saying:

"I was at Gordonsville, Bob, and hearing you were in these parts, I asked for you at the office. That's all there was."

I thanked him and he rode on. When it got too dark to work I threw a fodder stalk on the smouldering fire and opened my letter. It contained the account of my cotton merchant, and not only his account but his check for $350, balancing the same.

It was the one moment of my life when I seemed to be possessed of boundless wealth.

I had on my old Confederate uniform,—indeed these were the only clothes I had,—but I walked to the University that night and entered the law class next morning, under that prince of men and of teachers, John B. Minor. I had no resources whatever outside of my little fairy-story fortune, and I really do not see how, without it, I could have resumed and completed my professional studies.

I had shared my large capital to some extent with my brother, and about the time I began to be seriously troubled again with the ever-pressing question of ways and means, entering my almost barren room one day after lecture, I found on my table an envelope addressed to me and inside of it $75 in greenbacks, and—written in a hand with which I was not familiar, and entirely without date or signature—the words, "From an old friend of your father."

About the time this second supply of bread and water the ravens had brought was exhausted, at the minimum rate of college expenses, another envelope, addressed in the same hand, was left in the same place, and inside of it $75 more, but not even the scrape of a pen accompanying. I have never heard so much as one word that shed any light upon the identity of the kind donor, and this aggregate of $150 is the only money I owe to-day.

My sister, Josephine, who, with Mrs. Egerton, procured my release from prison, was quite intimate with General

Lee's family and a great favorite with the general. She is consequently something of an heiress in interesting mementoes of him given her by his own hand.

She has a lock of his hair and one of Traveler's, a star from his coat collar, the wooden inkstand, which he used generally in our war, and, if I mistake not, in the Mexican War also, and the remains of a pound of tea he gave her, asking that we should make tea from it the first time we were fortunate enough to have a family reunion. She has also the general's parade hat, or rather she and I have committed this to the keeping of the Confederate Museum in Richmond. The circumstances connected with this latter gift are strongly characteristic.

My sister had been spending the morning at the general's residence, 707 East Franklin Street, Richmond, Va., sitting most of the time with the ladies of the family in Mrs. Lee's room. The general was preparing for a trip somewhere, and was leisurely packing his trunk, that is, after the ladies had done what they could to aid him—and every now and then he would enter the room where they were bringing in his hand something which he thought would interest them. In one of these incursions he brought a wide-brimmed drab or gray-brown felt hat, saying:

"Miss Josie, has your father a good hat?"

My sister replied that she really did not know, as we had not seen him for some time.

"Well," said the general, "I have two good hats, and I don't think a good rebel ought to have two good articles of one kind in these hard times. This was my dress-parade hat. Take it, please, and if your father has not a good hat, give him this one from me."

Father would not wear the hat, deeming it too sacred a thing for common use; but after the general's death, by permission of his daughters, who were present, I wore it at two of our great Confederate reunions, with my dear old Confederate jacket, and I need scarcely say was the object of more intense interest than ever in my life, before or since. I made bold, too, to have my photograph taken with the hat on—of course, the jacket, too,—as a sort of heirloom for my family.

CHAPTER XXVI

My story is told. If it has failed to interest and to stir you deeply, the fault is in the telling. And yet I cannot but hope +that, in spite of feeble and inadequate portrayal, the great outlines of the picture have so impressed themselves upon you that you are ready to admit the life of Marse Robert's boys, from '61 to '65, to have been a higher and greater life than you had imagined.

It would seem as if this must be so, if you have credited the writer with a fair average of intelligence and conscientiousness. I can well understand, however, that, without reflecting upon me in any offensive sense, some of those who have done me the honor to read these reminiscences may feel that I have unconsciously and very naturally idealized my comrades of the long ago and the vivid life we lived together in our golden youth.

It is difficult to meet such a suggestion. I believe the strongest and most satisfactory way to meet it and, at the same time, the fittest way to end this book, will be to close with an analysis of the Soldier-Life, from which it will appear how natural and normal it is, that elements and forces, such as characterize that life, should produce men and deeds and scenes and incidents such as I have endeavored to portray in the foregoing pages.

It is also, just now, specially to be desired that the essential character and training of the military life should be better and more generally understood. However we may differ as to the advisability of the new career of foreign complication and conquest upon which this country seems to have entered, and which has resulted and must necessarily result in such an expansion of its military establishment, yet we must all agree that it is well the growing multitudes of young men who are entering and to enter the military service should have high and clear conceptions of that great life to which they have devoted themselves—a life, by the way, which, notwithstanding the horrors that often attended it, grew upon me every day I lived it; and to which, if the war had resulted in the establishment of the Southern Confederacy, I should have consecrated myself with whole-hearted devotion.

It will not be forgotten that I claim for the Army of Northern Virginia some peculiar characteristics, as well as a fuller and finer development of the soldierly character in general, because of the circumstances under which that army fought, and especially the leader, whose banner it followed; but, after all, the heroic story I have told is in no small degree the normal product and outcome of a grand system of physical, mental and moral training, which has been little understood and grossly misconceived and misrepresented.

What, then, is the training and what are the formative elements and forces of the Soldier-Life? I answer:

The essential character of the Soldier-Life is "Service;"

Its every employment, its all-pervading law, is "Duty;"

Its first lesson—Obedience unquestioning;

Its last lesson—Command unquestioned;

Its daily discipline—Accountability unceasing;

Its final burden—Responsibility unmeasured;

Its every-day experience—Hardships, Perils, Crises unparalleled;

Its social atmosphere—Freedom from Social Shams;

Its compensation—Fixed pay;

Its inspiration—Promotion from Above.

If you have measured these elements as I have mentioned them, there can be little need of elaboration or of argument. The compact analysis makes ample impression at once of theoretical soundness and of practical power. Beyond a doubt these are the essential elements and forces of the military life; they are such as must of necessity be unceasingly operative, and their influence in the development of character can scarcely be exaggerated. Let us briefly consider them.

The essential character of the soldier-life is "Service."

Can this be questioned? When a man enters the military profession, whether as an officer or a private soldier, by that very act he is cut off from the pursuit of his personal aims and purposes and devoted to the service of his country. Thereafter he has no home, no farm, no workshop, no business. He knows no self-directed future, attempts nothing, expects nothing, for himself. Every man outside the army regards him, and he regards himself, as a man relieved, separated from the entanglements and opportunities of the business world, and consecrated to a service which may at any time demand the sacrifice even of his life. Our English Bible, upon this, as upon so many practical phases of our human experience, rings wondrous true. Wrote the great apostle: "No man that warreth entangleth himself with the affairs of this life; that he may please him who hath chosen him to be a soldier."

The keynote which inspires and dominates and regulates all this life of "Service" is the single, simple majestic law of "Duty." No employment of the soldier is too trivial and none too great to be included in this all-embracing term and regulated by this all-pervading law.

Descriptive names and phrases express and impress conceptions, and thus frequently constitute a sort of connecting link between causes and effects, principles and results. "Service;" "the service;" "entered the service;" "discharged from the service;" promoted for gallant and meritorious service;" "duty;" "on duty;" "off duty;" "present for duty;" "absent from duty;" "shot to death for absence from duty"—how many times, during the four years from '61 to '65, do you suppose I read, wrote, uttered, heard these and kindred expressions? Is it not clear that, by his everyday's experience and intercourse, this one great figure—his life a "service," its employment "duty"—is burned in upon the soldier's soul?

In the light of these principles, and of his lifelong training, we gain a new conception of that sublime sentence in General Lee's letter to his son, "Duty is the sublimest word in the English language;" and of that groan of his mighty soul in the crisis and agony of defeat, "It is my duty to live."

The first lesson of the soldier-life is unquestioning Obedience.

No one will deny the justness of the analysis here. Undeniably, the first lesson of the soldier's life, logically and chronologically, is obedience. There is no department, no business, no station, in which instant, implicit, blindfold obedience is so vital to safety and success, or enforced by such terrible sanctions. In military matters hesitation is disobedience, disobedience is mutiny, mutiny is death.

The principle of the soldier's obedience is the principle of *obedience,* a principle very little understood and very much contemned in this day and land. It is this: authority is to be obeyed, not because it commands what is right, but because it has the right to command. One under rightful authority is therefore absolved from responsibility as to the policy or propriety or consequences of the command; his sole dignity, as well as duty, is to obey with unquestioning alacrity. This principle is not palatable to the republican sovereigns of this country, yet it is a principle notwithstanding—not exclusive, nor of universal application, but it has its place, and, in its place, is of vital importance. It is the principle on which God governs the world, the father his family, the soldier his subordinates; and it has other, many other, applications.

Its direct antagonism is *"higher law,"* that is, a law higher than the commands of rightful authority; in other words, authority is to be obeyed, not because it has the right to command, but because it commands what is right. This principle, too, has its applications, but it is not applicable to a subordinate under rightful authority. The harmony between the two is found, I think, in a limitation upon the principle of obedience. We pass from the law of obedience to the higher law when, but only when, the command is so palpably and grossly wrong that the authority can no longer be rightful and subjection to it no longer endured. This is the right of *revolution,* and is applicable by way of exception to every human relation and authority.

The soldier, however, has very little sympathy with the right of revolution, or any modification of or exception to the law of unquestioning obedience. His theory and practice in this regard find apt illustration in the reply of General Jackson to the brigade commander, who gave excellent reasons for having modified the order of march: "Sir, you should have obeyed the order first and reasoned about it afterwards. Consider yourself under arrest."

The last lesson of the soldier-life is unquestioned Command.

This analysis of the life and its lessons is not original with me; it is at least nineteen hundred years old, and rests on the authority of one who was a superb development of the most military nation of history, that grand old Roman centurian whose interview with the Son of God is perhaps the most striking of the Gospel narratives. Said he: "I also am a man set under authority, having under me soldiers, and I say unto one, Go, and he goeth; and to another, Come, and he cometh." Here are the two great correlative lessons of the life, obedience and command, and both are absolute. This is the soldier, not ashamed to obey, not afraid to command; knowing how to render, and thus learning how to exact, obedience.

The daily lesson of the life is unceasing Accountability.

The soldier breathes, as it were, an atmosphere of accountability. His daily routine is made up of inspections and reports. What he is, what he has, what he does, his person, his possessions, his conduct, are constantly passing under a scrutiny so searching that nothing escapes, however trivial, and all must conform to unvarying "Regulations." This is perhaps the most prominent and impressive feature of the life. I need not enlarge upon it. The fact is patent— can its influence be doubted? Apart now from your impression as to what the soldier is, what ought he to be as the result of such training? Can you conceive of anything tending more to develop regularity, reliability, promptness, accuracy, even in the smallest details?

In the upper grades of the soldier-life, mark how this accountability is retained and developed into Responsibility, which, in the case of the commander-in-chief, becomes absolutely awful, unmeasured and unmeasurable.

Responsibility! I had almost said no other human being can have any adequate conception of the meaning of the term. Responsible for what? For the lives of his followers, for the future of their bereft families; but it is not life or death, not victory or defeat alone, that trembles in the balance of his battles. It is the life and honor of his country, the weal or woe of millions yet to be. He orders the charge, and liberty and destiny and history flicker in the gleam of his bayonets.

The experiences of the life are unparalleled Hardships, Perils, Crises.

It would be superfluous to enlarge upon these, the most external and palpable features of a soldier's life, so shortly after a war which has overspread a continent and filled a land with veterans. Nor will we stay to prove what no one will deny, that robustness of character, dauntless determination, courage that saves from, if it does not hide, a multitude of sins, and a composure and balance of soul that no excitement can disturb, no terror overwhelm, are the legitimate fruits of the soldier training.

The social atmosphere of the soldier-life is Freedom from Social Shams.

The unconventionality and candor of student life are proverbial, and yet, though I stepped from the hearty, ideal student life of Old Yale into the ranks of the Confederate soldiery, it was not long before I felt that I had never before realized how unstudied, unconventional, and absolutely sincere human life could be. It was almost startling, the degree to which I knew other men, my comrades, and felt that I was known by them. All the little shams, insincerities, and concealments of ordinary society disappeared; until, for the first time in our lives, we seemed to be stripped bare of the disguises under which we had theretofore been accustomed to hide our real characters, not only from the world in general and from out most intimate associates and companions, but even from ourselves.

It was this which imparted to the religious life of the army a power and thrill unattainable, even unapproachable, in ordinary life. So close did men get to each other that I experienced no difficulty and no embarrassment in conversing with every man in the company on the subject of personal religion, and in these conferences have often felt that I was playing upon a naked human soul, between whom and myself there was absolutely no barrier and no screen. It was an experience thrilling and tremendous indeed. In view of it, I have more than once remarked that if my Maker should reveal to me that I had but a short time to live, and should permit me to choose a position in which I could accomplish most for the regeneration of my fellow-men, I should unhesitatingly say, "Let me be an officer in an army, in a time of active service."

The compensation of the soldier-life is Fixed pay.

The importance and influence of this feature cannot be estimated until you have answered this question: What is the most demoralizing of all human desires and pursuits? I know not how you will better answer than in the words of Holy Writ; for the wisdom of God has embodied the answer in a proverb, ".The love of money is the root of all evil." And the context is most impressive! "They that will be rich fall into temptation and a snare, and into many foolish and hurtful lusts, which drown men in destruction and perdition." A proposition thus enunciated needs no enforcement, and no one will contend that this terrific indictment is less true or less applicable to-day than when the noble apostle warned his "son Timothy" against this the greatest of all the lures of the tempter. And, so surely as opportunity makes temptation, the soldier, looking securely to his sufficient but fixed compensation, having his undivided services demanded and paid for by his country, and being consequently unable to devote himself to any lucrative employment, must be in great measure protected against the debasing passion of avarice.

The inspiration of the life is Promotion from Above.

Evidently the soldier's compensation is not the inspiration of his calling; and it is perhaps more true of him than of any other man that his chief inspiration is honorable advancement in his profession. Call it love of glory, if you please; even at that it is almost infinitely more elevating and ennobling than love of money, which is the ruling motive of much the larger part of mankind, certainly in this age and land. But the soldier does not call it love of glory. He is no moral philosopher or theorist; he is a practical man, and his inspiration, that of which he talks and dreams, that for which he serves and strives, is all embodied in one word —*promotion*. This is "the life of the service." So peculiarly true is this that the soldier's progress has well nigh appropriated the term "promotion," as the soldier's life has appropriated the title "service."

But it is not the desire for promotion, however inspiring, to which I wished chiefly to ask your attention, but rather the peculiar law of military promotion, namely, that it is promotion *from above*. Before you estimate the importance of this feature, let me ask you another question: What is the second great demoralizing influence of our age, and particularly of our country? I have not here the Word of God for answer; but in these days of unblushing demagogism I am sure of your concurrence when I say, it is flattery and service of the mob, cowardly concession to it, in order to secure promotion *from below*. I mean no reflection upon the right or principle of suffrage; but the practice of suffrage, and the means commonly resorted to to control it for personal ends are at once a disgrace to free government and a degradation of the candidate and the voter. No honest man can now pass through a political contest without being disgusted, if happily he be not also surprised, at the means employed against him.

The true soldier knows nothing of such contests or influences. He never dreams of promotion by any other power than that of his superiors, or on any other ground than gallant and meritorious service. No! the soldier's principle, the soldier's inspiration, is promotion *from above,* and it cuts off a world of temptation and demoralization thus to lift a man's eyes and efforts *up* for personal elevation and advancement.

We have finished our review of the root forces of the Soldier-Life. Where will you find principles of greater power for the development of character?

Is it objected that the soldier, as we see him in actual life to-day, fails to exhibit any close conformity to these elevated principles and lofty ideals? I answer that the like failure marks the embodiment among men of the principles and ideals of every lofty life—even of our holy religion. But balanced men do not on this ground question either the truth and beauty of these principles and ideals, or the sincere adoption of them by the followers of the Christ, or their moulding influence for good upon those who adopt them.

Is it objected further that, only the highest class of recruits could be expected to appreciate the philosophy of such a system? True, but the same is true of every high vocation—that only a few choice souls thoroughly grasp the inner philosophy, the root principles, the formative forces of the calling to which they have devoted their lives. But it is also true that intellectual appreciation, however much to be desired, is not indispensable to the operation and the moulding power of formative forces such as we have discussed. A young man who enters the military service and is subjected to its discipline and training may not have intellectual life and interest enough even to inquire what it is that is making a new man of him; notwithstanding, being compelled to conform his conduct to the regulations and to live the strenuous life we have just sketched, new habits will gradually be formed and the new man will unconsciously be made.

A touching and beautiful illustration of the justness of this soldier analysis, and the character-moulding power of its principles, occurred the first time I made use of it in public speech, applying it in that instance to a great soldier of the Confederacy, and showing how the mould prefigured the man. At the close of the address the son of another and one of the very greatest of our Confederate leaders, who had fallen in battle early in the war, pressed his way to my side, saying, with the deepest feeling: "Major, you have, in a very just sense, introduced my own father to me to-day. I have always admired the majestic outline of his perfect manhood, but never until I heard you just now have I realized where his qualities came from, nor sympathized, as I should have done, with my father's almost passionate love and reverence for his profession. It is all clear to me now."

I am not a blind enthusiast. I admit that the almost enforced idleness of the camp in time of peace, the absence of women and children and the lack of other refining and elevating influence of home, are blemishes in the life of the soldier. Nevertheless, I think we may, in the light of our analysis, begin to comprehend why great soldiers—Sir Philip Sidney, Henry Havelock, Hedley Vicars, Chinese Gordon, Stonewall Jackson, Robert Lee—have exhibited an almost unrivaled elevation, strength, and perfection of character, both as men and as Christians. The late Dr. T. De Witt Talmage never penned a truer or a stronger paragraph than the following:

"The sword has developed the grandest natures that the world ever saw. It has developed courage—that sublime energy of the soul which defies the universe when it feels itself to be in the right. It has developed a self-sacrifice which repudiates the idea that our life is worth more than anything else, when for a principle it throws that life away, as much as to say, 'It is not necessary that I live, but it is necessary that righteousness triumph.' There are thousands among the Northern and Southern veterans of our Civil War who are ninety-five per cent. larger and mightier in soul than they would have been had they not, during the four years of national agony, turned their back on home and fortune, and at the front sacrificed all for a principle."

In the light of all this, we begin also to understand why the writers of the Sacred Canon make use of the life of the soldier more frequently perhaps than of any other, as a figure of the Christian life.   Nor can it do harm in this connection to note that when the Son of God "marveled" at a Roman soldier's *faith,* pronouncing it the greatest he had found on earth, the man himself traced this faith to the teachings of his military life, saying substantially, with us— I have learned *as a soldier* the two great lessons of subjection and supremacy, of obedience and command; do you but issue the order, "Speak the word only, and my servant shall be healed."

INDEX